"Over the years, I've seen Maia's work transform the lives of hundreds of teachers and leaders. Maia is a teacher at heart and gets that a teacher has to give thought to hundreds of considerations over the course of the day. She helps us feel prepared, centered, and Together so that we can show up as our best selves for students."

> Chong-Hao Fu, CEO, Leading Educators

"Our job as leaders is to support our teachers to become superb educators so they can be at their best for our students and families. Too often we lose teachers with great potential because they become overwhelmed by the amount of information coming at them, that is, emails, texts, phone calls, student work, daily and weekly team meetings, and PD sessions. *The Together Teacher* provides the tools needed to equip teachers with specific strategies to process all that information and free up their minds to focus on honing their craft. We appreciate the tools provided and the humor and compassion that exudes from Maia, as it leads to all of us believing that being organized and being Together is 'cool' and something we all want to do."

> Kate Mehok, cofounder and CEO, Crescent City Schools

"Twenty years ago, I entered the teaching profession with good intentions and lots of enthusiasm. However, the impact I made was minimal because I lacked strong systems for managing all of my responsibilities. After implementing the strategies from *The Together Teacher*, I was able to stay on top of my daily priorities, utilize my calendar in a powerful way, and tame the email beast—and become a high-performing teacher. I'm a principal now, and I use *The Together Teacher* with my staff to help them plan ahead, get organized, and save time. *The Together Teacher* is one of the most transformative texts I've ever read as an educator."

> Eric Newcomer, principal, YES Prep Northbrook Middle School

"Through *The Together Teacher*, Maia leads you on a journey of self-reflection to create personalized organizational systems that work for your priorities and personality. In becoming a Together teacher, I began to use my two most finite resources – time and energy – more strategically, becoming a happier and more balanced person in my life both in and out of the classroom."

> Greta Gartman, elementary teacher, South Portland Schools, Maine

"Maia understands the reality of teacher life. Her work supports teachers across all grade levels and settings to ensure they have a clear, prioritized plan for their massive workload and laundry bag. Maia builds on her previous work and offers us new insights as we shift to a more tech-driven school environment. This book is required reading for school leaders looking to create healthy and sustainable working conditions for their staff."

Shawn Mangar, principal, Baychester Middle School

"I am SO thankful for being introduced to *The Together Teacher* during my first year of teaching. Maia's simple, efficient, and effective techniques saved me from many potential meltdowns! Now, six years later, I still think about these Together tips all the time. These techniques help me spend less time feeling overwhelmed and more time actually educating!"

Julia Ziac, STEM educator

THE
TOGETHER
TEACHER

THE TOGETHER TEACHER

Plan Ahead, Get Organized, and Save Time!

Maia Heyck-Merlin
Marin Smith
Maggie G. Sorby

Foreword by Ann Blakeney Clark

Second Edition

JOSSEY-BASS
A Wiley Brand

Jossey-Bass
A Wiley Imprint
111 River St, Hoboken, NJ 07030
www.josseybass.com

Jossey-Bass books and products are available through most bookstores. To contact Jossey-Bass directly, call our Customer Care Department within the U.S. at 800–956–7739, outside the U.S. at +1 317 572 3986, or fax +1 317 572 4002.

Wiley also publishes its books in a variety of electronic formats and by print-on-demand. Some material included with standard print versions of this book may not be included in e-books or in print-on-demand. If this book refers to media such as a CD or DVD that is not included in the version you purchased, you may download this material at http://booksupport.wiley.com. For more information about Wiley products, visit www.wiley.com.

Library of Congress Cataloging-in-Publication Data is Available:

ISBN 9781119542599 (paperback)
ISBN 9781119542605 (epdf)
ISBN 9781119542643 (epub)

Cover Design: Paul McCarthy
Cover Art: © Getty Images / RLT Images
Author Photo: © Courtesy of the Author

SECOND EDITION

SKY10025974_052421

To the Together Team (you know who you are)

CONTENTS

Foreword   xiii

Introduction   1

PART ONE: TOGETHER YOUR TIME   11

Chapter 1: Create an Ideal Week—And Build in That Self-Care!   13

Components of a Great Together Teacher System • Design Your Ideal
Week • Build Your Own Ideal Week • Let's Toss in Some Self-Care and Stress
Management • Self-Care and Stress Management Plan Examples • Let's Get
Started

Chapter 2: A Week's Worth of Readiness: Create a Weekly Worksheet   31

Setting the Scene • A Closer Look: What Is a Weekly Worksheet? • Weekly
Worksheet Examples • Select Your Weekly Worksheet Tool • Turbo
Togetherness • Maintenance Moves

Together Tour: Cassidy Cruz   57

Chapter 3: No More Missed Deadlines: Make a Comprehensive Calendar   59

Setting the Scene • The Multiple-Calendar Dilemma • The Comprehensive
Calendar: What Is It? • Together Teachers' Comprehensive Calendars • Pick Your
Tool: Where Will You Keep Your Comprehensive Calendar? • Build Your Own
Comprehensive Calendar • Keep Your Comprehensive Calendar Moving • Turbo
Togetherness • Maintenance Moves

Chapter 4: Corral the Long-Term To-Dos: Create Your Later List   **85**

Setting the Scene • The Later List: What Is It? • Together Teacher Later List Examples • Assemble the To-Dos: Build Your Later List • Select Your Later List Tool • Keep That Later List Fed and Happy • Carry Your Later List • Turbo Togetherness • Maintenance Moves

Together Tour: Laura Burrow   **105**

Chapter 5: Never Forget! Get on the Thought Catchers   **107**

Setting the Scene • What Is a Thought Catcher Exactly? • Together Teacher Thought Catcher Examples • Brainstorm Your Own Thought Catchers • Pick Your Thought Catcher Tool • Review Your Thought Catchers Regularly • Turbo Togetherness • Maintenance Moves

Chapter 6: Create Routines to Support Togetherness: Meet with Yourself   **123**

Setting the Scene • Build Your Meeting with Myself Checklist • Together Teacher Meeting with Myself Example Checklists • Logistics of Meeting with Yourself: Your When, Where, and What To Bring • When, Where, and What To Bring to Your Meeting with Myself • Daily Routines: Making the Most of Opening and Closing the Day • Turbo Togetherness • Maintenance Moves

PART TWO: TOGETHER YOUR SPACE, STUFF, AND STUDENTS   **143**

Chapter 7: Tidy and Together Up Your Teacher Workspace   **145**

Setting the Scene • Together Up That Workspace • Together Transport: Moving Materials Between Spaces • Contain the Instructional Chaos. Mean, Materials • Finding What You Need When You Need It • Carry It With You • Turbo Togetherness • Maintenance Moves

Together Tour: Angela Mu   **171**

Chapter 8: The Inbox, the Texts, the Messages: Tame the Communications Chaos   **173**

Setting the Scene • Set Up for Success • Establish Communications Routines or . . . Stop Checking Constantly! • Create Schoolwide Communication Agreements • Write To Be Heard, or Stop Sending Open-Ended Emails! • Email: Use It, Don't Abuse It! • Turbo Togetherness • Maintenance Moves

Chapter 9: Papers, Supplies, and Assignments: Support Student Togetherness 203

Setting the Scene • Displaying Class Schedules and Syllabi • Together Student Tools Created by Schools • Together Student Tools Created by Students and Families • Support Student Space Set-Up • Teaching Students Togetherness • Turbo Togetherness • Maintenance Moves

PART THREE: TOGETHER YOUR TEACHING 235

Chapter 10: Plan, Plan, and Plan Some More: Make Lesson Planning Efficient! 237

Setting the Scene • Together Teachers' Long-Term Planning Examples • What Is the Actual Work of Lesson Planning? • Materials Needed for Lesson Planning • Determine Day and Time To Plan • Where Should I Lesson Plan? • Turbo Togetherness • Maintenance Moves

Together Tour: Eric Nielsen 261

Chapter 11: Grading, Assessing, and More! 263

Setting the Scene • Determine What You Are Grading and Why • Determine How You Collect Student Work • Getting Efficient with the Actual Grading • Keeping Up with Student Progress • When and Where Are You Grading? • When and How Am I Sharing the Data with Students and Families? • Turbo Togetherness • Maintenance Moves

PART FOUR: TOGETHER YOUR TEAM 287

Chapter 12: Join 'Em and Lead 'Em: Make the Most of Meetings 289

Setting the Scene • Create the Meeting Agenda • Staying Together *During* the Meeting • Note-Taking During Meetings • Store and Retrieve Your Meeting Notes • Turbo Togetherness • Maintenance Moves

Together Tour: Veronica Urbanik 319

Chapter 13: Events, Projects, and Parties: Project Plan Your Way to Success!   **321**

Setting the Scene • Determine a Successful Outcome • Build Out Your Buckets • Create a Project Plan • Bring on the Team • Work the Plan • The Big Day—Or Night? • Celebration and Closeout • Turbo Togetherness • Maintenance Moves

Conclusion: Why the World Needs Together Teachers   337

Acknowledgments   347

About the Authors   349

Index   351

FOREWORD

Before you turn to the opening chapter of *The Together Teacher,* I invite each reader to think about the students who show up at your classroom door each morning. Imagine how those students would describe you. Would your students describe you as the teacher who consistently comes up a handout short or the teacher who has a handout placed on each student's desk before class begins? Regardless of where you fall on the continuum of un-Together or Together Teacher, Maia Heyck-Merlin brings her own classroom experiences as an amazing teacher to her readers and creates multiple trailheads for your Together journey.

The Together Teacher, however, is not just for teachers. As a former principal and school district superintendent, I have had the chance to visit many teacher classrooms over a 35-year career and see many incredible Together teachers still on the Together journey to hone their teaching practice. I have also visited classrooms of teachers just beginning their Togetherness journey. I have seen firsthand the extraordinary impact of Maia's work with teachers, assistant principals, principals and district office leaders. When I first met Maia, I felt I was well down the trail of Togetherness but was able to add many additional tools, systems, protocols and working habits to my leadership roadmap. I quickly learned that a culture of Togetherness in classrooms, schools and district offices can be transformational for a school district.

Imagine the experience of students across our nation if every principal handed each teacher hired a copy of *The Together Teacher.* Our students arrive in our classrooms each day with their own degree of un-Togetherness and Togetherness. These students deserve and need a teacher who tightly plans, utilizes tools and systems with discipline and consistency, declutters the learning space and avoids the reputation as the discombobulated teacher. The degree of commitment a teacher has to Togetherness will frequently impact the level of learning a student is able to experience. As educators we owe it to our students to make each precious teaching and learning moment count.

The teaching profession is challenging, complex and fast paced. The peaks and valleys allow little time for rest and rejuvenation. My wish for every teacher is the opportunity to take a slight detour on your teaching journey to read *The Together Teacher*. Give yourself permission to pause and take stock of your tools, structures, systems, routines, and protocols.

I am confident when you rejoin the trail you will be better prepared, energized and Together! Then share a copy of *The Together Teacher* with a teaching colleague, student teacher or mentor so that more and more students arrive at classrooms each day with a Together teacher. Let the journey begin. . .

Ann Blakeney Clark

Executive Leadership Coach

former Superintendent of Charlotte-Mecklenburg Public Schools

Introduction

Let's first picture the *not*-together teacher. This may be you on some days; I know it was certainly me. You race into the school parking lot, mug of coffee in hand (but lunch forgotten in the refrigerator at home) and backpack stuffed full of papers you intended to grade last night, but did not. As you sign in at the front office, stammer "hello" to the office staff, and walk quickly to your classroom (wait—why are there *children* in the building already?!), you realize you don't have copies of the unit test you are giving that morning and the copier is jammed. It's only 7:15 a.m. and you already feel overwhelmed.

Relate much? Then this book will help you plan ahead and work smarter so you are more prepared and less discombobulated. If this DOESN'T sound like you, this book will help you prioritize deeply and protect your time even more fiercely. No matter your entry point, this book will meet you where you are in your Togetherness journey.

The Together Teacher™ is the teacher who makes it *look* easy. You know, that person in your building who never scrambles to make copies at the last minute, has lessons planned a week or more in advance, turns progress reports in early, makes time for positive parent phone calls, conducts extra tutoring after school, *and* packs healthy homemade lunches. Don't stress—this teacher wasn't born that way. Countless routines, systems, and tools go into pulling off that level of Togetherness, and they are not achieved overnight. Throughout this book you will meet teachers with varying years of classroom experience, in multiple subjects and grade levels, who work in unique school environments. Some of them began their teaching career highly organized; others learned these skills on the job to deal with the demands of teaching. For some readers this book will affirm things you're already doing and provide ideas for refining your systems and coaching newer teachers. For others it will serve as a "how-to" guide on getting organized (enough) to be a great classroom teacher.

The Together Teachers I know execute their work with an incredible degree of intentionality. They rely on simple yet sophisticated systems that hold up under the complexity and fast pace of teaching. These systems require tremendous discipline, a little bit of time, and faith that planning and organization will actually free you up to focus on bigger, more fun, and more interesting things. To be clear, this is *not* a book that is going to tell you how to color-code folders and make picture-perfect charts. (Nor will it help you organize your closets at home!) It will not tell you precisely which planner or which app to use. **I will help you cultivate routines that help you become organized *enough* to get results for your students and make your life more fun and less stressful.**

PLANNING, ORGANIZATION, AND EFFICIENCY MATTER EVEN MORE FOR TEACHERS

As teachers, we face a unique set of challenges compared to the average professional. We have little to no discretionary time, stand on our feet most of the day, incur large amounts of take-home work, deal with mandated technology systems as well as old-fashioned paperwork, and manage constantly shifting schedules that allow for virtually no moments of concentration or focus. Let's not even talk about our rapid shift to online instruction during the pandemic (which, at the time of revisions to this manuscript, was hitting us all in full force). To-Dos come at us from a million different directions—email inboxes, phone messages, text messages, paper memos, and staff meetings.

Although the bulk of our role as teachers is to design and deliver outstanding instruction on a daily basis, there is a lot of other work that needs to be done in the background to ensure that those lessons are the best they can be. Given all of these demands, it is easy to understand how we may scramble to plan lessons, miss progress report deadlines, and hand back student essays two months after students turn them in!

Add to this complex set of responsibilities the additional duties involved in providing strong instruction—deeply analyzing student data, ensuring that lesson plans include high-quality rigorous questions, and making time for one-on-one tutoring with struggling students, all of which takes extreme focus and planning—and pile on the emotional toll of breaking up a scuffle in the hallway, calming the upset parent of a perpetually tardy student, and comforting a kid who is trying to comprehend a death in the family—and you have a recipe for stressed and undoubtedly less effective teachers.

Many resources are available to help you set ambitious goals and get your students invested in school. There are a ton of tools that will help you with unit planning, lesson planning, and making the right assessments to determine content mastery. However, there are very *few* accounts of how outstanding teachers actually spend their limited free time, plan ahead, and organize their work and classrooms to arrive at strong outcomes. As someone who has been a teacher, recruited teachers, hired teachers, trained and evaluated teachers, and worked like heck to retain great teachers, I believe that being organized is an invaluable skill to possess in *the* most demanding and important profession there is. Teachers MUST rely on solid organization and planning skills to meet the needs of their students.

WHAT DO I MEAN BY "TOGETHER?"

Together can take on a whole host of meanings. To some teachers it means having neat filing systems that allow them to find the exact manipulatives for a place value lesson. To others it means always meeting deadlines for lesson plans or using time efficiently to get more done in fewer minutes. To yet another group it means having the perfect plan for a field trip. Regardless of how each one defines it, Together Teachers all demonstrate seven essential skills.

1. **Prioritization.** This means you are focusing on the *right* things, not speeding through your day mindlessly checking any To-Do off a list just to get it done. You've determined what matters most at school and at home and your schedule reflects those priorities. The bulk of your time goes to what is most important. A teacher who does not prioritize well may focus too heavily on the aesthetics of his or her classroom at the expense of effective lesson design.

2. **Planning.** Planning well means you consistently look ahead to what is coming next and determine the steps you'll take to get there, often pausing to write them down. A teacher who plans well looks ahead on his calendar, notices that progress reports are due in three weeks, and diligently writes three per evening.

3. **Systems.** Organized teachers have a clear process and clear systems for all important classroom functions. For example, they have systems for collecting and handing back student work. Organized teachers can respond in 10 minutes when you ask to borrow a visual anchor from a poetry lesson a few weeks ago. Disorganized teachers often have

desks buried in papers—and maybe a car trunk full of still more papers they meant to return to students. Laugh, but trust me, it happens.

4. **Self-Awareness.** The ability to *do* your work with intentionality is a clear sign of a Together Teacher. Sometimes teachers make a lot of lists yet fail to accomplish their stated tasks. Teachers who execute well are aware of their energy levels, accurately estimate how long things will take to complete, and know what steps to take to check items off their lists. They enjoy getting things done!

5. **Efficiency.** Given the limited amount of discretionary time in a teacher's day, efficiency matters a ton. You can save a lot of time by making all of your copies for the week at once instead of running to the copier a few times per day. Efficient teachers take little bits of time and maximize them to the fullest. They send positive messages for parents while walking to their cars, thereby freeing up their evenings for personal priorities.

6. **Flexibility.** Flexibility is the forgotten part of Togetherness. The ability to adapt in the moment, respond to human needs, and switch gears when things go wrong is essential amid all of this planning. Too much Togetherness is a thing, people. We want to make the plans, even overplan, and then be ready to pivot as necessary to deal with emergencies, relationships, and crises. The era of COVID-19 has made us all the more aware of this need for systems resilience.

7. **Boundaries.** After conducting many interviews for the second edition of this book, we observed that our most Together Teachers all set clear boundaries for themselves—professionally and personally. These boundaries were not set arbitrarily but rather rooted deep in their values. It wasn't a matter of them just saying "no" to particular activities but rather constantly weighing trade-offs.

As teachers, we need to develop habits in all of these areas in order to be "Together." Here's why: If you are a person who loves organizing and making lists but you never refer to them, you will accomplish little. If you spend all of your time fiddling with perfect color-coded file folders that have every lesson categorized by day, but you don't use them efficiently, you will not move forward. Together Teachers take a balanced approach and hone each of the skills in this list in order to become their maximally Together selves.

WHY THIS MATTERS TO ME

When I started teaching fourth grade over two decades ago, I consistently worked 80 or 90 hours per week. In a last-ditch attempt at self-preservation, I read a ton about how professionals with tremendous volumes of work and lots of people to answer to managed their jobs. Although I found some strong resources to help me "get things done," "put in the big rocks first," and "not check email in the morning" (David Allen, Steven Covey, and Julie Morgenstern, to name a few of my favorite resources), nothing *totally* fit into my daily teaching life—the one during which I was consistently on my feet, had my precious planning time eaten up by student issues, was rarely in front of a computer, struggled to understand the announcements made over the garbled intercom, and dealt with more pieces of paper than I knew what to do with. There are some amazing resources out there in the vast field of productivity and time management, and more tools are made available each and every day online. The challenge, however, is that none truly address teaching, a unique profession that varies so greatly depending on how our schools function, what technology we are issued, and what expectations are set for our roles.

And very honestly, none of the existing materials addressed jobs as *complex* as mine was. I was responsible for 60 students (three sections of writing), communicating with the families of all of those students, and a fourth-grade teaching team. I received feedback from a literacy coach and homework from my own graduate classes; handled papers to collect, papers to grade, papers to return, papers to be filed, and professional development resources to be used now and later; and I needed an inordinate amount of *stuff* in my classroom. I spent a lot of money at office supply stores trying to find the perfect planner for teachers but was annoyed when I couldn't customize the templates that accompanied them. I put together a huge binder with tabs for every aspect of teaching, but it got too heavy to lug around school all day. I bought a PalmPilot with a nifty stylus pen (remember those?!) and started keeping an electronic calendar, but I couldn't find a way to enter stuff fast enough during the teaching day. I tried black-and-white composition books, graph paper, and Action Pads. Nothing could keep up with the pace and volume of my job teaching fourth grade.

In the meantime, I was slowly learning to teach, taking graduate classes, and picking up more responsibilities, such as tutoring my students on Saturdays. I quickly realized that fumbling for the right overhead transparency (ahem, #1999) or flipping through stacks of papers to locate copies for that day's lesson resulted in lost instructional time for my students and was an open invitation for them to misbehave. If I wasn't sure when my progress reports were due or when an important assembly was scheduled, I would enter the day unprepared and then become incredibly stressed when someone would remind me. I lost credibility when I gave a warning for talking out in class or told a student, "Great work on your spelling test! I am going to make a positive phone call to your parents tonight," and promptly forgot. When I spent too much time chatting with Mrs. Russell during a prep period, it meant I had yet another hour of work to take home. The only way I could survive was to be incredibly organized and super-efficient, and to plan as far ahead as possible in order to deal with the unexpected stuff, good and bad, that inevitably comes up in school environments.

After I stopped teaching, I was fortunate to spend a decade working in two other high-performing, disciplined environments—Teach For America and Achievement First. At TFA, many of us used a "Weekly Action Plan" to stay organized for the week, but we often found it was too short term a view of our work and duplicative of our electronic systems. At Achievement First, many teachers tried to use the Outlook tools but found it hard to organize their work in an exclusively electronic way while teaching. There had to be some way to take practices experts recommended, what I had observed my talented colleagues try, and what I had experimented with myself, and make it work for *teachers*!

I was fortunate that Achievement First, and then Relay Graduate School of Education, provided me with an informal research lab to develop approaches that would meet the demands and needs of teachers. Slowly, and with much trial and error, I eventually landed on the set of tools you'll find in the first half of this book. Over time, I learned there was no single system that all teachers could rely on to become magically more organized. What's more, individual teachers (and all people) have different work habits, particular affinities for paper versus digital systems, varied teaching loads, and different personal obligations and dreams. So, although there is no silver bullet, there is a practical set of tools, habits, and skills that can make teachers increasingly effective—and help them eradicate the perpetual feeling of being underwater and behind. And so was born the concept of The Together Teacher.

This book will not only teach you those critical organization skills but also provide you with tools, samples, and templates to support them. Throughout this book I feature many teachers at different stages in their careers, from a brand-new elementary teacher to an English teacher with twenty-plus years of experience. Some of the teachers I met once or twice in workshops or came to know through single thought-provoking conversations. Others I have had long-standing relationships with and know every detail of their lives. No matter how long you've taught, these Together Teachers will help you become a stronger and more organized planner.

HOW THIS BOOK IS ARRANGED

As we enter our second decade of delivering Together Teacher Trainings, we've updated our thinking and reorganized the second edition of the book in several different ways.

■ Because Togetherness is a journey—not a destination—we thought a better road map to implementation would make it feel less daunting. Hence, the *Twelve Months to Togetherness* concept. I begin with the tools that will have the most positive impact, and I encourage you to introduce just one new thing a month—and to evaluate if you even need it as you go along.

■ Look out for specific callouts for certain readers, like new teachers, teacher-leaders, or specials teachers. By no means does this book include callouts for every single variety of teacher out there, but there are some groups with special needs or challenges we've tried to highlight.

■ At the start of many chapters, you'll notice rubrics to assess where you are with each tool, as well as suggestions for differentiated starting points depending on the results of your assessment. You will also find end-of-chapter follow-up and practice activities.

■ We've included new chapters about planning, grading, communications, Student Togetherness, and event planning.

■ All online materials mentioned can now be found at http://www.wiley.com/go/togetherteacher. No more CDs to fiddle with!

This book is designed to help you deliver better results for your students and to make your important work more sustainable. I also share tips on how to adapt the tools to meet your particular work style and preferences. Most teachers build their own Together Teacher Systems as they read, starting with how to manage time, To-Dos, thoughts, and notes—and moving into how to juggle email, organize space, and deal with papers.

We have organized this text into the following five sections:

Introduction You are in it!

Part One: Together Your Time Time is a finite resource. It is all too common for our ideas, ambitions, and deadlines to come into conflict with the limited amount of time that life realistically allows. In the chapters in this initial section, I help you create your Ideal Week Template, track your time, and figure out how best to use the hours we all have in any given week. We'll use four practical tools to manage your time, track your To-Dos, and capture your thoughts and brainstorms.

Part Two: Together Your Space, Stuff, and Students Now that our time is all set, we move into our space. For many of us, working from home was foisted upon us during the COVID-19 years; some of us loved it, but many of us didn't. Regardless, we'll zoom in here on our workspace, communications, and Student Togetherness.

Part Three: Together Your Teaching Now we turn to the external environment. Emails, papers, classroom supplies, and student backpacks can bring either calm or chaos into our classrooms. In these chapters I share ways Together Teachers set up expectations and routines for themselves and their classrooms.

Part Four: Together Your Team In this section, we navigate team planning and meetings, school-based events, and extracurricular activities (Science fairs! Spelling bees!).

Conclusion In the book's final section, we'll test how your organization system will hold up under the stresses of daily teaching life and discuss ways to slowly implement the tools and habits introduced throughout the book.

Do I subscribe to a particular system, tool, or school of thought? Although I have opinions about EVERYTHING, I care most that your system is effective for *you*, and I'm indifferent about the exact tools you use to get there. I'm not here to force you to part with your paper planner or make you switch to an entirely electronic system. I promise to help you create and customize your OWN personal organization system.

FAQ: SHOULD MY TOGETHER TEACHER SYSTEM BE PAPER BASED OR ELECTRONIC?

Oh, the great debate! Paper versus Technology! Too much information is still kept in dusty file cabinets, there are still too many students who turn in handwritten five-paragraph essays, and in most family meetings it would still not be culturally acceptable to position your laptop between you and your students' parents. Increasingly, however, teachers are relying on iPads, notebook computers, Androids, and other gadgets to stay organized. Throughout the book and on my website (updated regularly through my blog), I recommend many helpful tech tools.

HOW TO USE THIS BOOK

You can read this book individually in one fell swoop (there are jokes! Fun! Encouragement), read a chapter per month, or just target the areas you need as you need them. Regardless of how you choose to read the book, you will want to engage with the content as you go. Below, we have outlined a few ways to interact along the way!

Follow these steps to create your own complete personal organization system:

- **Choose your Together Teacher System.** It could be a small binder, a beloved planner, a notebook with sections, a clipboard, a discbound notebook, or a tablet.

- **Use the Reader Reflection Guide.** Visit the Wiley website and download the free *Together Teacher Reader Reflection Guide*, which contains the learning objectives, reflection questions, key summaries, and next steps for each chapter. As you read, keep the Reader Reflection Guide by your side and make notes about each chapter. You can answer the reflection questions, reflect on your own habits, and select the tools that best match your needs and preferences.

■ **Check out other resources on the website.** It is full of Together Teacher sample templates for you to personalize, and other great resources. This process is really about customizing your own personal organization system, so I encourage you to start testing the templates and adapting them to meet your own specific needs.

■ **Explore the other resources on our own website,** www.thetogethergroup.com. You can also find us on Facebook at The Together Group, and on Instagram as @together_teacher.

Materials to Have on Hand as You Read

■ A writing tool and the Reader Reflection Guide

■ Access to the Internet to check out our Together templates on the Wiley website

■ Any current organizational tools you already use, such as planners, notebooks, Post-its, etc. Gather 'em all up! If you are beginning your Togetherness journey from scratch, you may want to grab a binder or some place to organize your various tools.

■ A computer or laptop if you are more digitally inclined or your school uses a digital calendar

■ Any pieces of paper you are lugging around with you in any folders

■ If you are so inclined, Post-it Notes, washi tape, and all the Flair pens in the world

And before we jump into all of the things, I want to pause and ask you why are you here? What will Togetherness GET you? No one needs to be organized just to be organized. Togetherness has to serve a larger purpose. Which leads me to ask you, What is your Togetherness intention?

Take a moment, a yoga-class moment if you will, and consider your Togetherness intention. In the examples provided, you will see the words "Balance," "Cheer," and "Ready."

These teachers believed Togetherness would help them achieve these things. So, go deep with me here.

PS Your intentions can change over various seasons of your life!

Like trying to live a healthier lifestyle (and isn't that on *everyone's* New Year's resolution list?!), getting organized is a process. No one *arrives* after just reading one book. You will find that some habits are easier to adopt than others and that some days we slip and rely on our old Post-it Note habits and on others we go on strict efficiency frenzies. Being organized is a learned skill, and, as with any other skill, takes time to become a habit. Throughout this book you will hear from teachers who have balanced their lives while remaining effective instructors; they've have paced their work to be sustainable for the long term.

I look forward to joining you on our journey. Let's begin with some vision-questing: Designing Your Ideal Week.

PART 1

Together Your Time

CHAPTER 1

Create an Ideal Week—And Build in That Self-Care!

As dedicated teachers we will always work long hours, but it *can* get easier. If you're intentional about how you use your time each week, more minutes will materialize. It may sound bananas, but as someone who taught and who has worked with thousands of teachers—from the most novice to the most experienced—I know it is possible to balance the professional with the personal. There are teachers who plan and execute awesome lessons and find time to train for a marathon. It requires discipline and diligence—and may not feel natural at first—but it will increase your effectiveness and make your life easier. I promise.

It's easy to fall back on available excuses: "My day is just planned for me by someone else," and "I have no free moments for the entire day." This is true: for the most part our days *are* dictated by others' demands. That said, there are large chunks of time (before and after school, during preparation periods and hallway transitions) when all of the other work outside of executing excellent lessons can get done. As Nilda V., a middle school English teacher, says, "There are a lot of distractions to the main 90% of my job—which is to design and execute excellent instruction every day. The massive amount of information that comes my way can easily take my eye off the main goal, and anything that can streamline [my work] can only help kids." We assume professionals know how to plan ahead, get organized, and sort through the daily deluge. And we assume that some people are born magically organized and that it's a lost cause for others. I'm here to tell you that organization is a learned skill that can fundamentally help you focus on the main 90% of your job that Nilda mentions.

In this chapter, you will self-reflect on your current organization systems, design an Ideal Week, and create a Self-Care Plan. This chapter is deliberately designed to be reflective and visionary. I promise the nitty-gritty stuff is right around the bend.

COMPONENTS OF A GREAT TOGETHER TEACHER SYSTEM.

Now that you have a clear view of your strengths and growth areas, let's consider *how* you will get there. Remember the Trapper Keeper you had in third grade? The one covered in Lisa Frank and Tonka Truck stickers? PS If you have NO IDEA what I'm talking about, please head immediately to YouTube. There was a *reason* you loved that thing so much. All of your spelling lists, homework assignments, field trip permission slips, pens and pencils, and classwork were in *one* neat place.

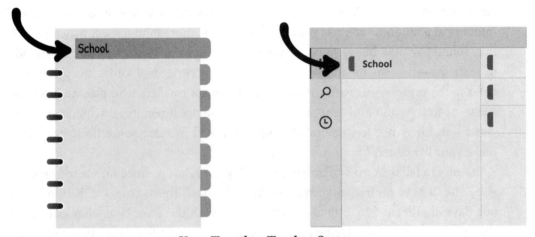

Your Together Teacher System

The problem is that most of us have not built an "adult" version of the Trapper Keeper. Instead we've allowed our organization system to spread out across pieces of paper, electronic notebooks, real notebooks, email inboxes, and real and electronic Post-it Notes. As you read each chapter of this book, I want you to keep the concept of the Trapper Keeper front and center in your mind. Although I'm not asking you to keep an *actual* Trapper Keeper, I am asking you to work toward clearly articulating each component of your organization system. For some of you that may be a one-inch binder containing all of your materials in hard copy; for others that may be a clipboard and a paper To-Do list; and for others that may be an iPhone. Throughout the rest of this book, I refer to the total system as your *Together Teacher System*.

As I ask you to select the tools that work best for you, keep in mind that I don't have a preference for what brand or medium you choose. However, to be effective and airtight, your system MUST:

- **Be portable.** Many of your To-Dos come flying in when you are on an innocent walk to the restroom. Whatever you use to stay organized, be sure it can be on you at all times as you move through your day. This means if you carry an iPhone you either have to wear clothing with pockets, carry a purse or wear a fanny pack (my favorite!), or wear an apron with big pockets. This also means that a fat two-inch binder is unlikely to work.

- **Be readily accessible.** If one of your colleagues stops you in the teachers' lounge and asks you to share a resource, I want you to have a handy place to immediately write down that request so you can be sure to follow up. For many people, paper entry is faster, but for others, entering a task into their smartphone works equally well. Whatever your weapon, make it swift and simple.

- **Quickly capture stuff.** Your Together Teacher System needs literal space in which you can grab the incoming work and immediately put it where it needs to go rather than recording different things across email drafts, notebooks, or pieces of scrap paper shoved in your pocket. For many teachers, this place is a pouch or folder they constantly carry.

As you venture on in your journey to create and customize your personal and classroom organization system, we will check your selection of tools against the components listed here.

READER REFLECTION

- **What tools or habits do you currently employ to stay organized?**
- **What already works well?**
- **Where do you need to improve?**

DESIGN YOUR IDEAL WEEK

Before we get into the details, it is important that you establish how you would *ideally* spend your time in any given week. When I have worked with teachers who are struggling, the first questions I ask them are, "What work do you have to do?" "Where is your time going?"

and "Ideally, where would you like it to go?" Many of them are not able to answer that last question. The following exercise will force you to consider how you would *ideally* like to spend your time each week. It's all you've got; let's spend it well!

Let's consider what your Ideal Week could look like. The idea here is that you want to have a philosophical, big-picture view of your time so you can manage your calendar—before your calendar manages *you*! Julie Morgenstern, author of *Time Management from the Inside Out* (who started her career organizing *stuff*!), says it well: "The time you have in a day, week, or month is like the space in the top of your closet: only a certain number of things can fit in it."

As you consider your Ideal Week, think about the following questions.

READER REFLECTION:

- When would you ideally go to sleep and wake up?

- When are you teaching and when are your preparation periods?

- What things must you do each week at a certain time, for example, student attendance submissions?

- What meetings or events occur regularly, for example, staff meetings and coaching sessions?

- What things must you do each week at a time of your choosing, such as grading or planning?

- When do you like to deal with communications like parent emails or student text messages?

- What are some personal priorities that would enhance your week, such as exercise, spiritual practice, and time with friends?

- When are you ideally *not* working (e.g. Saturdays or after 6 p.m. on weeknights)?

- What is something you *wish* you were better at planning?

- When is your energy highest? Lowest?

- When, if at all, do you find yourself procrastinating?

- What are some personal things you wish you had more time for?

- What do you find yourself never, ever getting done?

Now let's get more specific. We are going to review how MaryKate H., a middle school teacher in Virginia, plans her Ideal Week. Please note that this model was created at the beginning of the pandemic. As you review MaryKate's model (see Figure 1.1), consider the following questions:

■ When does she plan?

■ When does she grade?

■ When does she do personal routine activities, such as cooking, cleaning, and commuting?

■ When is she not working?

MaryKate's Ideal Week

As you can see, MaryKate's Ideal Week is very, very full. Here is what she did to build it:

■ **Set boundaries**—She put in the times her alarm goes off in the morning and her lights go out at night. These ensure that she is operating with the maximum amount of sleep she needs to teach well.

■ **Inserted her appointments**—teaching, grade-level meetings, schoolwide professional development, and so on—along with each meeting's time commitments.

■ **Added work time**—when she would do her lesson planning, grading, and classroom materials preparation. This scheduling allows some relief from feeling like she is *always* grading, planning, and copying—and helps maximize her limited prep time.

■ **Added buffer times**—such as showering and prepping for the day, and left some unscheduled time for not working or for doing whatever she felt like doing.

■ **Built in family time**—to work with her own school-aged daughters, walk the dog, and work out!

To be clear, MaryKate will not follow this plan to the letter each week. It simply gives her insight into when, ideally, she would accomplish all the work she has on her plate in a given week. Although you may feel that mapping out your time restricts you, I believe that this high degree of planning actually allows you to be *more* flexible. For example, one night a friend asked MaryKate to meet up at a park Wednesday evening with the kids. Although MaryKate had planned to listen to an audio book with her kids, she did a switcheroo and moved that to Thursday to take advantage of beautiful weather that Wednesday evening.

	Monday	Tuesday	Wednesday	Thursday	Friday	Saturday	Sunday
Super early							
6:00 am	workout meditate	workout meditate	workout meditate	workout meditate	workout meditate	workout meditate	walk dog
7:00	coffee shower dress make bed	coffee shower dress make bed	coffee shower dress make bed	coffee shower dress make bed	coffee shower dress make bed	walk dog	coffee shower dress make bed breakfast prep for day
8:00	breakfast prep for day	breakfast prep for day	breakfast prep for day	breakfast prep for day	breakfast prep for day	workout meditate	
9:00	online instruction		online instruction	online instruction	online instruction	coffee shower dress make bed breakfast prep for day	
10:00	student questions/ grading/ planning	team meeting	record/post next week's lessons	student questions/ grading/ planning	team meeting		
11:00	work with Maura	team leaders	work with Maura	work with Maura	finish grading; parent com- munication; prep for conferences		church
12:00 pm	work with Molly	email/student questions/ grading/planning	work with Molly	work with Molly			

Time							
1:00	lunch/games/read	lunch/games/read	lunch/games/read	lunch/games/read	lunch/games/read	family house clean (e/o week); family project time (e/o week)	food prep for SoCal
2:00	online instruction	online instruction	online instruction	online instruction	online conferences		
3:00							
4:00	walk dog	email	walk dog	meet w/ myself	close out the week		
5:00	prep dinner	walk dog	prep dinner (piano)	walk dog	neighbor time		
6:00	dinner	prep dinner	dinner	prep dinner			
7:00	clean-up/showers	dinner	clean-up/showers	dinner	pizza night		
8:00	family time: read	family time: shows	family time: audiobook	family time: games	family time: movie		
9:00	girls to bed; unwind	girls to bed; unwind	girls to bed; unwind	girls to bed; unwind	girls to bed; unwind		
10:00	bedtime	bedtime	bedtime	bedtime	bedtime		
11:00	sleeping	sleeping	sleeping	sleeping	sleeping		

Figure 1.1 MaryKate's Ideal Week

Kate's Ideal Week

Let's peek at a second model, an elementary school teacher, Kate M. We are going to block out how Kate, a new teacher, would ideally spend her time. As you review Kate's Ideal Week Template (see Figure 1.2), consider the following questions:

- When does she plan?

- When does she grade?

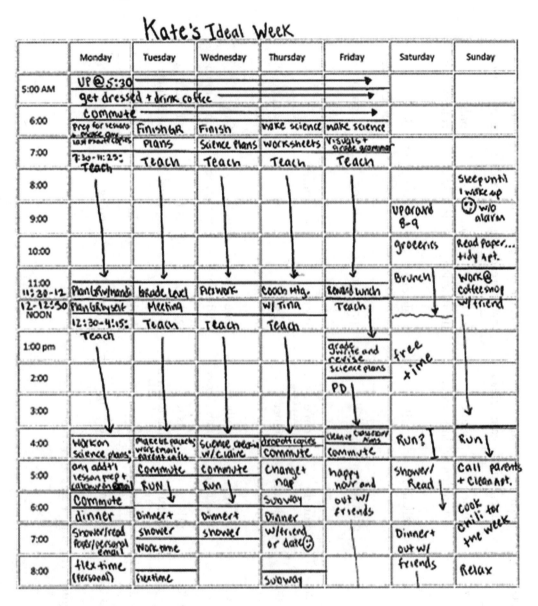

Figure 1.2 Kate's Ideal Week

■ When does she do personal routine activities, such as cooking, cleaning, and commuting?

■ When is she not working?

As you can see, Kate's Ideal Week Template is also very, very full. Similar to MaryKate, she set boundaries, added her work time, buffer time, and personal time! By knowing roughly what she would accomplish (or not accomplish) each evening, Kate could take advantage of opportunities that came her way.

The same can be true for you! By becoming extremely aware of how you use your time, and what you really need it for, you actually gain a great degree of flexibility and relief. When something unexpected comes up, you can relax because you know you have time set aside later in the week to deal. You can be more agile and spontaneous when you're aware of the work on your plate and how much time it will take to complete it.

BUILD YOUR OWN IDEAL WEEK

Let's build your own Ideal Week using the checklist. Do not worry about being very specific right now. Concern yourself only with including these essential components on your calendar as you complete the Ideal Week Template in Figure 1.3:

■ *Physical needs:* sleep, exercise, eating.

■ *Scheduled time:* teaching, lunch duty, staff meetings.

■ *Discretionary work time:* preparation periods, before and after school time.

■ *Big work (requires a high level of focus and brainpower):* lesson planning, grading papers, writing a weekly parent update.

■ *Little work (can be done during lower energy times):* entering attendance data, answering short emails.

■ *Discretionary personal time:* relaxing at home, reading, visiting a museum, exercise.

■ *Emergency buffer:* It's unavoidable—emergencies happen in schools. Save time here for urgent phone calls and the like.

Conflicts will inevitably arise between what you hope to accomplish and what you absolutely must get done. Conflicts will also arise between the ideal—watching the latest streaming binge with your partner and friends—and the real—the work you need to do to meet this week's deadlines.

All of this is to be expected. What's most important is that you provide yourself with a clear picture of your Ideal Week before you enter the weekly shuffle. You may not be able to make it to the gym three times because of meetings before and after school, but you'll be

	Monday	Tuesday	Wednesday	Thursday	Friday	Saturday	Sunday
Super early							
6:00 am							
7:00							
8:00							
9:00							
10:00							
11:00							
12:00 pm							
1:00							
2:00							
3:00							
4:00							
5:00							
6:00							
7:00							
8:00							
9:00							
10:00							
11:00							
Other Notes							

Figure 1.3   Ideal Week Template

aware of the choices and compromises you're making as you chug along, and you'll have a better idea of where you can fit things in at other times.

I'm Not a Dictator, But There Are Some Rules

Remember how I said we're creating a personalized organization system to meet *your* specific needs? Well, we are, *except* for a few critical commandments that must be followed. This is no matter whether you decide to keep an index card in your shirt pocket (yes, this was done by someone I used to date, and it proved highly effective for prioritization), an incredibly detailed paper-based planner, or a carefully synchronized Google Calendar.

Enter *The Rules*.

Rule 1: Get everything in one place. People tend to use too many tools at once: we have one notebook for meetings, another one for ideas, an online checklist for tracking tasks, as well as one or two electronic calendars. We have an abundance of systems, but this actually works against us. As much as you possibly can, keep your tools in as few locations as possible (ideally, one!). This means everything should sync to your smartphone or everything should be in one folder. You don't want to carry around a phone, laptop, two folders, one clipboard, and two legal pads to deal with all of your To-Dos. It's just too much to keep track of and things will inevitably fall through the cracks.

 Reader Reflection: In how many places do your To-Dos currently live?

Rule 2: Take it with you. You are on your feet in your classroom and moving through the hallways of your school all day. Whatever tools you use to stay organized, you must have them on you at all times. Whether you're in a staff meeting, parent conference, or classroom, you want to be able to record any To-Dos that fly your way in the moment. I recommend carrying no more than two tools. For some, this may be a smartphone and a clipboard. For others it may be a binder and a notebook.

 Reader Reflection: When another teacher asks you to do something as you walk down the hall, where do you currently record your next step?

Rule 3: Write everything down. I want you to write everything down. This way, you can empty your brain and focus on the hard work of teaching your students rather than wasting energy and time trying to remember and re-remember what you need to do. This is nothing revolutionary, but this concept was made popular by David Allen, author of *Getting Things Done*. I don't want you to experience that dreaded feeling in the middle of teaching when you realize, "Holy *&%, I forgot to [insert your own missing deadline

story here]." I don't want you to forget that brilliant idea for improving a unit in the coming year. I don't want you to lose credibility with your students because you promised them an extra-credit assignment but then forgot all about it.

READER REFLECTION:

- **What To-Dos still live in your head?**

- **When you have an idea for a colleague, what do you do with it?**

Rule 4: Make it bite size. Many To-Dos get stuck because it is not explicitly clear what needs to be done. To avoid a To-Do traffic jam, break down tasks as much as possible. Instead of writing "field trip" on your list, write "Call bus company to make field trip reservations." It may make your To-Do list feel longer, but ultimately it will articulate an aim for those five extra minutes you squeeze out of your prep period. David Allen calls this making To-Dos "actionable." This will help you avoid procrastination and make strides toward bigger, more important projects.

Reader Reflection: Think of one To-Do currently on your list (or in your head!) and consider how you would break it down into steps.

Rule 5: Keep like items with like items. A lot of old-fashioned To-Do lists fail because people keep big To-Dos, small To-Dos, short-term To-Dos, long-term To-Dos, and personal and professional To-Dos jumbled together in one place. Though this gets everything written down (see Rule 3), it is far from ideal because it's so hard to scan your list and pick out the right thing to do at the right time.

Reader Reflection: What changes can you make to your current system to distinguish between short term (today!) and long term (in a few months . . .) To-Dos?

Rule 6: Create a trigger for what you put away. Although it is easy to innocently set down a stack of papers on your desk or file an email carefully in a folder, remember that anything you "put away" has a way of never coming back to you. If you want to file papers, emails, or other items that truly require action, jot yourself a note about where you put those papers or emails and when you plan to return to them. Then you won't find yourself scrambling through the pile of mail at home looking for the wedding RSVP card or using the search feature of your email inbox in creative ways for that article you *had* to read!

 Reader Reflection: What papers, emails, or other items do you have buried on your desk or in a file cabinet that you wish you had time to return to?

Rule 7: Mind your energy levels. I am a morning person. To an annoying extreme. To the point where in college I used to call my girlfriends at 6 a.m. on Sunday mornings and ask if they were ready for brunch. Unsurprisingly, my inquiry was always met with a dial tone. I am beyond useless, however, after 8 p.m.

Have you ever tried to write a unit plan when you were incredibly tired? Or found yourself grading relatively simple student work when you were most alert? Save the smaller, mindless To-Dos, such as making charts and posters, for when your brain is fried. If you know you cannot get anything done right after lunch duty, reserve that time for making copies so that your low-energy time is not entirely wasted. Do the big stuff, like planning and data analysis, when you are most awake and energetic.

 ## READER REFLECTION:

■ **When are your energy levels highest? Lowest?**

■ **What times of day are you most productive? Least productive?**

■ **What tasks are good fits for each time?**

Rule 8: No tool is forever. Your job will change constantly. The organization system that worked in your last job or in college is unlikely to hold up under the demands of being a teacher. If you are just starting out in this profession, you may have graduate school or certification responsibilities to juggle. If you are further along in your career, you may have to balance department-head duties with your teacher-coaching obligations. Regardless of the responsibilities on your plate, you must consistently adjust your system to meet your ever-evolving roles and responsibilities.

 Reader Reflection: What organization systems have you already tried? What has worked about them? Not worked?

Rule 9: Own your schedule. There are certain things you have to do every day, week, and month. They should not routinely take you by surprise and

force you to stay up until 2 a.m. to complete them (let's save that scary situation for *real* emergencies, which should become few and far between). Grading, planning, and progress reports are known events. Why not reserve the time for them now? This will ensure that the known work doesn't creep up on you, and it will help you pace yourself to meet looming deadlines, such as report card completion or unit plan writing.

Reader Reflection: How/When do you currently reserve time for those big projects you *know* are coming, like progress reports or the next field trip?

Rule 10: Pause to plan. To maintain a high-functioning organization system, you will need to take a little time each week and each month to define what needs to be done in the weeks ahead. This may feel unnecessary at first, but it will ensure that you know what deadlines, personal activities, and meetings you have coming up. Most important, it will allow you to feel in control of your time instead of at the mercy of it!

READER REFLECTION:

■ **How much do you currently let yourself pause to figure out what you have to do before you start doing it?**

■ **When might be a good time to do this during your day or week?**

It is important to remember that it is these rules, not the concrete tools we are about to practice using, that are the fundamental keys to becoming a Together Teacher. In fact, over-reliance on a tool may give you a false sense of security. Sometimes teachers will come to me and say, "Maia, I tried everything you told me and bought what you said at Staples, but it just isn't working!" Often it is not the *tool* that is weak but the *habits* that need adjusting.

Lest you think I'm entirely about rules, fear not! We need to add in some self-care!

LET'S TOSS IN SOME SELF-CARE AND STRESS MANAGEMENT

I know, I know. The term self-care might be too buzzy for you. Or maybe you are all about it. But regardless of your feelings, I think we can all agree—especially during the pandemic—some semblance of self-care is essential if we want to keep helping our students. If you naturally build it in for yourself, feel free to bypass this section entirely. But if you feel like you need to recenter, take a peek at the Teacher Self-Care Menu (Figure 1.4), designed by

Self-Care & Stress-Management Plan

What can you do to take care of your...

	What is it?	How often do you wish to do it?	How long might it take you?
Physical Health?			
Mental Health?			
Spiritual / Emotional Health?			
Intellectual / Professional Health? (keeping well while at work)			
Social Health? (connections to friends & family)			
Other?			

Figure 1.4   Marin's Self-Care Planning Template

the cowriter of this book, former teacher and principal, and current clinical social worker, Marin Smith.

Are you excited to draft your own? Me too! Let's look at some examples first.

SELF-CARE AND STRESS MANAGEMENT PLAN EXAMPLES

Everyone's Self-Care Plan will look a little different—and will change over time—but it is helpful to have a starting point. The following examples (see Figure 1.5) show how different this can look for individual teachers. Whether it is walking the dog, calling friends, or exercise, let's articulate what will help us most during stressful times.

Remember: self-care can be as big and bold as a vacation, a hike, a special date-night, or a shopping trip. But it can also be as small and as quiet as having a cup of tea upon arriving home, journaling, cuddling, hydrating, or reading. Creating a balanced plan for yourself, that includes activities both big and small, special treats as well as daily routines, is key.

Let's peek at one more example, in Figure 1.6.

When we plan out our self-care times explicitly and get clear with ourselves about how much we can accomplish and when, rather than waiting or hoping for the just right amount

Self-Care & Stress-Management Plan

Given what you've learned about your stressors, coping style, developmental needs and changes, and strategies for self-talk...
What can you do to take care of your...

	What is it?	How often do you wish to do it?	How long might it take you?
Physical Health?	Play Basketball	few times a week	an hour
	Walk Anthony's dog	every day	20 - 60 minutes
Mental Health?	Listen to music	every day	at least 3 hours
	Meet a new person/friend	once every few days	30 - 60 minutes
Spiritual / Emotional Health?	Talk with 1 FAM about my classroom	every day	15 - 30 minutes
Intellectual / Professional Health? (ing well while at work)	Read newspaper	few times a week	≈ 30 - 45 minutes
	Eating lunch away from school	every day	30 minutes
ocial Health? (ons to friends & family)			
Other?			

Figure 1.5   Self-Care Plan Example

of time to magically open up, self-care is MUCH more likely to happen. And we're MUCH more likely to feel more sustained, capable, and empowered—in all parts of our life.

READER REFLECTION: GO AHEAD AND ADD AT LEAST FOUR THINGS TO YOUR SELF-CARE PLAN.

■ Try to fill in at least four boxes in the "What Is It" column (you needn't fill in every section!)

■ Think about how often you *realistically* want to engage in each activity

■ Give yourself a clear estimate of how long each activity might take

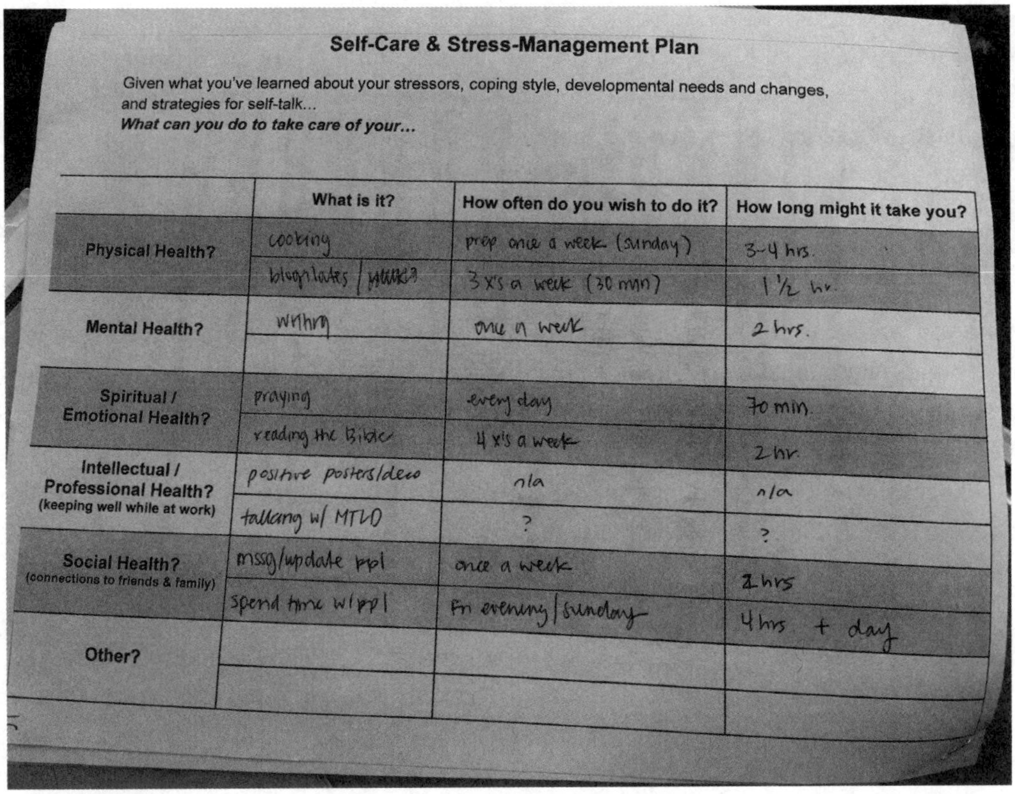

Figure 1.6   Self-Care Plan Example

It's important to remember that your Ideal Week and Self-Care Plan are dynamic tools, and they will change as your circumstances or priorities change. For example, everyone's Ideal Week pivots multiple times, mine included. And you've adjusted the ways you care for yourself and your families during the pandemic as well. Think about your Ideal Week and Self-Care Plan as the anchor you return to, adjust, and revise when the waters get choppy.

LET'S GET STARTED

Let's get started on your journey to becoming a more Together Teacher. Remember, our purpose is *not* to become an overscheduled robot who focuses only on their To-Do list all day and can never relax. Our goal is to give you a clear view of all of your work—big and small—and to create a system that supports you in synthesizing everything as it comes in.

As Gilbert C., a pre-K teacher, puts it, "When you start to look at your day a little differently, through the 'I have this amount of time, I could get something done' lens, it makes you more productive and more relaxed at the same time. I set deadlines for myself, and I reserve the last two to three hours per day for my girlfriend. I have literally blocked time for not working, and I force my schoolwork into the allotted time."

As you will see in the multiple examples throughout this book, careful planning of your time, organization of your To-Dos and stuff, and figuring out what simply can be done faster or at different times of the day can make you noticeably better at your job—and a lot less overwhelmed and stressed.

Let's get started with our first tool—the Weekly Worksheet—to give you a practical way to record your appointments, deadlines, and personal events.

And now we are moving on to the Together Tools in earnest. Hooray!

CHAPTER 2

A Week's Worth of Readiness: Create a Weekly Worksheet

SETTING THE SCENE

It's 4:30 p.m. on a Friday afternoon. Your kids have left the building (or virtual classroom!) and your fellow teachers are pressuring you to join them for a much-needed happy hour. You look at the bottomless pile of papers to grade and the incomplete lesson plans and think: *I'm exhausted, but there's no way I'm going to make progress on this stuff in an hour.* So you shove everything into your tote bag and pray you will get to it all on Sunday.

Now let's fast-forward to what typically happens to most of us. Sunday comes around and by the time you eat breakfast, go to the gym or spend time with your family (or both), do laundry, and shop for groceries, it is past 3:00 p.m. The tote bag taunts you from the corner of the living room. Eventually you open it and try to comb through its contents. You have no idea where to begin. It takes an hour just to sort everything into piles—papers to grade, scraps of paper with scribbled notes on them, grades that need to be recorded, agendas from staff meetings with notes scrawled across the page, and graphic organizers to copy for next week's lesson plans. Once you've sorted through everything, it's 5:30 p.m. By the looks of it, you still have about five more hours of work left and your alarm will go off at 5:15 a.m. tomorrow. For most teachers this is the weekly challenge: How on Earth do I get it all done?

This is not because you are doing anything wrong. For most of us teachers, our preparation periods allow us to take a breather, deal with an unexpected kid situation, or catch up on email. Given that prep periods are often the *only* bit of discretionary time within our professional day, it is a constant challenge to determine how to use them wisely. However, I would encourage all of us to think about that little chunk of time as an opportunity to get more done at school—so you can take less work home! As we get more specific and talk about how to prepare for a week, we'll be thinking together about how to maximize times like these so the Sunday Scaries are, well, less scary. The Weekly Worksheet is typically the tool we teach first during our in-person and online workshops because it will provide the most immediate positive impact on your week. Trust me, try it!

IN THIS CHAPTER, YOU WILL LEARN TO:

- ◾ Identify and plan time for your professional and personal priorities
- ◾ Plot your time and To-Dos in advance of the week
- ◾ Determine your best use of time based on energy levels and physical location
- ◾ Capture unforeseen To-Dos and adjust accordingly

This process will help you plan ahead, get stuff done, and capture incoming work. We'll discuss how to take your appointments, teaching time, and meetings, *plus* your To-Dos, and put them all in one place: on your fancy-schmancy list for—you guessed it—*this week only!*

Weekly Worksheet: An hour-by-hour view of your time and To-Dos for the week ahead.

There are probably lots of things you instinctively do to get ready for a week of teaching. You plan lessons, make photocopies, create charts, make phone calls, and so on.

Preparing your Weekly Worksheet is not about *doing* the work; it is about *defining* the work and planning your week so that you can maximize your time and *make the best choices* to move things ahead. For *most* teachers, this requires a *highly* portable, always accessible, and constantly reviewed tool that gives a view of your time and your To-Dos.

Reader Reflection: Rate your current capacity to maintain a mission-supportive, effective, and efficient balance between your time, your big picture priorities, and the urgent and unplanned To-Dos that inevitably arise.

0	1	2	3
Priorities?! Ha! I have no time for priorities. Every day is like a game of whack-a-mole and I'm just trying to stay afloat. My To-Do list just grows and grows. I keep a calendar or a To-Do list, but not both; or, I don't use either.	I'm not really sure of my big priorities but I feel like the work I am doing probably supports them. I have a To-Do list but I'm never really sure *when* I'll actually get tasks done; I just hope I do!	I have some sense of my priorities, but my work toward them depends on what else comes up that week. I keep a clear schedule and use a To-Do list regularly but the two are not always in synch. Sometimes I have time I'm not sure what to do with, and other times my To-Dos stay undone because of my schedule or how it changes.	My big priorities are clear to me, and I have time to work toward them each week. I plan my week with both a schedule and a To-Do list, with a clear picture of what I'll do and when. When emergencies arise, I am prepared to shift gears and rearrange tasks.

- If you rate yourself a 3, peruse the Together Teacher examples to see if there any ideas you want to steal or modifications you wish to make. You can also check your system against the checklist later in the chapter to ensure it's totally up to standard!

- If you rate yourself a 2, start with the Weekly Worksheet sections on Teacher Examples and read on to learn more about improving your system to better align your time with your To-Dos. Focus your attention on the practice exercises before synching up on your systems.

- 1 or 0? You've come to the right place! Read on!

Before we dive into the nuts and bolts of this chapter, I want you to take a quick unscientific quiz to get at your general orientation of What-ness and When-ness. Taking this three-question "quiz" will unearth habits and build self-awareness to help you discover your natural orientation AND what your environment may require of you. We can then use this information to select the Weekly Worksheet model that will work best for you.

Quick Quiz: What-er or When-er?

1 **When you need to grade a huge stack of papers or review a ton of exit tickets, do you:**

    a. Write on your To-Do list: Complete Grading

    b. Create a calendar appt to complete grading (e.g. Wednesday afternoon from 4 to 6 p.m.)

2 **Are you more likely to be overheard saying:**

    a. "I never have enough time to get everything done!"

    b. "I can't change my plans because I need to get something done then."

3 **Would your colleagues describe you as:**

    a. Flexible but overcommitted

    b. Reliable but rigid

What-er and When-er Answer Key

	Mostly answer a's? You're a What-er!	Mostly answer b's? You're a When-er!
Definition	What-ers are more oriented toward their lists. They prefer choice in how they spend their time, and they have a strong need for flexibility.	When-ers prefer to lock their To-Dos into time slots. They consider their energy levels and physical locations when planning.
Benefits	Flexibility Optimism Helpful	Reliable Organized Account for time and place
Drawbacks	Overcommitted Tasks can take too long to get done	Lack flexibility Can become flustered when things go off track

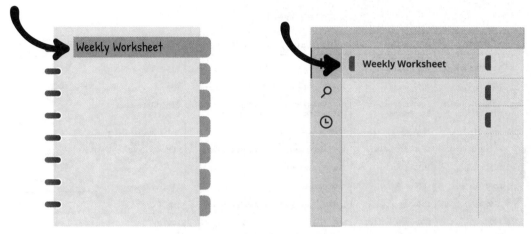

Your Together Teacher System

Regardless of your overall orientation toward What-ness and When-ness and your propensity for paper versus digital, let's pull out that Together Teacher System and create our first section.

A CLOSER LOOK: WHAT IS A WEEKLY WORKSHEET?

One thing I want to be very clear about is this: the *process* matters more than the product. Depending on whether you are biased toward paper products or electronic systems, your final outcome may look very different. Regardless of tool, you'll go through the same thinking process each week. Your Weekly Worksheet should allow you to do the following:

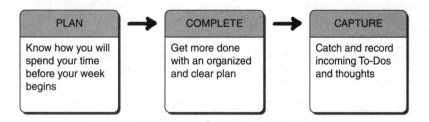

Let's start by examining common features of all Weekly Worksheets.

The template in Figure 2.1 is designed to give you a full view of your work each week—your time mapped against your To-Dos. Let's walk through the specific pieces of this template.

Sections of a Weekly Worksheet

Your Weekly Worksheet will contain the following criteria:

1 **Names Priorities Clearly.** This is where you fill in the priorities for the week for both work and home; these are high-level priorities, not specific To-Dos.

Anna's Week 10.25

	Monday 25	Tuesday 26	Wednesday 27	Thursday 28	Friday 29	Sat 30 Sun
①		6:45-7:10 Coach A/S				SATURDAY
	7:15-7:30 Arrival	7:15-7:30 Arrival	7:15-7:30 Arrival	7:15-7:30 Arrival	7:15-7:30 Arrival	9:00 Prospect
	7:30 Tardies	7:30 Tardies	7:30 Absences	7:30 Absences	7:30 Morning Circle Prep.	18 miles
	8:00-9:10 Attendance	8:00-9:10 Attendance	8:00-9:10 Attendance	8:00-9:10 Attendance	8:00-9:10 Attendance	
	9:15-10:05 GR	9:15-10:05 GR	9:15-10:05 GR	9:15-10:05 GR	9:15-10:05 GR	
	10:05 Math LP -finish-	10:05 ▓▓ GR	10:05 ▓▓-GR check GR LPs	10:05 JK-DJ	10:55 Lunch w/ 1st Gr.	5:00 Teacher U Graduation
	11:15-11:35 Recess	11:15-11:35 Recess	11:15-11:35 Recess	11:15-11:35 Recess	MATH 11:55 ▓▓▓, Edgar	9:00 Halloween
	11:35 Lunch	11:35 Lunch	11:35 Math w/ ▓▓	11:35 Lunch	Zion, ▓▓, Johaara, Destiny	
	12:00 Culture Blast	12:00 CB	12:00 Lunch	12:00 CB		SUNDAY
	12:30 ▓▓, ▓▓	12:30 ▓▓, ▓▓	12:30 ▓▓, ▓▓	12:30 ▓▓, ▓▓	12:45 Read Aloud	
	1:00	1:00 ▓▓ - Math	1:00 CB	1:00 ▓▓ - math	1:00 CB	12:00 Rock Climb
	1:50 Lunch	1:50 Lunch	1:50 Lunch	1:50 Lunch	2:30 PD	▓▓, ▓▓
	2:30 Math	2:30 Math	2:30 Math	2:30 Math	MAKE-UP	
	3:35 Issa/Ron-Math	3:35 ▓▓/▓▓-Math	3:35 ▓▓/▓▓-Math	3:35 Issa/Ron-Math	▓▓	
	4:00 Elijah P-Writing	4:00 ▓▓ P-Writing	4:00 ▓▓ P-Writing	4:00 ▓▓ P-Writing	▓▓	
	4:20-5:00 TLM SNACKS	4:30-5:30 GLM	4:20-5 Coaching Pod		▓▓ ▓▓	
② DEADLINES	SEND GIFT ☑		Send LPs ☑ ★★★ Permission Slip ☑	★★★ CALL MOM ★ MOM'S B-DAY ☑ ★★★ ★	Call parent chaperones ☑	
	5 miles ☑	5 weights ☑ miles ☑	8 miles ☑	5 weights ☑ miles ☑	2 miles ☑	

Lesson Plans		Materials to Prepare		Emails/Calls/Follow-Ups	
Math ☑		Parent letter -Culture Night ☑		Ms. ▓▓ - reading ☑	
MM ☑				Ms. ▓▓ - tardies ☑	
GR ☑		Permission Slip ☑		Ms. ▓▓ - attendance ☑	
				Ms. ▓▓ - stay after ☑	
				▓▓ - Garden Guerillas ☑	
		Saturday ☺ -oreo truffles - dip/pepper pumpkin bread - veggies			

Errands/Home/Personal		People		MUST DO!	
		▓▓ - ▓		⊕ ⊕ ⊕ Run	
				⊕ ○ Weights	
		Thank You Notes- Dad		⊕ Speedwork	
		Erica			
		Emily			
Fresh Direct ☑		Coach			

Figure 2.1   Anna's Weekly Worksheet

WHAT IS A PRIORITY?

Great question! If improving your classroom culture is important for this week, that priority will land in this section. If hosting a bachelor party for a close friend is important personally, you will note this here too.

Later on, you'll write specific To-Dos associated with your priorities. For example, for the above priorities, this might sound like "Create a Student of the Week recognition system and criteria" or "Make dinner reservation."

The best way to come up with your priorities is to review your overall goals and simply close your eyes and ask yourself, "What could I do that would have the *highest* level of impact, both personally and professionally?"

The end goal is for your time and To-Dos to align with your priorities.

2) **Lets You Plan Ahead for the Week.** All good Weekly Worksheets include some kind of schedule where you write any appointments, meetings, and deadlines for the week.

3) **Shows All Time Commitments AND To-Dos.** It is important that we see our Time and To-Dos in a singular location. Too often our time commitments live in a calendar and our To-Dos live in a notebook, thus creating a situation in which our plan for the week lives in multiple locations.

4) **Includes Personal AND Professional.** Although it can be very tempting to keep your life and work entirely separate, there are many benefits to knowing what is for dinner tonight and when you have an after-hours work event.

5) **Captures Incoming Work.** Nothing about our work is bundled neatly. It comes at us at all times of day and in all directions. Whatever you use for your Weekly Worksheet, you will want to make sure it is with you at all times to catch that work on the fly.

Let's take a look at several examples of Together Teacher's Weekly Worksheets. We will look at What-ers, In-Between-ers, and When-ers. As you look at these samples, consider what your natural orientation is and what your school environment requires of you.

WEEKLY WORKSHEET EXAMPLES

In this section you will have a chance to see exactly how other Together Teachers plan for a week to really maximize every moment.

And if you want to jump right to it:

- If you are a paper person and a What-er, peek at Sam's Weekly Worksheet.

- If you are a make-your-own-Together-Template kind of human, check out Meghan.

- If you are a gentle "When-er," peek at Katie. She locks most of the To-Dos into time slots.

- If you are all digital and a serious When-er, jump to Laura.

With each example, feel free to keep this mini Weekly Worksheet checklist by your side to see how the model works!

Weekly Worksheet Checklist

Criteria of a Weekly Worksheet	Example
How are the priorities named?	
Is the entire week mapped out?	
Are Whats and Whens joined in one location?	
Are the professional and personal considered?	
Is there a place to capture To-Dos that "come up"?	

Sam's Weekly Worksheet

Sam B., a math teacher in Queens, shared the notebook What-er model shown in Figure 2.2 during the pandemic. Who loves notebooks? [my hand goes up!]. So portable, so full of possibility! Sam falls squarely in the What-er camp, but, but, but there is a little bit of WHEN sprinkled on the lists. For example, she lists when her work time is happening and what she will get done. Bonus points for tracking water intake too! Note that Sam creates the Weekly Worksheet by making a notebook page per day. No planning by the day around here!

Now, for my favorite part, the "10-Minute Quick Hits." Sam takes the time to list the "quicker" work (Figure 2.3). I think of this work as the equivalent of the thoughtless supermarket grab of the tempting stuff at the end of the aisles. Sure, it would be easy—and perhaps efficient—to just complete the quickies as they come to mind, but by carefully saving them for later, Sam can conserve her energy for bigger cognitive lifts for when she really needs it!

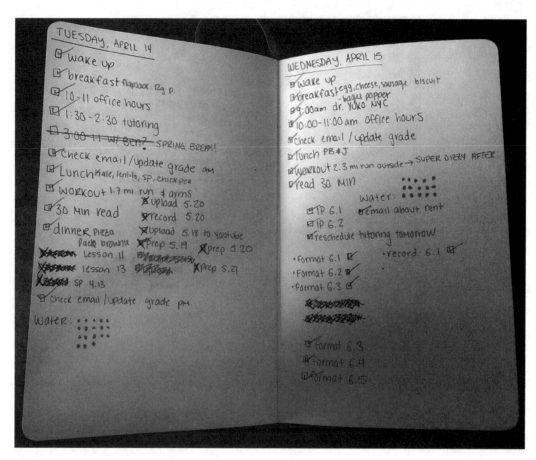

Figure 2.2 Sam's Weekly Worksheet

Weekly Worksheet Checklist

Criteria of a Weekly Worksheet	Example
How are the priorities named?	
Is the entire week mapped out?	
Are Whats and Whens joined in one location?	
Are the professional and personal considered?	
Is there a place to capture To-Dos that "come up"?	

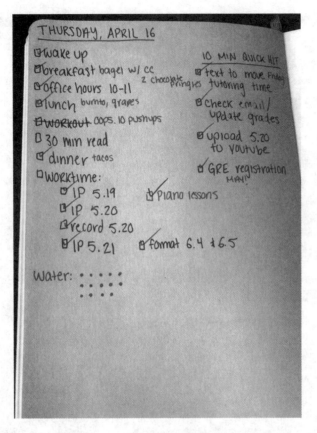

Figure 2.3 Sam's Weekly Worksheet – With Quick Hits!

 Reader Reflection: What is a benefit of using a notebook or other paper-based tool?

Meghan's Weekly Worksheet

Meghan, a teacher in White Plains, New York, took a slightly different approach and created a Weekly Worksheet (Figure 2.4) with preset Whens but left room to add in her Whats.

(If you want to build your own like Meghan, check out our free templates that accompany this book at http://www.wiley.com/go/togetherteacher.) I like to call this example "What-Leaning" or "What-Forward." In Meghan's case, she created a template that worked for her (note this is a pandemic model) and then added things as they came up. She took time each evening to reprioritize and "When" things up. We love a good contained Post-it Note to capture additional work!

Weekly Worksheet Checklist

Criteria of a Weekly Worksheet	Example
How are the priorities named?	
Is the entire week mapped out?	
Are Whats and Whens joined in one location?	
Are the professional and personal considered?	
Is there a place to capture To-Dos that "come up"?	

I love how Meghan includes a section to prompt her to glance ahead at the following week. And, of course, love those checkboxes!

 Reader Reflection: What is one benefit of being a bit more "What-y?"

Meghan's Action Plan

	Monday 4.13	Tuesday 4.14	Wednesday 4.15	Thursday 4.16	Friday 4.17
Notes					
8	8:30 Call Betsy				
9		9:00-10:30 Schoology Basics	Kinder GLM		
10					
11					
12				Reading Meeting	
1			1:30-3:00 iRead Webinar		
2					
3					
4					
5					
6					
To Do	□ daily work check □ list to contact	□ daily work check □ list to contact	□ daily work check □ list to contact	□ daily work check □ list to contact	□ daily work check □ list to contact

Monday To Do	Tuesday To Do	Wednesday To Do
□	□	□
□	□	□
□	□	□
□	□	□
□	□	□
□	□	□
□	□	□

Thursday To Do	Friday To Do	Next Week's Plans
□	□	K| □M □T □W □Th □F
□	□	1| □M □T □W □Th □F
□	□	2| □M □T □W □Th □F
□	□	3| □M □T □W □Th □F
□	□	4| □M □T □W □Th □F
□	□	5| □M □T □W □Th □F
□	□	EMT| □M □T □W □Th □F

Figure 2.4   Meghan's Weekly Worksheet: Before & After

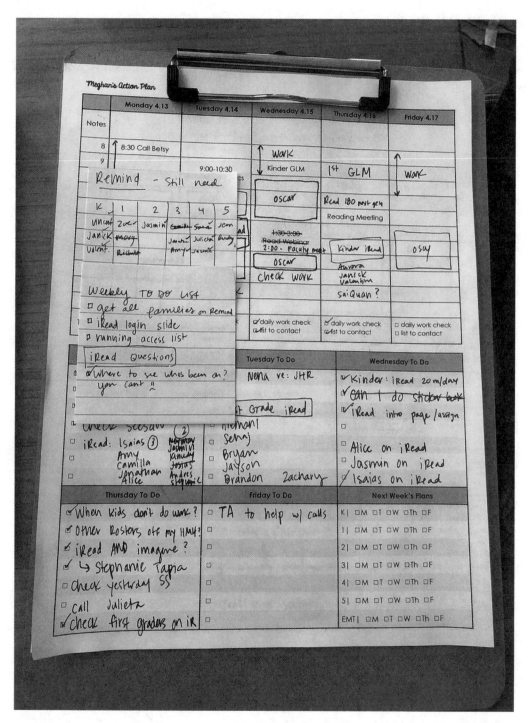

Figure 2.4   (*Continued*)

Drew's Weekly Worksheet

Drew, a teacher in Washington, DC, continues a hybrid What-When approach (Figure 2.5). He lists his priorities and he creates To-Dos associated with priorities. Let's review this model in more detail.

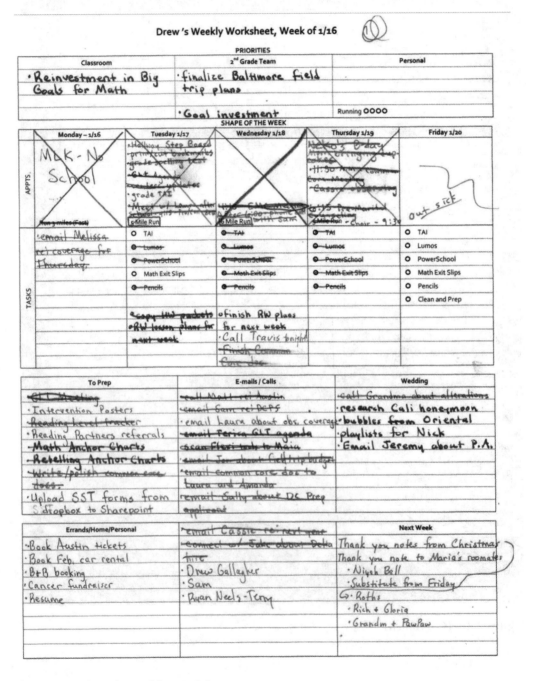

Figure 2.5 Drew's Weekly Worksheet

Weekly Worksheet Checklist

Criteria of a Weekly Worksheet	Example
How are the priorities named?	
Is the entire week mapped out?	
Are Whats and Whens joined in one location?	
Are the professional and personal considered?	
Is there a place to capture To-Dos that "come up"?	

What makes Drew's model awesome is:

- His priorities are named very clearly at the top (reminder: "Priorities" just means what is most important that week!).
- Much like Meghan, the recurring daily tasks are permanently part of Drew's Weekly Worksheet.
- He is actively engaged in crossing things off, moving items around, and adjusting on the fly!

Katie's Weekly Worksheet

Katie B., a teacher in Milwaukee, shifted even a bit more into When Territory, in Figure 2.6. She took her recurring To-Dos for the week and considered the time she actually had available to use. For most of us, this is before school, prep periods, lunch, and after school.

Weekly Worksheet Checklist

Criteria of a Weekly Worksheet	Example
How are the priorities named?	
Is the entire week mapped out?	
Are Whats and Whens joined in one location?	
Are the professional and personal considered?	
Is there a place to capture To-Dos that "come up"?	

Katie's Daily Planning Worksheet

	Monday	Tuesday	Wednesday	Thursday	Friday
Before School	☒ Do Now copies ☒ Post LPs ☒ Put up obj. ☐ M-Th reading copies ☒ Check for prog.	☐ Record + enter grades	☐ Correct + record R1	☐ Correct + record R2	☐ Correct + record R3
Lunch	☐ Fact practice copies for wk ☒ Email Robb about group ☒ Email group ☒ Email Kari - obs.	☐ Alphabetize assessments	☐ PDF recaps and travel docs for All-staff Conference	Lunch w/ Chaniya ✕	Lunch Bunch
Prep	☒ LW sheet ☐ Post vocab ☒ email to Kari ☐ Exit slips for wk ☒ SS + Writing copies	☐ Correct ☐ Assess packets	☐ Correct remaining work	☐ Reading LPs ☐ Writing LPs	☐ Reading copies ☐ AR
After School	☒ Desks ☒ Board ☒ Tutor ☐ Correct - SS - Reading (2) ☐ RTI Paperwork ☒ Class @ 5:30	☐ Staff meeting ☐ board ☐ desks ☐ Write Fri. Assessment	☐ Board ☐ Desks ☐ Tutor ☐ Check-in w/ Robert @ 5PM ☐ Reading LW	☐ Board ☐ Desks ☐ Tutor ☐ Class @ 5:30	☐ AR ☐ M-Th copies ☐ W Copies ☐ SS copies ☐ Principal Panel 5:30-6:30
Home	Relax + spend time w/ Ky ☐ Lesson visions for Annie	☐ Critical Incident Journal ☐ Email feedback ☐ email Lowe notes ☐ Main @ 7:30 ☐ Prep for Institute check-in ☐ Task 8.6	☐ Critical Incident Journal ☐ Email Bender	Thursday TV w/ Ky	☐ Drinks @ the Hamilton w/ Kourtney @ 9PM Relax!

Saturday: ☐ Summary statements	Sunday: ☐ Correct Fri Assessments
☐ Workout ☐ Clean apt. ☐ Research for paper ☐ Outline paper + write 1-2 pgs.	☐ Workout ☐ Finish + submit paper ☐ review portfolio

Figure 2.6 Katie's Weekly Worksheet

There are a few things I appreciate about Katie's Weekly Worksheet:

- Delineation between evenings doing school work and evenings relaxing

- Careful planning of before and after school time

- General attention to what can be done in each prep period

 Reader Reflection: When might a What-er want to visit When-er World?

Speaking of, let's head to When-er World together right now!

Angela's Weekly Worksheet

Angela M., a middle school teacher in Queens, created a live Google Doc (Figure 2.7) that outlines her teaching responsibilities, office hours, and more. Angela is a clear When-er but the magic here is that she's not constrained by a digital calendar, which often don't have times that match a teacher's schedule.

Weekly Worksheet Checklist

Criteria of a Weekly Worksheet	Example
How are the priorities named?	
Is the entire week mapped out?	
Are Whats and Whens joined in one location?	
Are the professional and personal considered?	
Is there a place to capture To-Dos that "come up"?	

There are a few things I love about Angela's Weekly Worksheet.

- Angela uses color coding to show different kinds of tasks.

- Checkboxes! Many When-ers' Weekly Worksheets don't include that satisfying ability to check things off. Angela's got the best of both worlds!

- Hyperlinks. In an era of too many tabs, it is helpful to be able to jump to regularly used documents.

Time	Monday	Tuesday	Wednesday	Thursday	Friday
7:45 AM					
8:00 AM	Huddle / Advisory IB				
8:15 AM	Advisory IB	Advisory SM	Advisory AM	Advisory JP	Advisory IB
8:30 AM	Assign Posts for today's lesson	Assign Posts for today's lesson	Assign Posts for today's lesson	Assign Posts for today's lesson	Assign Posts for today's lesson
8:15 AM	Create SM for next Mon	Create SM for next Tues	LL Materials	GC: Weds Posts	Create SM for next Thurs
9:00 AM			LL GC/Videos		
9:30 AM			BB Materials		
10:00 AM			BB GC/Videos		
10:30 AM			Send feedback to LL		
10:30 AM	GC: Mon Posts	GC: Tues Posts	Send feedback to BB	Boulton 1:1	Lucksavage 1:1
11:00 AM			Create SM for next Weds		
11:30 AM					Community Meeting
11:30 AM	Lunch	Lunch	Lunch	Lunch	Lunch
12:00 PM	Create SM for next Mon	GC: Tues Posts	Grade Level Meeting		GC: Thurs Posts
12:30 PM	Arts Class in Session (hangout)	Arts Class in Session (hangout)	Arts Class in Session (hangout)	Arts Class in Session (hangout)	
1:00 PM	GC: Mon Posts	Grade Assignment 1/3	Create SM for next Weds	Create SM for next Thurs	
1:00 PM	GC: Mon Posts	Send Lessons to JS			
1:30 PM		Input Grade 1/3		FILM Video	FILM Video
1:30 PM	FILM Video	FILM Video		FILM Video	FILM Video
2:00 PM	FILM Video	FILM Video + Post		FILM Video + Post	FILM Video + Post
2:30 PM	FILM Video + Post				
2:30 PM	Office Hours	Office Hours	Office Hours	Office Hours	Friday PD.
4:00 PM	Office Hours		Grade Assignment 2/3	Grade Assignment 3/3	
5:00 PM			Input Grade 2/3	Input Grade 3/3	

Figure 2.7   Angela's Weekly Worksheet

Reader Reflection: How can you make your own Weekly Worksheet useful to you? What do you need to personalize?

Now let's head into a final model that is far more When and definitely more digital.

Laura's Weekly Worksheet

Laura B., a middle school teacher in Austin, and her school, are pretty darn digital. This has been especially true in pandemic times, with the Zoom and Google Meet invites flying. Laura simply adds her To-Dos into her existing Outlook calendar (Figure 2.8) by giving herself time for Unfinished Tasks and by using her All-Day Appointments feature to list her To-Dos.

Weekly Worksheet Checklist

Criteria of a Weekly Worksheet	Example
How are the priorities named?	
Is the entire week mapped out?	
Are Whats and Whens joined in one location?	
Are the professional and personal considered?	
Is there a place to capture To-Dos that "come up"?	

I love a lot about Laura's approach, namely:

■ The efficiency of using a digital calendar to create recurring time blocks each week

■ The portability of always having your phone and calendar with you

■ The ability to "catch" a To-Do and enter it into your calendar

 Reader Reflection: What is one benefit of being this digital with your weekly planning?

Before we begin to brainstorm the contents of your own Weekly Worksheet, let's keep our big goal in mind: to create a view of your week that also helps you plan how you want to spend your time. If we put in the effort to be intentional before the week begins, our Weekly Worksheet will guide us like a grocery list guides us through the supermarket. We start with a set of priorities (healthy food!) and some ingredients to get there. We will be flexible and make substitutions as needed, but without the list in hand, who knows what we'd end up

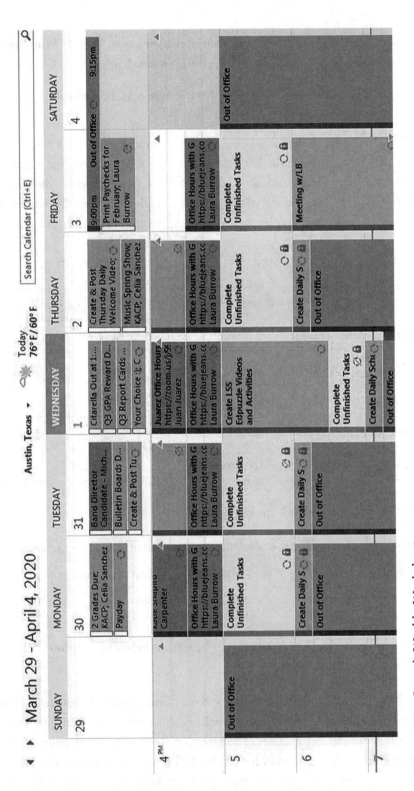

Figure 2.8 Laura's Weekly Worksheet

buying! The goal here is to have a point of view about our time before our week is inevitably filled with adrenaline-filled decision-making!

 Reader Reflection: Brainstorm the content of your Weekly Worksheet.

Before you build your own, let's take some time to brainstorm exactly what might end up on your Weekly Worksheet.

	Personal	Professional
What are your recurring standing meetings or events each week? (e.g. teaching time, coaching meetings, lunch duty, prep periods, exercise classes, coaching slots, etc.)		
What are the meetings and events for next week, in particular?		
What are your recurring deadlines each week? (e.g. lesson plan due dates, attendance reports, parent phone calls)		
What are your other weekly To-Dos?		

Not sure if you've captured it all here? Trade with a Together Colleague to gather their feedback and gather additional ideas for things that will end up on your Weekly Worksheet.

HELP! I CAN'T DECIDE!

If you are searching for *the* perfect template to use for the rest of your life, you may as well just buy a sleeping bag and move into the local office supply store. It doesn't exist. What *does* exist is a tool that is good enough for a period of time in your teaching life. This tool will need to be adapted and modified over the course of your career. Your iPhone may crash and you may revert to paper for a year. During the pandemic, you may wish to go more paper based. Or more digital. The point is that you *want* your system to evolve over time.

That was the easy part of customization! Now let's select your actual Weekly Worksheet tool.

SELECT YOUR WEEKLY WORKSHEET TOOL

Now that you have brainstormed the contents of your Weekly Worksheet, it is time to select where it will actually land. In the next section, we have outlined some of the most common tools used.

- **Option 1. Modify/update an existing planner or notebook.**

  If you have a planner you love or a notebook you are super into, don't change it. But make sure it contains all of the elements of a Weekly Worksheet. This may look like adding priorities into your weekly view of your planner pages or putting "Whens" into your notebook, like Sam did previously. If you're more of a visual person, check out Bullet Journals or hand-drawn options. You can peruse our blog for lots of ideas for planners or notebooks!

- **Option 2. Download a Together Template.**

  Review the Together Template examples in this chapter and the next and see what appeals to you. There are also multiple templates on the accompanying website. Note that nothing will be perfectly designed to meet your needs, but that is the point. We are on a careful customization journey together. This process is reflected in Meghan's example earlier in the chapter.

- **Option 3. Choose and experiment with an existing app.**

  You may already use an app and wish to expand on the list option. The key here is to not just let your Weekly Worksheet become a laundry list. You will want to "sprinkle" a little bit of When in here somehow!

- **Option 4. Make the most of your digital calendar.**

  If you already work in a fairly digital environment and you are kind of "When-y," then you may want to rely on the weekly view of Outlook or Google. You may want to add in your personal stuff or subscribe to your personal calendar from here as well.

TIME BLOCKING:

If you use a digital calendar, you might also "time block" a few key activities—paying careful attention to your energy levels and physical location:

- Sacred nonwork activities, such as exercise, family time, relaxing
- Lesson planning at a particular time of the week when your energy is high
- Routine data entry when your energy is lower

READER REFLECTION:

- What tool will I use or update?
- How will it help me be more effective?

Making My Weekly Worksheet TOTALLY Digital?

Some teachers may prefer to make their Weekly Worksheet entirely digital. Your Weekly Worksheet can follow an inordinate number of digital formats.

- Google Doc (simply upload one of our templates) that is always accessible and ready for updates
- Take advantage of Outlook or Google Calendar. This method is especially efficient if your school already sends invites this way.

Check Your Work! Do on your own or trade with a colleague, to make sure your Weekly Worksheet plan includes the following:

☐ My priorities are clearly located and visible

☐ My appointments and meetings are either:

    ☐ Already hanging out in my digital calendar

    ☐ Written in a separate location

    ☐ Listed in my planner

    ☐ Captured on my Weekly Worksheet

☐ My To-Dos for the week are:

    ☐ Listed separately from my calendar (for the What-ers)

    ☐ Listed within my calendar (for the When-ers)

☐ A clear place to capture incoming To-Dos, appointments, and work

☐ Other sections you'd like to include (optional):

    ☐ _____

    ☐ _____

KEEP LIKE ITEMS WITH LIKE ITEMS, AKA PROCESS IN BATCHES

We all know it is easier to make copies ONCE a week instead of every single day! Whenever possible, complete as much of the same type of work all at once. I'm sure you all have heard the news that shifting gears and multitasking actually slow us down. Try to get in a lesson planning groove and crank out as much as you can. Get comfortable in a grading groove and complete a whole set of papers. This way you can be surrounded by the right materials at the right time, complete what you start, and not divide your time by checking email, calling parents, grading, planning, and procrastinating!

TURBO TOGETHERNESS

Ready to get to it? I thought so. The Weekly Worksheet is typically the tool we teach first during our in-person and online workshops because it will provide the most immediate impact on how you spend your time.

☐ Brainstorm your weekly priorities, timed commitments, and To-Dos.

☐ Select a template that best meets your needs, taking note of What-ness/When-ness and preference for digital or paper-based options.

☐ Print or carry your Weekly Worksheet around with you to make the most of your time.

Nadia A., an elementary school teacher in Austin, reminds us of the power of the Weekly Worksheet: "At the beginning of my teaching career, I was staying at school until 9:00 at night. Now, I'm prioritizing what has to be done for tomorrow. If I don't have the next day set, my whole day is off. During my prep periods, I'm very purposeful about what I'm hitting. Because of this, during weekdays, I don't allow myself to leave past 5:30. I'll take some things home to read over—like skimming and scanning lesson plans—but I don't have to do in-depth work after school."

MAINTENANCE MOVES

Use your Weekly Worksheet for two weeks. Share it with a Together peer and ask them to evaluate you according to the following rubric and to share their rationale. Or, use it to check yourself!

0	1	2	3
When I sit down to make a Weekly Worksheet, I still feel totally overwhelmed.	My Weekly Worksheet is not well connected to my priorities, but it gives me a pretty good sense of my schedule and To-Do list. I'm still not sure how to balance both personal and professional, or where to capture incoming work.	My Weekly Worksheet lets me make a plan for my week, but priorities are not as clear. My time commitments and To-Dos are easy to see, professional and personal are included, and I capture incoming work using this tool.	My Weekly Worksheet clearly names my priorities, shows all my time commitments and To-Dos, includes personal and professional obligations, and has space to capture incoming work.

How is your Weekly Worksheet working for you? What do you want to . . .

Keep?

Add?

Change?

Together Tour:

Cassidy Cruz

Cassidy Cruz is a middle school science teacher in New Braunfels, Texas.

What is your favorite office supply you use in your classroom? Why?

I love my planner. It is carried around with me all day!

What is your most used organizational tool to keep YOURSELF Together?

I keep a paper calendar that I copy things down from Google calendar. The reason I do this is copying it over allows me to internalize a lot of my deadlines.

How do you re-Together yourself when unexpected things pop up?

I tend to do a one-minute meditation/breathing exercise to manage my emotions. I then work out the necessary details that I need to change by creating a To-Do list. I then tackle the task!

What is a time you had to adjust your Together practice and why?

During the pandemic, I had to quarantine for 14 days and then teach my students remotely with a sub.

What is your top Together Trick to share with other teachers?

On Sunday night, go over your Weekly Worksheet so that you can internalize your upcoming week. That includes thinking about lunches, dinners, errands, etc.

What is your favorite teaching snack?

Cooler Ranch Doritos

Why does Togetherness matter to you?

Taking care of my daughter and having quality time with her is the most important thing in my life. I need to make sure my teaching is sustainable and does not take away from family time.

No More Missed Deadlines: Make a Comprehensive Calendar

SETTING THE SCENE

We do not intend to miss deadlines or forget things. It just *happens,* because there is a *lot* coming at us from so many directions every minute of the day. At times it can feel easier to just go with the flow and hope (pray!) someone reminds us if we miss something. However, at some point this habit takes a personal and professional toll. You miss the memo from your principal telling you when to start reading assessments and end up testing 20 first graders in two days. You don't realize that Mother's Day is early this year and spend a stressful hour calling your sister and begging her to tack your name onto the gift she purchased. We seek to be Together Teachers so we can eliminate the frenzy that so often accompanies forgetting a deadline.

IN THIS CHAPTER, YOU WILL LEARN TO:

- ▨ Consolidate multiple calendars into one singular view of the year
- ▨ Ensure that all professional and personal deadlines, events, and meetings are recorded
- ▨ Select the most efficient tool to plan ahead for the academic year
- ▨ Determine when and how you will review your calendar to look ahead for upcoming events

The calendar. The mainstay of our day-to-day, month-to-month, and year-to-year life. In this chapter you'll find tools to help you determine what sort of calendar to keep, how to input the various dates flying in from a million directions, and finally how to maintain your calendar so that it can sufficiently guide you from month to week to day. What follows may push you a bit out of your comfort zone—it *will* require some up-front time. But I promise the payoff is tremendous. Plus you'll uncover a terrific batch of calendars from Together Teachers who will help you figure out what works best for you.

Comprehensive Calendar: A **complete** consolidation of all calendars, resulting in a monthly snapshot of deadlines and events for the **entire year.**

Reader Reflection: How do you currently organize incoming deadlines, events, and information? By the end of this chapter, how do you hope to improve your system?

And for those of you building your Together Teacher system chapter by chapter, we are moving on to the second "tab." Section 2, here we come!

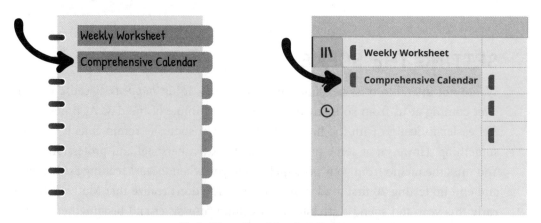

Your Together Teacher System

THE MULTIPLE-CALENDAR DILEMMA

Multiple calendars—a hard-copy testing calendar placed in your mailbox by your principal, an emailed syllabus outlining graduate coursework, or a special services calendar listing days for speech therapy—can lead to collisions (a field trip scheduled on picture day, report cards due the same day as your thesis) when they are not synchronized and put in one place. No one has time to review multiple calendars to identify overlaps and competing deadlines. Nonetheless, we often find ourselves juggling multiple calendars, dreading the night when our students' basketball playoff game is the same as Grandma's ninetieth birthday party.

Most of us have not taken the time to put all of our time commitments and deadlines into one place. That ends today! Or whenever you finish this chapter!

Reader Reflection: Assess yourself.

Rate your current calendar systems below

0	1	2	3
I regularly miss deadlines or appointments, and depend on others for reminders. I have multiple calendars in multiple locations. I don't have a consistent calendar system.	I often don't see collisions ahead of time on my calendar. There isn't a clear sync between my personal and professional commitments.	I rarely miss deadlines or appointments, but sometimes collisions catch me off guard. I have a "good enough" calendar system.	I never miss any deadlines. My calendar system captures both personal and professional commitments for the entire year in one portable, easy-to-access location.

How did you rate yourself, and where should you go next?

0 or 1	2	3
Read on from here! We'll have you clearly calendared in no time!	Review the Together Teacher examples and then jump into guided practice on pages to see what improvements you can make to streamline your process or make your calendar more accessible.	Explore the Together Teacher Examples to compare and contrast them against your own and borrow any updates.

The best way to deal with the multiple-calendar dilemma is to keep one master calendar—the Comprehensive Calendar—on which you record dates from all sources (work, family, graduate school, and so on) that generate deadlines and events. This is the only way you can tell if a late night of coaching might bump into the deadline for your progress reports. Combining multiple calendars takes an up-front investment of time, particularly at the beginning of the school year, but it pays off hugely when you can save time (and oh so much mental energy) by finding what you need in just one place.

THE COMPREHENSIVE CALENDAR: WHAT IS IT?

The overall goal is to consolidate all of your important deadlines and time commitments into *one place* so that you can record deadlines clearly, know where you need to be and when, and regularly check for scheduling smashups. The Comprehensive Calendar is exactly what it sounds like—a calendar that presents a comprehensive view of your time. Most of us already keep some form of calendar, but most of us have not made it truly comprehensive. Your Comprehensive Calendar may be digital and backed up in the cloud, a straightforward paper calendar, or a hybrid—the printed version of what you keep online. Your choice of digital or paper will determine the level of detail you can put on your Comprehensive Calendar, because each option allows a different amount of room to write and edit.

At the minimum, your Comprehensive Calendar should contain a monthly view of the following items:

- Deadlines, one-time and recurring (turning in attendance records, due dates for report cards)
- School holidays and special events (assemblies and field trips)
- Standing meetings (grade-level meetings and professional development)
- Personal events (appointments, social events, and birthdays)

A strong Comprehensive Calendar is:

✓ Portable

✓ Accessible

✓ Truly Comprehensive

✓ Usable through the end of the academic year

✓ Unique (there can be only one!)

✓ Different from your Weekly Worksheet (though it may be in the same tool if you are digital)

Some teachers initially view calendar consolidation as extra work, but the reduced stress and increased effectiveness it yields will make the time you devote to it well worth the effort. Imagine how good it will feel to see a snapshot of your life laid out month by month. Imagine pushing aside the constant worry that you're forgetting stuff because you know you have captured all of your important milestones in your Comprehensive Calendar! Unfortunately, getting the important dates *onto* a Comprehensive Calendar is not enough. Once you have set up your calendar, you must block time to review it regularly (more on that when we get to the Meeting with Myself in Chapter 6).

NEW TEACHER ALERT: WHAT IF YOU ARE NEW TO YOUR SCHOOL—OR NEW TO THE PROFESSION—AND HAVE NO IDEA WHAT TO ANTICIPATE?

■ Does your school regularly use a digital calendar? If so, it may be easier to adopt whatever platform your school uses.

■ Check the district website for any important districtwide dates and note them in your calendar. These may include holidays, building closures, testing dates, and so on.

■ Check any bulletin boards in the office or teachers' lounge with important dates posted for staff, parents/families, or students. These may include field trips, special celebrations, and birthdays.

■ Review any calendars or handouts from staff meetings or ancillary teachers at your school. There may be things like an individualized education plan calendar, a calendar distribution schedule, or a music lesson list.

■ Ask grade-level or content leaders and coaches for other important dates. Make sure you understand deadlines and expectations for progress reports, midterms, and parent conferences.

Let's read on to see how Together Teachers have created all different kinds of Comprehensive Calendars.

TOGETHER TEACHERS' COMPREHENSIVE CALENDARS

As we review these examples, I recommend you:

1 First glance at the sample calendar and make your own observations

2 Next, read the description and answer the questions following each calendar.

We start with paper calendars and move into digital versions after that.

Chineka's Planner-based Comprehensive Calendar

Many of us have planners we know and love, and we don't want to give them up! Nor should we. If you are a planner-person to your bones, let's peek at Chineka's Comprehensive Calendar in Figure 3.1. Chineka J., an English teacher in Seattle, has a blend of Bills/Due Dates, Teaching Responsibilities, and Personal Time.

There are many things we love about this model:

- **Portability.** Paper-based tools, and this is in a discbound planner, are easy to carry around the school building.

- **Consolidation of Deadlines and Events.** Everything from Father's Day to Chineka's own birthday to eighth-grade graduation is right in one place.

- **Ability to Look Ahead.** Chineka can record and plan ahead for future months because it is all in one place.

And some of us just love to write things down and cross them off, am I right? Of course, if you select a model like this and your school is super digital, you will need to move items from your school calendar over to your paper-based model. No Competing Calendars, please!

 Reader Reflection: Why is it helpful to put personal and professional in one location?

Anna's Paper Calendar

Anna T. is an elementary school teacher who's in the classroom half time and takes responsibility for attendance, student behavior, and teacher coaching for the remainder of the day. Anna is also a marathoner and very devoted to her family.

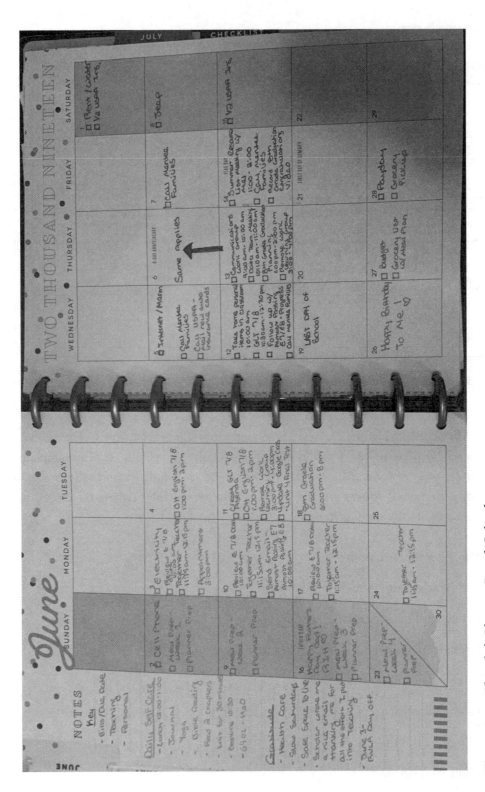

Figure 3.1   Chineka's Planner-Based Calendar

November

SUNDAY	MONDAY	TUESDAY	WEDNESDAY	THURSDAY	FRIDAY	SATURDAY
	1 ⑦ 5 miles TLM PD Practice —	**2** Coach GLM	**3** Coach 5 miles SG	**4** 3 miles	**5** 6:30 Victor's ⑧ Dad comes! → 8:00 MM	**6** 1 mile 5:30 Malatesta
7 🏃 MARATHON	**8** Leadership Story TLM PD Practice —	**9** Coach → Snacks to GLM	**10** Coach SG	**11** Air Hockey ½ Day 'till 6:00 Report Card Night →	**12** AF PD Day	**13** ④ 9:00 Leadership Fellows
14 12:00 Rock Climb ⑤ LP FD	**15** Send Andrea's present TLM	**16** Coach P6P Meeting ③ GLM	**17** Coach SG	**18** Attendance ① Dinner w/ Nibette 7:00	**19** - call families meetings ⑥	**20** Prepare sister girl ✈
21 LP - Thanksgiving FD Dinner!	**22** TLM Analyze math ② Hadiyah's Party	**23** Coach Vet: 11:00 am GLM	**24** Coach SG ½ Day	**25** Andrea's B-day **Thanksgiving Break** EAT!!	**26** **Thanksgiving Break** Nayeem's parents	**27**
28 LP FD	**29** Attendance Awards → Prepare TLM	**30** GLM				

Figure 3.2 Anna's Comprehensive Calendar

As you can see in Figure 3.2, Anna used her paper Comprehensive Calendar to keep a high-level overview of her personal and professional responsibilities. (The template for her calendar was created in Microsoft PowerPoint and is included with the resources that accompany this book.) Anna notes the "big stuff" on her calendar (where the circled numbers correspond to the numbered items in the following list):

1. Dinner plans with friends

2. Veterinarian appointments for her pets

3. Grade-level meetings (GLMs)

4. Special group membership meetings, such as the Leadership Fellows event

5. Weekend lesson planning (LP)

6. Calling families

7. Marathon training

8. Visits with her dad

At first glance, this looks like a very full month. Notice, however, that Anna has carefully looked ahead at the entire month (and beyond!) to ensure that she can fulfill the obligations that make her a great instructor *without sacrificing her personal goals*. Anna plotted her work so she could hang out with her dad *and* run the marathon the first weekend of the month, by moving her lesson planning to earlier that week. Without a thoughtful plan in place, Anna could have easily gone into the teaching week after the marathon unprepared because her family and marathon commitments ate all of her weekend work time. Instead she thought ahead and reserved time to complete this work during the week before.

It is important to note here that the Comprehensive Calendar is not an hour-by-hour list of everything Anna does each day. She limits it to the big stuff. Her daily play-by-play is covered by her Weekly Worksheet. The Comprehensive Calendar is meant to give an overview of deadlines, events, and big commitments—both personal and professional. Anna starts by listing big events for the school year on her printed copy of her academic calendar, broken down by month. Then, she fills in additional appointments as they come up.

READER REFLECTION:

■ **What are the benefits of a paper-based Comprehensive Calendar?**

■ **Why is it important to include personal commitments on your Comprehensive Calendar?**

Brendan's Digital-Paper Blend Calendar

Now let's look at another Together Teacher, one who admits that organization was a real challenge in his first year as a middle school special educator. Brendan C. juggles massive amounts of paperwork and deadlines. Because he first updates his calendar by hand and later types the updates into his computer template (see Figure 3.3), his Comprehensive Calendar is slightly more digital than Anna's and counts as a hybrid. Each is equally effective. If you choose this option, it is worth noting it takes a tremendous amount of discipline to do this at the end of each day.

You can see Brendan typed in the "big predictable stuff," such as:

1. Teach For America (TFA) events on weekends (from his TFA calendar emailed to him at the beginning of the year)

2. School holidays (from his district calendar)

3. State discipline monitoring (from a calendar circulated by his principal)

(Here, too, the circled numbers on the calendar correspond to the numbered items in the list.)

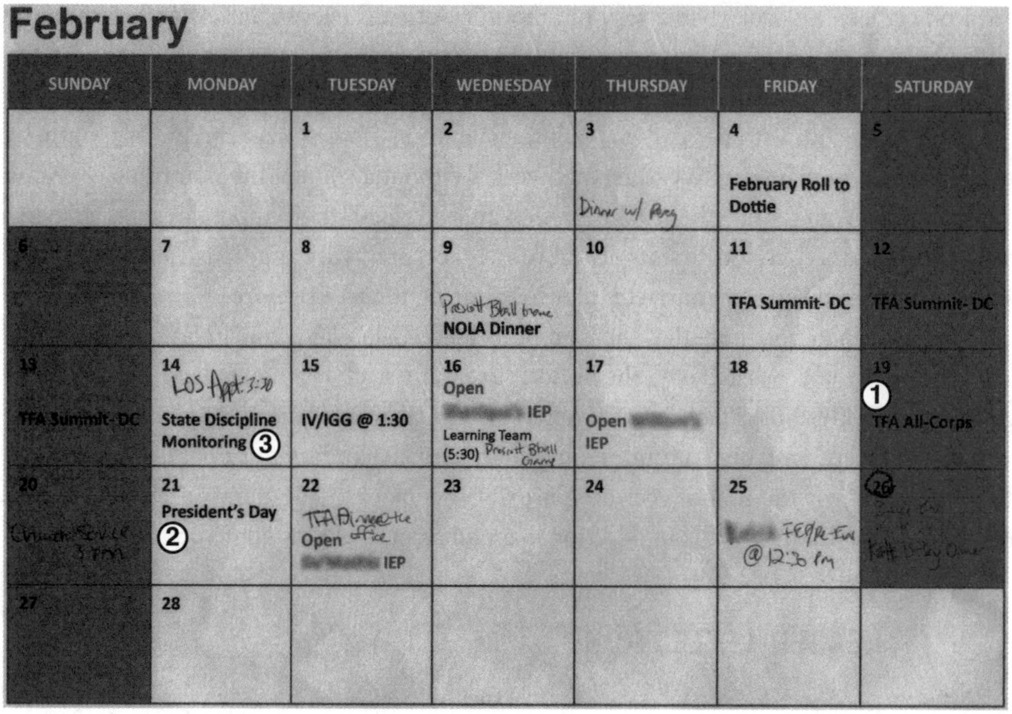

Figure 3.3 Brendan's Comprehensive Calendar

After capturing those key dates, Brendan took the following steps:

■ Printed out a copy of his Comprehensive Calendar and inserted it into his Together Teacher System (a small, flexible binder).

■ Throughout his teaching day, as new calendar items, like church service on the 20th and a basketball tournament on the 9th, come up, Brendan handwrites them into his Comprehensive Calendar.

■ During his Meeting with Myself (don't worry, we'll get into this in Chapter 6), he updates his digital calendar and reprints it for his Together Teacher System.

Warning: This method requires a very strong commitment to the disciplined habit of transferring handwritten notes into a digital system. Otherwise, you run the risk of having two calendars with different information!

If you choose to go digital and it is not culturally acceptable to whip out your phone, laptop, or tablet during a staff or parent meeting, then I recommend you print out at least three months of your Comprehensive Calendar and keep it in your Together Teacher System, as Brendan does. This will allow you to capture deadlines and appointments that come your way when you do not have your tech handy or aren't able to use it. Then, each week during your Meeting with Myself you can transfer the information captured on this hard-copy calendar to your digital Comprehensive Calendar so the two do not become desynchronized (a scary word, and rightfully so!).

READER REFLECTION:

- **What are the benefits of a hybrid calendar system?**
- **What's important about calendar consolidation?**

Now let's move to looking at some increasingly digital calendars.

Gilbert's Digital Calendar

Gilbert C. is a pre-K teacher. He has a lot of hobbies and interests outside his classroom and prioritizes spending time with his friends and girlfriend.

Gilbert's Comprehensive Calendar (see Figure 3.4) is similar to Brendan's but uses a different format. Gilbert records everything *outside* his routine teaching schedule on his calendar. It contains a combination of events, deadlines, and meetings. Similar to Anna and Brendan, he does *not* put his exact teaching schedule and prep periods onto this calendar. But unlike Anna and Brendan, Gilbert uses color coding to separate his various responsibilities. Gilbert noted the following items (again, the circled numbers on the calendar correspond to the numbered items in the list):

1. Hard deadlines, such as when his lesson plans are due (November 19), are listed at the top of each day.

2. Personal commitments, such as when he needs to drive someone to the airport (November 26 at 5 p.m.), are listed as specific times.

3. School events that he needs to be aware of, such as a fire drill on November 9th, are also listed.

How does Gilbert actually make this happen? When he gets a memo outlining when lesson plans are due, he inserts the deadline into his online Comprehensive Calendar as soon as possible.

Option A: If he is in front of his computer and online, he enters the information directly into his Google calendar.

Option B: If he is not in front of his computer, he enters the information into his Google calendar using his phone.

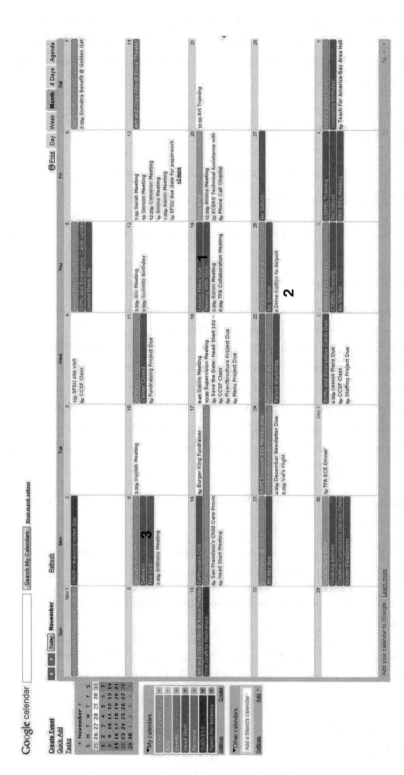

Figure 3.4   Gilbert's Digital Calendar

Option C: If he is not in front of his computer or his phone, he records the deadline on a printed version of his Google calendar that he keeps in his Together Teacher System (a small binder). He then needs to insert that handwritten item into his actual digital calendar at the end of the day.

This method prevents him from having to find his deadlines in multiple locations. Let's talk through one example in detail.

Using a digital calendar and keeping it on your phone will help ensure all dates are synchronized and you can view your calendar on the fly. If you keep a digital calendar but do not keep it in your phone, I recommend that you print out your calendar up to six months in advance and put it in your Together Teacher System.

Emily's Digital Calendar

Emily S. is a high school history teacher, grade-level chair, and graduate student. Before we go any further, I want to warn you not to stress out when you see Emily's Comprehensive Calendar (see Figure 3.5). At first glance it will appear very, very full. This is because Emily takes the additional step of Time Blocking everything up front. Many teachers take this step week by week when building the Weekly Worksheet, but Emily completes it further in advance because of the flexibility of her digital calendar.

Emily color codes her calendar in Outlook and records a greater level of detail than the three previous teachers. For example, all of the work related to AP US History II is in the same color. Color coding allows her to easily see if her time is aligned with what's most important.

Note how Emily does the following (again, the circled numbers on the calendar correspond to the numbered items in the list):

1. Records one-time events, such as a dentist appointment and manicure

2. Inserts Time Blocks from her Ideal Week Template, like setup and copying on Fridays

3. Assigns Time Blocks for tasks with deadlines, like turning in attendance each morning

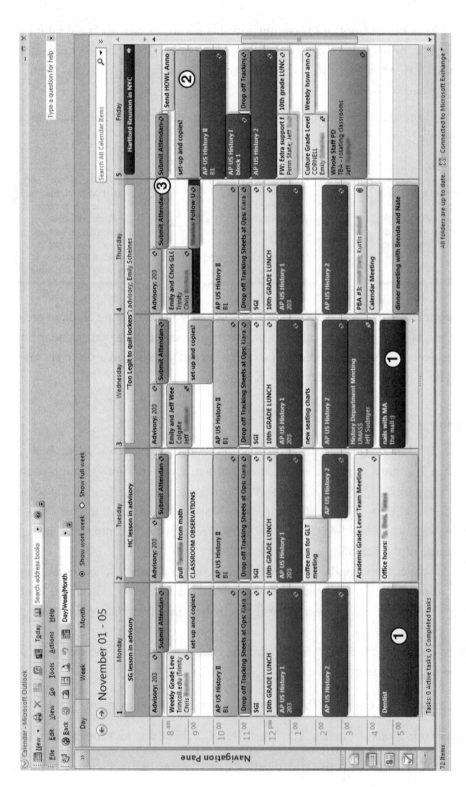

Figure 3.5   Emily's Digital Calendar

Emily's high school also uses Microsoft Outlook, so on Emily's calendar you can also see events like classroom observations and grade-level meetings.

At first this level of detail might seem overwhelming, but it ultimately shows how much (or how little) free time Emily has throughout the week. This enables her to determine precisely how she will use that time to accomplish everything she needs to do. Emily plots her recurring weekly commitments and then adds in specific items for each week, such as a coffee run for the grade-level team meeting or creating new seating charts, around those routine responsibilities. Emily's Comprehensive Calendar also shows how she incorporates personal appointments into her week.

READER REFLECTION:

- ■ **Would you prefer to put your teaching schedule in your Comprehensive Calendar? Why or why not?**

- ■ **What are the pros and cons of keeping a highly detailed Comprehensive Calendar?**

Together Teacher Comprehensive Calendar Summary

Although Chineka, Anna, Brendan, Gilbert, and Emily each include a different level of details on their calendars, all of them record both personal and professional activities, deadlines, and meetings.

The elements shared by ALL Comprehensive Calendars are:

- ■ The professional and the personal are in one place.

- ■ One-time events or deadlines are shown.

- ■ Meetings and appointments are noted.

- ■ Regularly repeated deadlines are recorded.

- ■ Optional: If digital, Time Blocks are inserted.

FAQ: Do I REALLY need to write everything down?
Often people ask whether it is truly necessary to record *everything*. Isn't that taking "Togetherness" a bit too far? I tend to disagree. Putting everything in your Comprehensive Calendar enables you to be more productive and efficient during your limited discretionary time each day. The only things that do *not* need to be written down are To-Dos that have automatic triggers, such as changing the cat litter. I do not need to write this down because there is a clear "reminder" built in for that one! Jenny C., a kindergarten teacher, says, "By my

fourth year of teaching it started to hit me that I needed to be more organized. I don't know why it took me so long. At first it wasn't a huge deal, but then I became grade-level chair and it started to get to the point where I could no longer keep it in my head. It just got to be too much, and I never wanted to be the person, particularly as a leader, who had to say, 'I'm sorry I missed this meeting' or 'I missed this deadline.' From that point forward I committed to writing everything down."

 Reader Reflection: What is a Comprehensive Calendar? How can it help me?

Check for Understanding

For each calendar item, decide if it belongs on your Comprehensive Calendar or your Weekly Worksheet. Circle your answer and explain your rationale.

1. Book hotel for next summer's vacation:

   Comprehensive Calendar or Weekly Worksheet?
   Why?

2. Respond to evaluation feedback by Friday:

   Comprehensive Calendar or Weekly Worksheet?
   Why?

PICK YOUR TOOL: WHERE WILL YOU KEEP YOUR COMPREHENSIVE CALENDAR?

It is now time to decide what your single source of calendar truth will be. Consider the following questions.

■ How much detail do you want to include?

■ What is your preferred way to enter items onto a calendar? By keyboard or by hand?

■ What appealed to you from Chineka, Anna, Brendan, Gilbert, and Emily's examples?

■ Some teachers find themselves drawn to color coding, whereas others like neat places to check off boxes for completed To-Dos. What visual cues do you want to include?

Remember that whichever tool you choose, it must be:

✓ Easy and efficient to add new information, deadlines, and meetings

✓ Portable so you can take it with you around school each day

✓ Readily available in multiple locations, meaning you can see it at home and at school

✓ Visually pleasing to you, allowing you to enter the degree of information that you can handle

Let's look further at the options that teachers most commonly prefer.

Comprehensive Calendar Options

	Options	**Benefits**	**Drawbacks**
Paper	• Various paper planners • Bullet Journals • The UnCalendar • Moleskine planners • Levenger calendars • Self-created versions in Microsoft Word, Excel, PowerPoint Additional commentary on each of these calendars can be found at www.thetogethergroup.com. Whatever kind of paper planner you use, be sure that it includes the following: **A monthly view.** Without this, you will lose sight of the big picture. **A weekly view.** Most paper-based planners also have a daily view. We discuss this more in an earlier chapter when we talk about creating a Weekly Worksheet.	• It is more culturally acceptable to record deadlines on a paper calendar when walking down the hall. • Many teachers find paper calendars more visually appealing.	• They can be easy to lose. • You have to reenter recurring events, such as birthdays and deadlines for paying bills, multiple times each year—and again the following years.

(*Continued*)

	Options	Benefits	Drawbacks
Digital	• Google Calendar • Outlook Calendar • iCal	• Easily synchronizes to your smartphone or tablet • Available when you move throughout your school during the day • Easy to insert recurring events, like birthdays and deadlines for paying bills • Easy to switch between day, week, and month views	• Pesky reminders: A lot of teachers prefer electronic or web-based calendars because of the reminder feature on their smartphone. I would caution you to use this option very, very carefully. What often happens is we set reminders for everything in our calendar; they accumulate and then we find ourselves "snoozing" or "dismissing" 38 reminders at one time, thus becoming blind to our calendars and following up on nothing! • It's so easy to get distracted by other notifications or content on your phone or computer.

FAQ: What if I love my wall or desk calendar?

Many teachers prefer a wall or desk calendar. If you need it for the visual appeal, please use it, but you must also maintain another fully portable Comprehensive Calendar like those described in this chapter. If you take the wall/desk route, you run the risk of having dual (and dueling!) calendars, neither of which is fully comprehensive.

READER REFLECTION:

- ■ **What tool will you use for your Comprehensive Calendar?**
- ■ **Why did you make this selection?**
- ■ **What pitfalls do you need to watch out for?**

BUILD YOUR OWN COMPREHENSIVE CALENDAR

OK, let's do this thing! Gather up any and all calendars or pieces of paper that hold deadlines or appointments. Think of every place you look for deadlines, including online calendars and work and home email inboxes, and every piece of paper on your desk or kitchen counter. Check for testing schedules, unit plans, ancillary schedules for your students, ongoing due dates, and personal deadlines like when your grad school papers are due. You want to be ready to record everything you can for the duration of the academic year!

Step 1: List Your Calendars

List all of the calendars you need to consolidate (e.g. personal, grad school, testing dates, field trips, family events, kids' school, etc.) as well as the other places events and deadlines like to lurk (e.g. email inboxes, faculty room bulletin board).

1. *My school calendar*
2. *Team Meetings calendar*
3.
4.
5.
6.

Step 2: Put in Your Hard Deadlines

Insert each *hard deadline* into your Comprehensive Calendar on the appropriate date. By "hard" deadline I mean work that you would stay up until midnight to accomplish. Each deadline should go at the *top* of the due date on your Comprehensive Calendar (as shown in the earlier examples) so it is clear that the deadline falls on that particular day and doesn't get lost amongst other calendar traffic.

Hard Deadline: A must-do-at-all-costs-because-other-people-are-counting-on-you deadline.

Hard deadlines include the following:

- Completing your taxes by April 15
- Turning in your lesson plans on Thursday evening at 7 p.m.
- Birthdays, bill due dates, and the like

Reorganizing your classroom library and painting your kitchen are *not* hard deadlines. These are tasks you would *like* to accomplish—but you are not *required* to accomplish them by a specific date. They are "soft" deadlines. Do not clutter your calendar with soft deadlines or you will quickly become blind to them. Your brain is very, very astute and knows *exactly* what is a fake, arbitrary, I-would-like-to-do-this-but-I-may-lose-steam deadline. We address soft deadlines with your Later List in an upcoming chapter.

Reader Reflection: List the next three months of hard deadlines you need to add to your Comprehensive Calendar.

Date	Hard Deadline
9/15	*Due date for license renewal application*
12/18	*First semester grades due*

Step 3: Insert Events and FYIs

If you know that your coteacher will be out attending a literacy conference in two weeks, that event should land at the top of your Comprehensive Calendar so you can be sure you are sufficiently prepared for his absence. In this vein, your calendar should also capture events like earthquake drills, family Thanksgiving dinner, and your mom's birthday. If you use a paper calendar, just note these at the top of the monthly view.

Tech Tip

If you keep a digital calendar, use the all-day appointment feature to note deadlines.

Record events with specific times on your schedule in their actual time slots—for example, special field trips or assemblies, book fairs, and career days. If you are using a paper calendar, you can record these events in both the monthly and weekly views (where the layout often includes times of day).

 Reader Reflection: List the events and FYIs for the next 3 months you need to add to your Comprehensive Calendar:

Date	FYI or Event
4/6	*Susan out for PD*
6/20	*Donuts with Dad event*

4. Record Recurring and One-Off Meetings

Many teachers find it helpful to insert both recurring and unusual events such as professional development sessions, special staff meetings, and parent workshops on their Comprehensive Calendars.

Reader Reflection: What meetings do you need to record on your Comprehensive Calendar?

Recurring	When
Weekly Grade-Team Meeting	*Every Wednesday, 4:15 p.m.*
Coaching Meeting with Xavier	*Every other Tuesday during prep*
One-Off	**When**
Check-in with Jocelyn's parents	*Tues 4/26, 7:30 a.m.*
Feedback Meeting re: new English language arts curriculum	*Weds 5/15, 4:30 p.m.*

FAQ: Should I insert my teaching schedule into my Comprehensive Calendar?

Most teachers who use paper Comprehensive Calendars, like Chineka, Anna, and Brendan in the previous examples, choose not to include every detail of their daily teaching because most things remain the same each day. But given the ease of entering events electronically as recurring events, teachers who use digital calendars, like Emily, often *do* include their detailed teaching schedules. It is truly a matter of preference. What I care about is that you have a system for figuring out the best way to use your nonteaching time. In an upcoming chapter, we will discuss ways to make a plan for your "free" time at school.

5. Get the Personal Stuff in There

Let's not miss this important step. Personal stuff matters. Some people balk at the thought of putting personal stuff into a calendar because it feels like every part of their life is planned.

I think the opposite! For many years my friends and had a standing Thursday night date to watch *a favorite show,* eat good Brooklyn pizza, and share a bottle of wine. I really valued this time with my friends, so it was blocked on my calendar. I worked my tail off during the week so I could have this weekly time with very important people in my life. Did I make it every week? No. Sometimes I had to attend work events or had other personal conflicts and could join them for only the last half hour. Nonetheless, that time remained blocked so that I knew to schedule around it as best I could.

Many of the Together Teachers in this book have blocked time for family, church, exercise, and time with friends. Robby, a third-grade teacher, notes the kickoff times of his favorite football team so he can be sure his lesson plans are done in time to enjoy the game! If you are selecting a paper-based tool for your Comprehensive Calendar, note you will have to enter the activities multiple times, like Chineka's model. And if you are going digital, it is easy to enter the items as recurring appointments.

 Reader Reflection: List some personal events or sacred time you want to reserve for yourself on your Comprehensive Calendar:

What	When	For How Long
Exercise	*M, W, F*	*45 mins each day*
Church	*Sundays*	*10–11:30 a.m.*

Tech Tip: What if I have MULTIPLE digital calendars?

Indeed, many of us do have multiple digital calendars. For example, if you have a school Google calendar and a personal Google calendar, it is simple to subscribe to one from the other. This lets you see everything in one singular view.

Now let's take all of this info you just listed and enter it into your Comprehensive Calendar of choice.

We get it. All of these dates in one singular location can feel overwhelming. But trust us, when you don't have to pull an all-nighter to finish report card comments, you will be thankful you took time to look around the bend.

KEEP YOUR COMPREHENSIVE CALENDAR MOVING

Whew. You *did* it. By now you should have a complete Comprehensive Calendar. It may have taken a few hours, but doesn't that feel great? All of your other calendars can now be thrown away! You have only *one place* to refer to for all your deadlines and events.

Now that you have transferred all of your calendars into one Comprehensive Calendar, you must keep it alive and update it regularly. Let's talk about what this looks like. Here's how we gather information, record it, review it, and act on it!

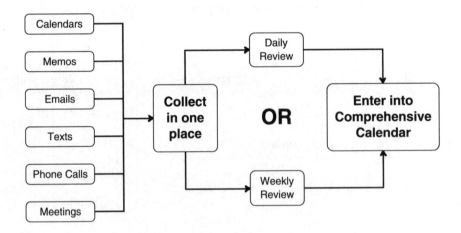

Let's look at how this plays out in an average day in the life.

For each scenario below, fill in the third column to list some Together action steps you could take using your Comprehensive Calendar.

TURBO TOGETHERNESS

1 Select the Comprehensive Calendar tool that best meets your needs and preferred work style.

☐ Paper—planner or notebook

☐ Digital—Outlook, Google Calendar, iCal

The Scenario	When we're Together, we. . .
You receive an email from your principal including four different deadlines in the upcoming month.	*Read that email during a designated time, and then transfer the deadlines to your Comprehensive Calendar. Bonus points for deleting the email after!*
You are sitting in a staff meeting and there is a special presentation where they list a few upcoming half-days.	
You receive your child's school calendar for the upcoming year.	
You receive a syllabus for your graduate school course, along with due dates.	
You receive a text from a group of friends giving you a concert date for two months away.	
You are in a parent conference, and you agree to follow up with the parent in a month on reading progress.	

2. Gather all of your calendars and transfer all items into your Comprehensive Calendar.

3. Continue to add both personal and professional items into your Comprehensive Calendar.

4. Add major tasks and events at the top of the day as an all-day task.

After both creating and then by faithfully maintaining your Comprehensive Calendar you will feel a great sense of relief and an increase in your effectiveness. Anna, whose calendar we looked at earlier, exclaims:

"Holy moly, it is really hard to remember when I didn't write everything down on a calendar. I had a basic calendar, but it was only weekly, nothing long-term. I used a lot of Post-it Notes for deadlines, which was not the best system. It's been so helpful to plan so far ahead and not have to worry about those long-term deadlines until I need to."

No longer will you read, reread, and then frantically search for an email with To-Dos buried in it. No longer will you scramble through papers on your desk to unearth the calendar that the speech therapist dropped off. No longer will you pay the overnight shipping fee to get that gift basket for your sister's birthday to arrive in time. You can now confidently review one calendar, see what is coming up, and plan ahead accordingly for those deadlines and events.

MAINTENANCE MOVES

After using your Comprehensive Calendar for a few weeks, let's see how you do against our big criteria.

My Comprehensive Calendar is. . .

	Always	Sometimes	Rarely	Never
Portable				
Accessible				
Consolidated				
Reviewed Regularly				

What's working best about your Comprehensive Calendar?

What is one small tweak you can make to your Comprehensive Calendar to improve your Togetherness?

CHAPTER 4

Corral the Long-Term To-Dos: Create Your Later List

SETTING THE SCENE

As teachers, we are bombarded with a million things to do from multiple directions all day long. As we discussed in the last chapter, some of these things have hard deadlines or are appointments or meetings: they must be done or attended to at an explicit time. These must be noted on your Comprehensive Calendar. Most other items we come across, however, do not have clear deadlines. These are most often the things we would *like* to do. So where on Earth should we note the following:

- Your principal's book recommendation for teaching students with autism?

- The fleeting thought you had during a read aloud about repainting your kitchen walls?

- The idea you had during a staff meeting for teaching point of view?

- The realization that you need to return that birthday gift your great-aunt sent to you?

You may be inclined to jot these thoughts down on a Post-it or in a notebook (or even on your To-Do list if you already keep one), but often they get jumbled and forgotten about in the midst of the day-to-day deluge. You want just one place where you can capture your To-Dos so you can easily refer to and complete them in an appropriate time frame. Enter the Later List:

IN THIS CHAPTER, YOU WILL LEARN TO:

◼ Identify the locations of all of your multiple lurking To-Dos

◼ Create a Later List that tracks To-Dos over the long term, organized by start date

◼ Transform a Later List item onto your Weekly Worksheet

 Later List: A *long-term and total* list of To-Dos, categorized and grouped in some logical fashion

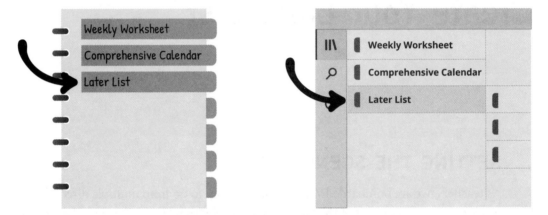

Your Together Teacher System

The instinct to keep a written list is the right one. This chapter focuses on how to make that list more effective by organizing it by start date so it is easier to sort through. The Later List is for work that needs to happen at some point but does not yet have a specific day—or even week—assigned to it. Keeping this list allows you to hold on to reminders about future events, and prevents you from having to recopy long-term projects over and over and over again.

And for those of you building Together Teacher Systems—whether paper or digital—we have moved on to our third tab!

THE LATER LIST: WHAT IS IT?

There will always be more to do than we can accomplish in any given day or week. Most of you are familiar with the old-fashioned To-Do list: that list you write in your notebook, on which you cross off what you can and then recopy the next day. The challenge with this traditional system is that it fails to hold up as your role grows increasingly complex (and I rank teaching as arguably the most complex job out there). As your work becomes more complicated, your basic list becomes impossible to tackle because the To-Dos on it are so disparate, vast, and long term. Additionally, the list may be long enough that it is not worth your time to recopy the same dratted item over and over each day or week. You may have "Buy baby shower gift" and "Write *Roll of Thunder, Hear My Cry* unit plan" on the same list. You may clutter it with things you would *like* to do but don't have the time to actually get done. Last, there may be some tasks need to be done today mixed up with others that need to be done this week mixed up with yet more that can be done later in the month. You get the picture.

 Reader Reflection: Rate your current system for keeping track of long-term To-Dos that float through your head each day:

0	1	2	3
I don't write anything down. I'll get to it when I get to it! (But sometimes I wake up in the middle of the night in a cold sweat.)	I jot down notes for myself in lots of different places—whatever is most convenient at the time, be it a piece of scrap paper, a Post-it Note, or a reminder in my phone.	I keep track of this stuff in one place, that's accessible and portable, but it's more like a running list than a clear plan.	I note these items in one accessible and portable place, and keep ideas organized with categories or due dates.

How did you rate yourself, and where should you go next?

0 or 1	2	3
Read on from here! We'll have you literally listed in no time!	If you rate yourself a 2, peruse the following examples, then focus in on some practice exercises. Feeling ready for more? Build your own Later List toward the end of the chapter.	If you rate yourself a 3, check out some ideas and examples from other teachers and then get started with building your own Later List at the end of the chapter.

Let's say you have a Later List item to reorganize your classroom library.

As you can see, the template in Figure 4.1 is simply boxes with months of the year in them.

January	February	March

April	May	June

Figure 4.1   Later List Template

As you have thoughts about To-Dos or projects that need to be started in particular months, you can simply record them in the appropriate box on your Later List. Let's play through the "reorganize classroom library" example mentioned in the previous paragraph. Here is how your thought process could work:

You are sitting beside a colleague before a staff meeting starts and you begin talking with them about the Classroom Library situation, shall we call it.

I really need to reorganize it before we start book clubs. However, my brain is so full right now with updating my classroom management systems, preparing homework packets for February vacation, and report card night.

I don't want to forget about this though, and I don't know enough about my schedule to just pick any old day in March.

I'm going to open my Together Teacher System and record this as a Later List item for the month of March.

Boy, oh, boy, my classroom library is a *mess!* Books are mixed up in boxes, some are totally worn out, and some belong to other teachers.

When we approach March during a Meeting With Myself (discussed later in Chapter Six), I'll consider making 'Reorganize classroom library' a Weekly To-Do.

January	February	March
		Organize classroom library

April	May	June

Figure 4.2   Later List with Classroom Library To-Do

In Figure 4.2, this teacher has recorded her thought in a place where it does *not* risk getting lost.

Now that you've seen how a Later List can help keep track of the far away stuff for far away, let's peek at some real-life teacher Later List examples.

TOGETHER TEACHER LATER LIST EXAMPLES

These examples are a variety of paper and tools, all of which work equally well. As you look at these examples, keep track of both the method and the tool each teacher uses.

Planner Model

Some of you already use a planner you know and love, but in my experience, we often use planners to CAPTURE incoming work, but not PLAN. Take a look at the model in Figure 4.3 and you will see how this teacher took advantage of the notes column displayed in the monthly layout of this planner. Way to get ahead for Oktoberfest in September!

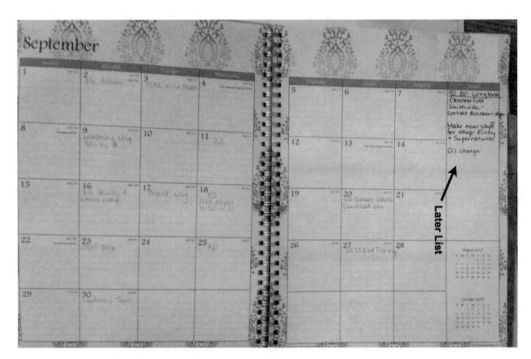

Figure 4.3 Planner-Based Later List

Or, if you don't want to pop the Later List near the calendar view in the planner, you could always go for some old-fashioned Post-it notes popped in the back of a planner or notebook (Figure 4.4). We don't have to overthink this!

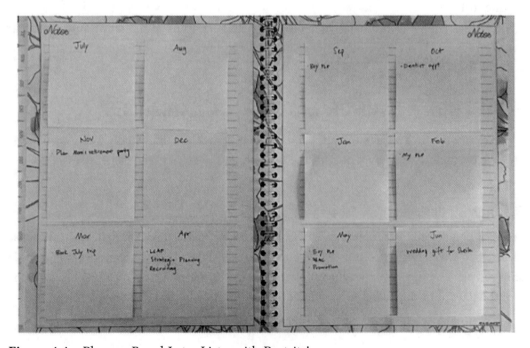

Figure 4.4 Planner-Based Later List—with Post-its!

Reader Reflection: Do you have an existing tool that a Later List could easily slide into?

A Together Template Later List

Let's look at the simple yet elegant way Cloi C. organizes her Later List, in Figure 4.5. Cloi, an elementary educator in Washington, DC, keeps her Later List in simple boxes created in Microsoft Word. You can find all of these templates on the Wiley website: http://www.wiley.com/go/togetherteacher.

July		August		September	
Create class blog create parent blog for school yr	purge clothes detail car	organize Book Room create clasrm libraries for school CLASSROOM	Beth boarding reservations	B2S Night Folders/Materials Thank yous to parents for B2SN	plan B-day

October		November		December	
PT Conference Info Sheet Thanksgiving Activity Plan	Thanksgiving Plans	Plan for "Deck the Halls" Activity	Advent Celebrations	Guided Reading Catalog	Mom Bday Dad Bday

January		February		March	
100th Day of School Prep Scholar Valentine's Day Gift Prep Field Trips Plan for Rest of Year organize all electronic files Science Fair Prep	Emily's 19th Nanee Bday	Read Across America Plan Scholar St. Patrick's Day Gift Prep	Plan Spring Brk	Fix Book Hospital Books Create IEP Meeting Tracker Start Scholar Portfolio Assembly Earth Day Activity Plan	organize closets

April		May		June	
Mother's Day Activity Plan Memorial Day Activity Plan Get Career Day Speakers	CSS Wedding	Spirit Week Activity Plan Prep	Kelsi's Bday	End of Year Scholar Gifts	Vacation!

Figure 4.5   Cloi's Later List

Cloi includes columns for both personal and professional long-term To-Dos. For example, in July she wants to get ahead on starting her class blog! And in February, she is going to START thinking about Spring Break—because then you can plan the fun!

Reader Reflection: How can having personal and professional in one location help you?

Example 3: Later List in Google Keep

Our next teacher works in a school that uses its Google calendar to the max, and therefore, it makes sense for him to stay in the Google-verse. Google Keep (Figure 4.6) is essentially a

December

- [ ] Work
  - [ ] Review second semester change-over plans
  - [ ] Update bulletin board
  - [ ] Review progress toward each admin goal
  - [ ] Discuss parent-teacher conferences
  - [ ] Mail appointment for all HS grad checks
- [ ] Personal
  - [ ] Book Feb travel

March

- [ ] Work
  - [ ] Meet with NHS to review selection process
  - [ ] Collect summer curriculum development requests
  - [ ] Complete draft of master schedule
  - [ ] Begin orientation / transition for new freshman
  - [ ] Send 3rd qtr honor roll for elementary students
  - [ ] Complete draft of master schedule
  - [ ] Work on annual awards assembly
- [ ] Personal
  - [ ] Book reservation for July vacation

January

- [ ] Work
  - [ ] Review plan for Pre-K screening
  - [ ] Coordinate an alumni day
  - [ ] Complete all non-instructional staff evaluations
  - [ ] Review teacher and student grades
  - [ ] Send honor roll letters
  - [ ] Attend support staff mtg
  - [ ] Textbook inventory check
- [ ] Personal
  - [ ]

April

- [ ] Work
  - [ ] Circulate recommendations for student placements
  - [ ] Revise building close-out checklist and teacher checkout form
  - [ ] Established summer vacation / work schedules
  - [ ] Secretaries Day
  - [ ] Complete Admin Evaluations
  - [ ] Contact parents of students not graduating
  - [ ] Conduct elections for student government
- [ ] Personal
  - [ ] Eyeglasses / contacts

February

- [ ] Work
  - [ ] Begin work on next year's master schedule
  - [ ] Begin Pre-K screening
  - [ ] Work on budget recommendations
  - [ ] Host staff recognition day lunch
  - [ ] Begin hiring process for new teachers
- [ ] Personal
  - [ ] Car inspection

May

- [ ] Work
  - [ ] Prepare list of capital improvements projects
  - [ ] Complete senior exit interviews
  - [ ] Sign diplomas
  - [ ] Complete and distribute school-closing procedures
  - [ ] Graduation ceremony
  - [ ] Organize awards ceremony
  - [ ] Run early registration for summer school
- [ ] Personal
  - [ ]

Figure 4.6   Later List in Google Keep

Chrome extension (with an accompanying phone app) that works like digital sticky notes—only better because it synchronizes across all of your devices. You can read more about Google Keep—and many other digital options—on my website. Similar to the previous two models, this teacher organizes by month and then sorts by personal and professional. Notifying parents ahead of time about graduation requirements? YES! Getting that car inspected well before the deadline? Absolutely!

 Reader Reflection: Do you prefer the paper-based or a digital Later List? Why?

As you can see, each of these teachers chose different tools for their Later Lists, but each one is organized by the month in which the teacher wanted to *start* the To-Do.

ASSEMBLE THE TO-DOS: BUILD YOUR LATER LIST

Before you build your own Later List, let's practice with a few examples of Later List tasks. Remember, these are things you need or want to get done at some point but that do not have a specific due date. However, they do have start dates—when you would ideally like to begin them.

Step 1: Stuff We Need to Do Eventually That We Don't Have the Mind Space to Deal with Right Now

What happens: It's September. Your principal asks you to present a professional development (PD) workshop to your entire staff in December. You agree!

The context: Most of us find it easy to agree with a request to do something two or more months in the future because our calendars are not very full that far in advance. However, we are very busy right in the moment and we know we cannot turn any attention to designing that PD until November.

The next steps:

First, I'll enter the hard deadlines associated with this PD session into my Comprehensive Calendar. My principal wants to review the materials on November 20th. I'll also enter the date of the actual PD into my calendar.

Next, I'll put this project on my Later List in the month in which I want to *start* thinking about it. In September, I'll be fully devoted to starting off the school year correctly. In mid-October, I can turn my attention to this PD session. I'll enter "Begin Planning PD session for December" into the October box on my Later List.

FAQ: WHAT IF YOU ARE NOT CLEAR ABOUT WHAT AN ACTUAL DEADLINE IS?

Ask! Many times teachers receive To-Dos from various directions without a clear understanding of when things may be due, what priority they have, or what is expected. It's helpful to really try and understand what is being assigned by asking a few questions like:

- When is this To-Do actually due?

- Would you like to see any examples along the way?

- When will we revisit this project together?

- Do you have any other expectations?

 Reader Reflection: Your turn! Try these two examples, one professional and one personal:

	Professional	Personal
The Situation	In the middle of the school year, your coach recommends you read *Guiding Readers and Writers* by Irene Fountas and Gay Su Pinnell. This isn't an urgent To-Do, and it doesn't require a specific due date.	You want to rent a beach house with friends and their families. Each summer, you get very fired up about booking a great house for the following summer. However, in July most rental companies do not have their listings posted for the next summer. At the same time, if you don't plan ahead, you may lose out on a great house at an affordable price.
What deadlines, if any, do you assign yourself?		
What month do you want to START thinking about this? Why?		

READER REFLECTION:

List some To-Dos, personal and professional, that you want to accomplish a few months down the road—things you don't need to think about for a while:

(1)

(2)

(3)

(4)

(5)

Setting up your Later List may take a while, but it will prove to be completely worth the initial investment of time. I assure you: the sense of relief you will feel once you get all of these items in one place will be worth the hours you spend getting them out of your brain and off scraps of paper.

Step 2: Deadlines That Need a Longer Lead Time

By categorizing your To-Dos by start month you can give yourself more time to meet upcoming due dates and plan backward to meet deadlines. For example, if you owe promotion-in-doubt lists to your principal on February 1 (a deadline you will have recorded on your Comprehensive Calendar), you will need to do some planning in the months prior to meet that deadline. So how does this work?

Promotion in Doubt Thought Process

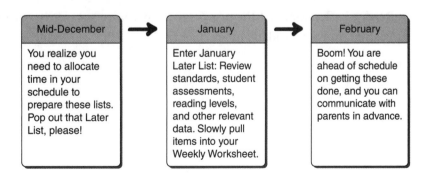

Reader Reflection: Look ahead on your Comprehensive Calendar. What's one To-Do for LATER that you want to start preparing for now?

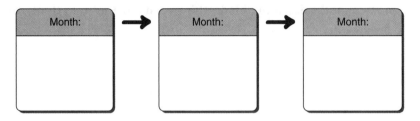

Step 3: Stuff You May Want to Do Someday But You Cannot Even Assign It a Month Right Now

As you move about during your busy school day you will often have ideas about things you *want* to do in the future, but you're too busy to even imagine when you could ever start. For most of us, these are a lot of larger personal and professional aspirations that exist in the back of our heads. Let's talk about a few samples of these *rainy-day To-Dos*:

I would like to get all of my digital photos in one single spot. They are EVERYWHERE across apps, devices, the Internet, and so forth. But I just can't seem to prioritize getting them all in one place. Too much work. For now. However, when I have an important event, like maybe my kids graduating from high school, perhaps I will make them an album with these photos! Aha! Then that puppy will come off my Later List and land on my Weekly Worksheet.

Many teachers would like to reorganize their lesson plan files on their computers. For most of us, finding the time to do that will not be easy, nor will it ever be the most important thing to do. However, you don't want to lose sight of the thought altogether. Eventually (perhaps during summer vacation when you're preparing for the coming school year) you will want to set aside four hours on your Comprehensive Calendar to watch some good TV and reorganize your lesson plan files.

 Reader Reflection: List the rainy-day ideas you've got rattling around on Post-its, in your head, or in your journal:

1
2
3
4
5

In sum, you need a place to dump and organize *all* of your To-Dos that do not require your immediate attention but that you do not want to "lose" or inefficiently copy over day after day. Don't worry; these items will land on your Weekly Worksheet through a routine we teach in an upcoming chapter.

 FAQ: When should I "Roll Over" or "Undate" a To-Do?

This happens! And it is okay! If you find that you are carrying over a To-Do month after month or that you keep giving it a Time Block or a deadline on your Comprehensive Calendar week after week but never achieve it, you might decide to "undate" it. What I mean by *undate* is that you might decide to keep the To-Do on your Later List but assign it to the Rainy Day category. When it becomes important, it will be assigned to a particular month or week.

And for any additional stuff, the first step is to get every piece of relevant information out of your head, out of your email inbox, off of any scrap pieces of paper, off the back of your hand, and onto one Later List. Wait! You may be thinking, "But Maia, that will be *soooooo* many things!!!" You're right—this exercise will force you to face up to a lot of notices and reminders. This list should be so thorough that it should include items you may need in a week, a month, or perhaps never. Regardless of the exact timing of a task, it should be captured! No more rattling around in your head!

I advise you get situated comfortably on your couch over a weekend or in the evening, with all of your papers, accounts, school bags and folders, notes from parents, lesson plans, memos from your principal, voicemails, and anything else where your To-Dos lurk—including your brain. Then, step by step, dump all of the relevant items into your Later List.

Now, go get 'em all. That's right, round 'em up! Yep, go get them and make a big pile of them in front of you. Go on! Scoot! We are ready to choose the best tool for you!

SELECT YOUR LATER LIST TOOL

Now that you know what you need to put on your Later List, let's give it all a home. There are a number of tools that can house your Later List. This is one of those times that habit matters so much more than the actual tool, and there are multiple ways you can construct your list. Here are a few options.

Later List Tool Options

Table 4.1 Later List Tool Options

	Tool Choices	Benefits	Drawbacks
I'm a planner person to the bitter end!	• Use the sidebar of the monthly pager of your planner • Use Post-It Notes in the back of your notebook or planner	It is right there with you.	It could be lost. You have to redo it each year.
I'm old school! I love paper!	• Use one of the modifiable Together Templates from http://www.wiley.com/go /togetherteacher • Print it out and put it in your Together Teacher System • You might also try building your own like Cloi.		
I'm traditional *and* cutting edge! I want to store electronically but capture on paper as I go!	• Keep your Later List in table or list form using Microsoft Word or a Google doc, so it can be sorted easily • Print out a copy each week and capture incoming Later List items with a pen as they come your way • Once a week, type up the new items you captured into your electronic copy, and print out a new version	Don't have to be online or on your device! Less likely to lose!	Need to maintain a regular routine and habit for synthesizing new and old each week!

Table 4.1   (Continued)

	Tool Choices	Benefits	Drawbacks
Get with the times, people, and go digital!	• Make sure your Smartphone is synchronized to your Comprehensive Calendar. • Favorite Later List apps of Together Teachers include Google Keep, and many others reviewed frequently on The Together Group blog.	Your tech may not always be available during the school day.	Make sure your app is designed for viewing on your computer, too. You will enter many items into your Later List and you'll want to see them on the big screen!

Tech Tip: Dealing with Being Digital When It Isn't Easy to Open Your Gadget on the Fly

Teachers who use a hybrid organization system keep hard copies with them, either because they don't carry a smartphone and cannot access their computer while teaching, or because it is not appropriate to pull out their iPad in a parent meeting. If this is you, we suggest you print out copies of your Later List once per week so you can add in your thoughts by hand as you move around your school each day. This step is critical to capturing everything that comes up. If you can avoid taking a paper system around with you to capture stuff, by all means skip it. However, I continue to find it easier to write a note quickly on paper than to open a laptop or app when walking down the hall with 30 children. Similarly, putting a screen between you and your students' parents at meetings can be seen as inconsiderate. If you are *very* fast with your thumbs and keyboard, however, *and* you work in an environment where having open laptops or tablets is considered culturally appropriate, by all means enter your To-Dos into your gadget on the spot.

READER REFLECTION:

■ **What tool will you select?**

■ **Why is this the best tool for you?**

FAQ: Do I include personal and professional items in the same place?

I don't know about you but I do not have time to keep and maintain two To-Do lists. Therefore, I keep only one Later List with *everything* on it, including a ton of personal stuff—everything from "book summer beach house" to "take cats to veterinarian" to "order new sippy cups." Hey, it all has to get done too, right? And I have found it is a mental relief to have it all in one place.

KEEP THAT LATER LIST FED AND HAPPY

Now that you've created your Later List, you need to keep it alive, by feeding it To-Dos so it can help you regulate your workflow. Let's discuss how to do this.

As To-Dos come your way from many directions, you'll need to decide how and where you want to categorize them on your Later List. Let's practice with a few examples:

The Incoming To-Do	Where will you put this on your Later List?	Why?
You're organizing a community-building event for your grade-level team three months from now.		
You receive an email from a parent with suggestions for improving the first day of school.		
Your partner asks you to research day care options for next year.		

What's an incoming To-Do that came your way this week?

Where will you put it on your Later List?

Why?

Regular Weekly Review

This list will be too big to review every day. It is too scary, and it will inevitably clutter your focus and execution. I recommend reviewing it only once per week in your Meeting with Myself (we'll cover this in an upcoming chapter) and scooping out what you *must* get done that week only. Similar to how you would not stand in front of the freezer eating your Ben and Jerry's ice cream straight from the container (right?!), you don't want to eat up all the To-Dos at once. You need to scoop out a reasonable amount at a time for one week only. Everything else can be tucked neatly away for the future. When you review your Later List each week, you have a few choices about what you can do with them.

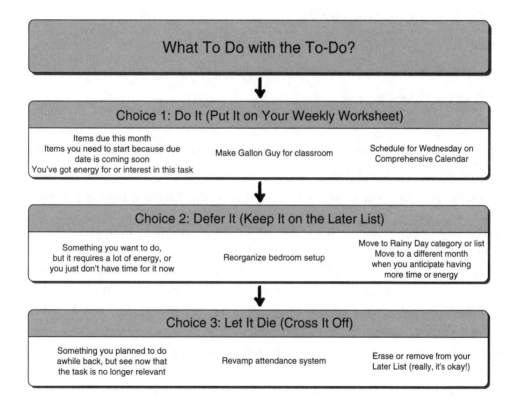

CARRY YOUR LATER LIST

You're familiar with this theme already. You guessed it: I recommend printing your Later List each week and putting a copy in your Together Teacher System. Although stressful and unnecessary to review daily, it is helpful to have your Later List on hand in order to capture updated or future actions that pop into your mind. If you choose to keep your Later List completely digital, make sure you have a device with you at all times that's poised and ready to receive your To-Dos.

TURBO TOGETHERNESS

☐ Where do you want your To-Dos to land? For example, Excel, Word, Google Doc, Google Keep or Tasks, paper table, sidebar of planner, or another app?

☐ Begin building your Later List using your tool of choice!

☐ Set aside time on your Weekly Worksheet to corral all of your To-Dos for both the short and long term.

☐ Make the initial investment:

　☐ Go through your email inbox(es).

　☐ Review any scraps of paper you have collected.

　☐ Go through all of the papers on your school desk.

　☐ Review any memos.

　☐ Empty your brain.

☐ Review your Comprehensive Calendar to work backwards from any known deadlines to plug in tasks to your Later List.

☐ If needed, print out your Later List and put it into your Together Teacher System.

Sometimes you may come to the end of a month and find many things have not moved off your list, but don't beat yourself up for not accomplishing everything you'd planned. The larger point is that you make conscious choices about what to do and what not to do. You may have had every intention of reading the book *Yardsticks* in April to learn more about what your kids should learn during each grade, but that month may have become busy with preparation for the upcoming state test. *This is okay* because you made the choice to prioritize the state test over *Yardsticks*. You can always move this item to May on your Later List.

"The Later List allows me to empty my mind of all the things that I would love to accomplish but just can't take on at the current moment. For example, it allows me to know that I *will* paint my kitchen and frame my photos in July so I don't have to feel guilty about not doing it all winter. It also reminds me about all the things I *can't* do yet—for example, my doctor doesn't make appointments more than four weeks in advance, so if I want an October appointment I put it in my September list so that making the appointment doesn't get lost in the shuffle of my life." – Kate

MAINTENANCE MOVES

Use your Later List for 4 full weeks. Share it with a Together peer and ask them to evaluate you according to the following rubric and to share their rationale.

0	1	2	3
I'm still feeling totally swamped. I tried building a Later List but I'm not really using it. I'm still not sure what goes where.	My Later List is not always completely accessible. I use it occasionally, but also resort to Post-it Notes and other reminders when I can't get to it. I'm not yet able to synthesize all the incoming info in one place, but I like the idea of it.	My Later List is mostly portable and accessible. I find it helpful to have a place to store longer-term ideas but I'm not sure the categories and due dates are helpful to me just yet. I return to it sometimes, but not yet consistently.	My Later List is always portable and easily accessible. It is well-organized with useful categories. It is helping me keep track of ideas and longer-term To-Dos in projects in effective new ways. I have a clear routine for returning to it regularly.
Suggestion: Print a Together Template and simply record items as they come in.	Suggestion: Make sure your list is portable. Brain dump items as they come and sort during your Meeting with Myself.	Suggestion: Double down on reviewing during your Meeting with Myself.	Suggestion: None! Keep on keeping on!

How is your Later List working for you? What do you want to. . . .

Keep?

Add?

Change?

Together Tour:

Laura Burrow

Laura Burrow is an assistant principal of instruction and former eighth-grade social studies teacher in Austin, Texas.

What is your favorite office supply you use in your classroom? Why?

I love my personal laminating machine because it allows me to create and save things year to year to help me work smarter, not harder!

What is your most used organizational tool to keep YOURSELF Together?

My Outlook calendar for meetings, task deadline reminders, etc.

How do you re-Together yourself when unexpected things pop up?

I have planned my daily classroom prep time each week with routine tasks that need to happen. This allows me to adjust tasks and my calendar as needed.

What is a time you had to adjust your Together practice and why?

During the pandemic, I had to adjust my calendar to include off-screen time, lesson recording time and time to make family engagement phone calls. I also moved to a digital weekly worksheet since I had no access to a printer.

What is your top Together Trick to share with other teachers?

Save everything! Use clear and detailed conventions on all digital documents you create. You will be so happy you did this each year!

What is your favorite teaching snack?

Popcorn

Why does Togetherness matter to you?

Togetherness means more time with my friends and family.

CHAPTER 5

Never Forget! Get on the Thought Catchers

SETTING THE SCENE

It's 2:00 p.m. on Thursday. You've just taught your social studies lesson and transitioned your kids to PE. While teaching the American Revolution, you had an idea for an end-of-year field trip. After class you walk over to your colleague's room and notice she is also on her prep, engrossed in grading tests. You stop in to see what she is up to and share your idea. She tells you about her interest in an end-of-year trip to Boston. You discuss the possibility of taking kids biking on the Minuteman trail to Concord. By the time you check the clock, 25 minutes have passed, and it's almost time to pick up your students.

What just happened here? Despite your best intentions, you lost a good chunk of your prep time and you crushed someone else's desperately needed prep with an important but nonurgent brainstorming session. Uh-oh!

IN THIS CHAPTER, YOU WILL LEARN TO:

■ Identify various Thought Catchers you may need in your current role

■ Determine how to use your Thought Catchers in the middle of a busy day

■ Provide yourself with structure and accountability for communicating nonurgent ideas

Reader Reflection Rubric: What do you currently do when you have an idea to share?

0	1	2	3
Anything I can to get the thought out of my head! Sometimes I send a quick email or pop by a colleague's classroom. I really don't want to forget my idea! Sometimes I hear back, and sometimes I don't. Sometimes I lose my own time or take time away from others, but hey, we've gotta chat!	Write the thought down in a notebook, on a Post-it, or on my To-Do list. Sometimes I remember to bring up my ideas, but sometimes I don't. I try to be respectful of my time and others', so sometimes ideas get lost.	Make a calendar invite or reach out to my colleague to set up a time to chat about my idea. This way I am protecting my time and theirs, and we'll eventually find time to talk it through.	Write it down in a portable and accessible place that's devoted to tracking running thoughts. I also have a clearly established routine for returning to these thoughts and bringing them up with others in a timely way.

If you rated yourself a 0, just keep reading. We got you!

Those of you who self-rated as 1s can jump to the actual examples.

2s and 3s, go ahead and just ensure your system is in shape.

New Teachers	Jump right to plan more effective communication with your colleagues.
Teacher Leaders	Review the sections to use Thought Catchers to prepare for meetings and written communication with your team.
Specials Teachers	You might start Thought Catchers for grade-level teams or departments, as your work is more spread out across your building.
Fall somewhere between these categories?	Start with creating Thought Catchers for the various individuals you interact with throughout your week.

WHAT IS A THOUGHT CATCHER EXACTLY?

Now that we have discussed how to master a week with the Weekly Worksheet, manage long-term commitments via the Comprehensive Calendar, and outline tasks using a Later List, it's time to deal with another set of issues that can clutter our brains and litter our inboxes—our thoughts.

What do we do with those great ideas about teaching fractions that pop into our heads while we're in the shower, or that lightbulb that pops on when we're walking down the hall about a book we want to share with our grade team?

For most of us, these thoughts are either scrawled onto the agenda of a professional development (PD) session or found littering a To-Do list. Or we forget about them altogether. This chapter is about using a quick and dirty tool, the *Thought Catcher*, to help you capture your thoughts so you can return to them at the appropriate time without creating unnecessary urgency for others, firing off a half-baked email that may or may not come back to you, or forgetting them completely. We will see how some Together Teachers store their thoughts in various locations so they can easily return to them as needed.

 Thought Catchers: A place to record and revisit your thoughts for people, teams, or topics for future reference.

In general, these ideas are **not** time sensitive. They are collected in boxes or digital lists, without dates. Figure 5.1 shows one example:

Person _____	Person _____	Person _____
Person _____	**Person** _____	**Person** _____
Person _____	**Person** _____	**Person** _____

Figure 5.1 Thought Catchers Template

So, how does this work? Let's say you meet weekly with a literacy coach who helps you design lessons to support your struggling readers. You frequently have thoughts you'd like to share with her when you are moving around the school or even *while* you are teaching lessons. You do not want to barrage her all day long by busting into her office or firing off 10 emails. Instead, you'll do this:

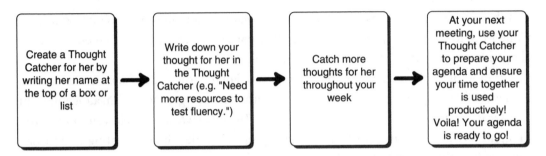

| Create a Thought Catcher for her by writing her name at the top of a box or list | → | Write down your thought for her in the Thought Catcher (e.g. "Need more resources to test fluency.") | → | Catch more thoughts for her throughout your week | → | At your next meeting, use your Thought Catcher to prepare your agenda and ensure your time together is used productively! Voila! Your agenda is ready to go! |

In addition to individual people, Thought Catchers can also be used to store thoughts and ideas for:

- Teams, such as grade-level teams, committees, or departments
- Written memos and communication
- Ideas for future events, such as an end-of-year class celebration
- Feedback for others, if you are coaching or taking notes on students
- Fun personal lists (e.g. restaurants, books, movies to try!)

READER REFLECTION:

List some benefits you can imagine will come from using Thought Catchers. How could this tool help you with your:

- Colleague interactions?
- Email inbox?
- Meeting preparation?
- Written communication?

And you guessed it! This becomes another section in your Together Teacher System. And if you are getting tab fatigue, remember how much easier it is to go to the grocery store when your list is organized by aisle. Same concept. We promise you it will get more time back in your day.

Now we are clear on how Thought Catchers will help us. (Even personally! Imagine me not bombarding my friends with ALLLLLLL of my random thoughts throughout the day.) If you are capturing your ideas as you have them, you will be more prepared to meet with people and write regular updates, and you will avoid those slapdash visits and emails that

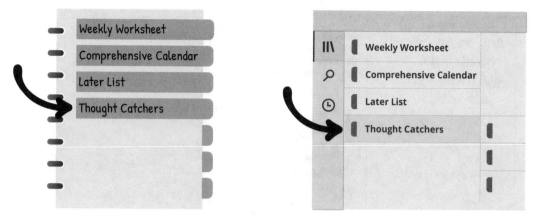

Your Together Teacher System

often prove so ineffective. Let's move ahead and look at some examples from teachers who use Thought Catchers in a variety of ways. As in the previous chapters, a number of tools are presented from which you can choose, but the practice of recording your thoughts in a unique and organized place is the habit we want to hold firm.

TOGETHER TEACHER THOUGHT CATCHER EXAMPLES

In this section we will look at a variety of Thought Catchers. As you review, consider the purpose of the Thought Catchers—and how these are different from actual To-Dos!

Thought Catchers for Coteachers and School Leaders

Here's how Kate M., a third-grade teacher, uses her Thought Catchers to jot down nonurgent thoughts to share with her colleagues when the opportunity arises (see Figure 5.2).

Kate keeps Thought Catchers for three people with whom she interacts regularly:

- Annie is her coteacher. Kate wants to mention something to Annie about grit (character) rewards for their students.

- Gerrie is Annie's principal. You will notice Kate had an idea to share about "Smart Board clickers" and "Moving Funtastic Fridays to Thursdays."

- Tracy is Kate's instructional coach. You can see that Kate has important topics to discuss with Tracy, such as support for guided reading classroom management and questions about student reading levels.

When Kate has a thought for one of these people in the midst of her busy day, she writes it in the appropriate box on her Thought Catchers and saves it for the meetings she routinely has with each of them. As you can see, her captured thoughts range from the straightforward (Where a good place is to put up the FDR assignments?) to the more complex (How and when to shift a choice chart?).

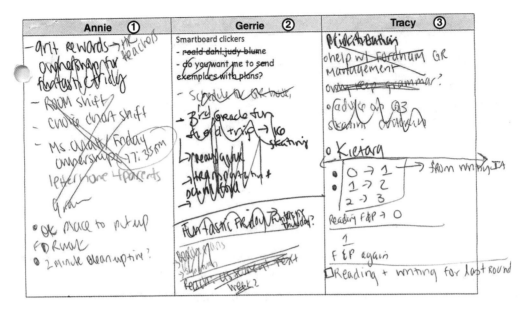

Figure 5.2   Kate's Thought Catchers

FAQ: WHAT IF I DO NOT HAVE STANDING MEETINGS WITH SOME OF MY ADMINISTRATORS OR COLLEAGUES?

Teachers are often guilty of inundating their school leaders with one-off questions that would be more easily addressed during face-to-face time. If Kate wants to ask her principal, Gerrie, about getting a Smart Board clicker, she is going to wait until they have a regular meeting, *or* she is going to compile that clicker inquiry with a few other quick questions in a single email so that Gerrie can review all of Kate's thoughts at once.

If you do not have regularly scheduled meetings with colleagues, you have a few options.

- The first is simply to ask for some regular time with your instructional coach, coteacher, or other individuals.

- If this is not possible, then consider saving up ideas until you have three or four. Then set up a time to meet, or bundle those ideas into one email. If you go for this option, be sure to peek at Chapter 8 on writing effective emails to make it very easy for your principal to reply!

Thought Catchers for Observation Notes

Let's look at another example from Nilda, a middle school writing teacher and teacher-leader. Nilda uses her Thought Catchers to capture notes for other teachers she coaches at her school (see Figure 5.3). Her Thought Catchers help her keep all of her observation notes in a single location, so that her feedback is already prepared when she meets with each teacher.

While she was observing in Esme's classroom, she took two notes—"Strong Voice" and "Marathon Mile Push"—about Esme's lesson delivery. (The first is one of Doug Lemov's highlighted techniques for effective teaching in his book *Teach Like a Champion*.)

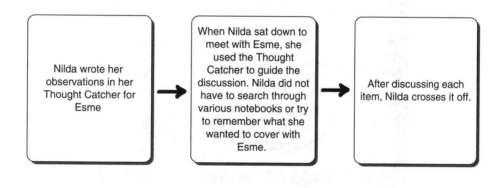

People Boxes

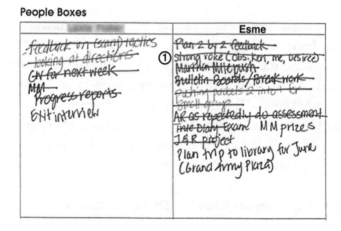

Figure 5.3   Nilda's Thought Catchers
Source: Nilda, a middle school writing teacher and teacher-leader

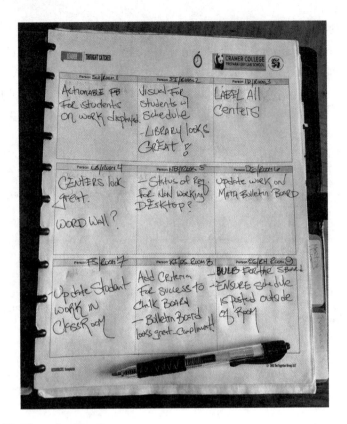

Figure 5.4 Jeff's Thought Catchers

Jeff G., a teacher-leader in Camden, also shares his Thought Catchers per classroom. He can quickly move around the school building and jot notes like, "Room 2, Library looks great!" or "Room 4—Word Wall?" Structuring by groups of colleagues also ensures Jeff doesn't miss anyone! Jeff notes, "Thought Catchers are extremely helpful because they allow me to walk the building and have what each teacher needs at my fingertips on one or two pages. This is helpful in both PLCs (Professional Learning Communities) and coaching. In some cases, what I captured in my Thought Catchers can influence what is covered in PD."

 FAQ: What happens when my Thought Catchers fill up?

Great question! That depends on whether you are paper based or digital for this tool! If you are paper based, you will likely find once the section fills up, you print out another template for yourself. If you are digital, you can simply clear out as you go.

Like Nilda and Jeff, Anna uses Thought Catchers to collect instructional feedback for colleagues, but goes digital (Figure 5.5).

Anna keeps a tab for each person she coaches in Microsoft OneNote. A list of all past interactions are also listed vertically down the right-hand side of her screen. You could do

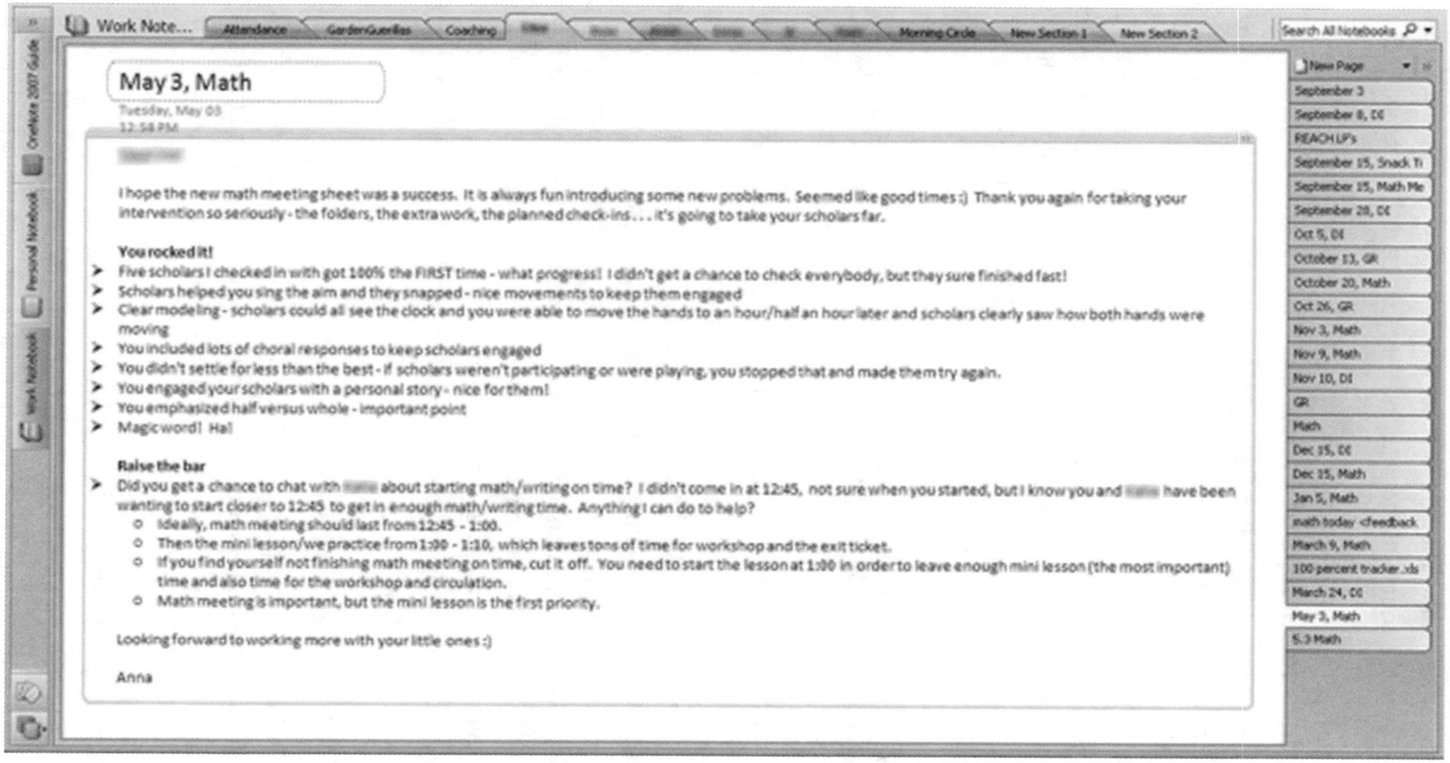
May 3, Math

Tuesday, May 03

12:58 PM

I hope the new math meeting sheet was a success. It is always fun introducing some new problems. Seemed like good times :) Thank you again for taking your intervention so seriously - the folders, the extra work, the planned check-ins . . . it's going to take your scholars far.

You rocked it!

- Five scholars I checked in with got 100% the FIRST time - what progress! I didn't get a chance to check everybody, but they sure finished fast!
- Scholars helped you sing the aim and they snapped - nice movements to keep them engaged
- Clear modeling - scholars could all see the clock and you were able to move the hands to an hour/half an hour later and scholars clearly saw how both hands were moving
- You included lots of choral responses to keep scholars engaged
- You didn't settle for less than the best - if scholars weren't participating or were playing, you stopped that and made them try again.
- You engaged your scholars with a personal story - nice for them!
- You emphasized half versus whole - important point
- Magic word! Ha!

Raise the bar

- Did you get a chance to chat with about starting math/writing on time? I didn't come in at 12:45, not sure when you started, but I know you and have been wanting to start closer to 12:45 to get in enough math/writing time. Anything I can do to help?
  - Ideally, math meeting should last from 12:45 - 1:00.
  - Then the mini lesson/we practice from 1:00 - 1:10, which leaves tons of time for workshop and the exit ticket.
  - If you find yourself not finishing math meeting on time, cut it off. You need to start the lesson at 1:00 in order to leave enough mini lesson (the most important) time and also time for the workshop and circulation.
  - Math meeting is important, but the mini lesson is the first priority.

Looking forward to working more with your little ones :)

Anna

Figure 5.5 Anna's Thought Catcher

the same with Evernote, Google Keep, or any number of other handy apps. Anna's notes for all of the teachers she supervises are in one place and she can easily refer to them. One benefit of keeping an electronic Thought Catcher is that Anna can maintain a running record of conversations over the course of the year and look back on them as needed.

Thought Catchers for Groups of Colleagues

Thought Catchers can also be an effective way to prepare for group meetings or to capture thoughts for teams of people. Let's look at how Nilda records thoughts for her writing team in her Thought Catcher (Figure 5.6).

Nilda was in a PD session about assessment when she realized she had a thought for the writing team about "aligned scoring and rubrics." Although she could have just scribbled it down on the workshop agenda, she instead noted it in her Thought Catcher. The benefit to this additional layer of intentionality is that when Nilda goes to plan her writing team's meeting agenda, she can refer right to her Thought Catcher and see her ideas all in one place.

TEACHER-LEADER ALERT!

This tool is particularly helpful for teachers who are juggling leadership roles. For example, you may realize during your weekly staff meeting in February that you want to talk to the science department in April about aligning end-of-year assessments. Rather than forgetting that thought or shooting a panicked email out to your team, you capture it in the section for the science department on your Thought Catcher and put "April" in parentheses beside it. This thought would sit on your Thought Catcher until April, when you build the agenda for April's meeting. Extra points if it also lands on your Later List! You can even encourage other members of the science department to brainstorm topics in advance of the meeting and maintain a shared list of meeting topics and ideas for the year.

Thought Catchers for Written Updates

Many teachers write updates for parents or students to keep them informed about important events or initiatives at school. Let's look at a sample (Figure 5.7) from Darci S., in Idaho, to see how she keeps track of announcements for her weekly staff update.

Thought Catchers for Fun!

The Thought Catcher concept can also extend to your personal life—an idea popularized by David Allen in *Getting Things Done*. For example, I often struggle to think of thoughtful

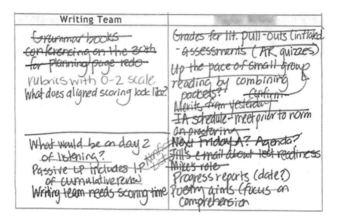

Figure 5.6 Nilda's Thought Catchers for the Writing Team

gifts for important people in my life. By keeping a Thought Catcher for gift ideas, I can easily jot down an idea if I read a review of a book or product that might be a good future gift, or if I see a website or store to which I may want to return. I can then refer to this list when I am trying to buy my sister a gift the week before her birthday. You can also keep personal Thought Catchers for things like books you want to read, restaurants you want to visit, and movies you want to watch.

FAQ: How are Thought Catchers different from the Later List?

Each tool captures different types of thoughts.

The **Later List** keeps track of your To-Dos for later (e.g. set up classroom library). The Later List helps you store long-term tasks until the time comes to schedule them on your Weekly Worksheet.

Thought Catchers are NOT To-Dos— just information to discuss and share with others. They might become To-Dos later on, but not yet! Thought Catchers help you consolidate, filter, and distribute random thoughts and ideas more effectively.

READER REFLECTION:

■ **What are Thought Catchers?**

■ **How can they help improve my overall Togetherness?**

Forge International School engages students within an inclusive international learning community, challenging all members to take risks and contribute locally and globally through open-minded inquiry.

Empowering learners to shape the future.

To-Do	Thought Catcher	Shout-outs
Office Garage Order: The Art of Coaching, Diane Sweeney's Student-Centered Coaching and Results Coaching by Karen Kee Brene Brown: Dare to lead		
Questions and Notes	**Newsletter Topics**	**Team Meeting Topics**
	MYP Community monthly/bimonthly newsletter: (Fireside/S'mores/Bonfire) ***Why MYP, unit spotlight, community/personal project/learner profile focus/ATL skill/video	Focus on Learner Profile Teaching ATLs First week Inquiry Units

Lisa Lit/Lang	KH Math	CD Science	KNS Indiv. Soci.
Walk Through	Walk Through	Walk Through	Walk Through
AC Lang Acq.	**JE Design**	**Art**	**MR PE/Health**
Walk Through	Walk Through	Walk Through	Walk Through

Figure 5.7   Darci's Thought Catchers

BRAINSTORM YOUR OWN THOUGHT CATCHERS

Let's plan for building your Thought Catchers by figuring out who needs them. After that, we'll select the right tool.

Set Up Your Thought Catchers	
Individuals. With whom do you meet regularly? Who "deserves" a Thought Catcher?	
Teams. What teams and groups do you meet with regularly?	
Written Communication. What regular communications do you write?	
Personal. What fun personal lists would you like to keep?	

Now that you have considered the content of your Thought Catchers, let's take that final step and load them into a usable tool. We want to catch and contain those good thoughts, right?!

PICK YOUR THOUGHT CATCHER TOOL

You can keep your Thought Catchers in a number of different locations. Let's review the various choices and their pros and cons. By the end of this section, you will have a clear sense of the best tool for you.

Paper Thought Catchers	Digital Thought Catchers
Some teachers prefer hard copies in their Together Teacher System so they can jot down thoughts throughout the day, like during a staff meeting or when they're walking down the hall. Many teachers print out a Together Template Thought Catcher and store it in their Together Teacher System. When the pages fill up, they simply throw them away after all the thoughts have been dealt with, or they type up the information and reprint new versions if the thoughts need to be carried over into the following week.	For the more electronic among us, there are a few other ways to maintain your Thought Catchers. You may want to use an electronic option if your Thought Catchers tend to get really full. Here are some of our favorite options: • Google Keep or Tasks • Microsoft OneNote • Evernote • Microsoft Excel (some teachers like to make a tab for each person) Even if you are biased toward digital options, it is helpful to have a paper backup of your Thought Catchers because it is often cumbersome or inappropriate to pull out your technology in the middle of a class or meeting.

 FAQ: Can I consolidate tools?

Absolutely, and we encourage you to do so whenever possible. For example, if you use a paper-based planner, then think about adding a section in the back for your Thought Catchers. If you already use OneNote to keep your Later List, then just add a section for your Thought Catchers. Simplify and synthesize, people!

 READER REFLECTION:

■ **What tool will I use for my Thought Catcher?**

■ **How will this tool help me be more effective than I am right now?**

REVIEW YOUR THOUGHT CATCHERS REGULARLY

Now we could get all excited building our Thought Catchers, and then . . . never look at them again. But no, no, no, our thoughts are too valuable for that!!! We want to make sure we review them regularly and either pass them on to someone else, turn them into action items for ourselves, or simply let them go. It is easiest to return to your Thought Catchers at a few natural points. Most likely you will peek at them each day, and you will also systematically review them during your Meeting with Myself—to be discussed in our next chapter!

"It is time to write my weekly update to the math department. Let me peek at my Thought Catcher!"

"Oh, I'm preparing for a meeting with my coach! Let me check my Thought Catcher!"

 Reader Reflection: When and how will you regularly review your Thought Catchers?

 FAQ: Is there a limit to the number of Thought Catchers I can have?

No, there is really no limit. You may end up with 5 to 10 for individuals, 1 or 2 for colleague groups, 2 to 3 for future ideas, and 2 to 3 fun ones. You may also realize that some people need a whole *page* rather than just a box! That is totally fine. Of course, if you start reaching upwards of fifty, you may have gone too far! (Unless you are a secondary teacher using them for your students!)

TURBO TOGETHERNESS

Picture a world in which you have a place to capture the many, many thoughts that pop into your head as you are teaching, walking down the hall, or in a staff meeting. No longer will they be quickly forgotten, scrawled on a piece of paper, distracting to your colleagues, or creating an email collision course. You will calmly jot down your ideas in your Thought Catchers and then wait for a good time to raise them or handily refer to them when you need to reference something.

- ☐ Select the Thought Catcher tool that best fits your preferred work style (and keeps your system simple).
  - ☐ Paper
  - ☐ Digital
- ☐ Create headings for your Thought Catchers—consider individuals, groups, written communication, and future events.
- ☐ Populate your Thought Catchers with thoughts about the various topics.
- ☐ Print and carry in your Together Teacher System, or ensure it's available to you electronically to record thoughts as you move around your school and home.

Nilda, introduced earlier, reflects on how using Thought Catchers makes her a more effective communicator. "Thought Catchers allow me to free up my 'brain space' on that random yet brilliant idea that my principal doesn't necessarily need to hear during Monday's breakfast rotation! I can safely tuck it into my Thought Catchers and know that it will be waiting there for our weekly check-in. I also use Thought Catchers to avoid email abuse with those one-off messages that don't usually lead to much action anyway. Sharing my thoughts with a colleague seems to resonate more when we're face to face and we can have a dialogue that results in next steps!"

MAINTENANCE MOVES

Use your Thought Catchers for a month and observe their efficacy. Are your meetings more efficient? Are your emails—incoming and outgoing—reduced? Are you more purposeful and speedy writing that parent update? Pay attention to anything you scribble in the margins. If your grocery list is getting chicken-scratched around the edges or emailed to yourself, it may be easier to get a Thought Catcher in place!

CHAPTER 6

Create Routines to Support Togetherness: Meet with Yourself

SETTING THE SCENE

Congratulations! You are the new owner of four key tools to help you do the following:

- Plan your schedule (Weekly Worksheet)
- Meet your deadlines (Comprehensive Calendar)
- List your To-Dos (Later List)
- Track your ideas and thoughts (Thought Catchers)

Now it's time for us to discuss *how* to actually use all of these tools together on a regular basis and how to keep them current and working for you! This chapter is about building habits and routines to MAINTAIN your new Together system. As teachers we have a very, very limited amount of discretionary time available to us. When you ritualize your planning routines, your brain is freed up to think about the harder work of teaching kids.

IN THIS CHAPTER, YOU WILL LEARN TO:

■ Prepare systematically for a week by creating a Meeting with Myself agenda

■ Determine where, when, and how to Meet with Yourself weekly

■ Create Opening and Closing Routines to maximize time before and after school

READER REFLECTION: BEFORE WE JUMP IN, IT'S TIME FOR OUR USUAL SELF-REFLECTION!

■ **Describe what makes you feel completely ready for a week. Sleep? Food prepped? Copies made?**

■ **Describe what your friends, family, and students say about you when you are totally ready.**

Feeling pumped to achieve this vision? Me too! Let's get to it!

Sue H., a middle school teacher, describes her teaching life *before* she implemented a weekly planning routine: "It was day by day. I would show up at school each morning and hope that Joe (a colleague) wasn't hogging the copier as usual. I had a rough sense of where things were going, from point A to point B, because of our interim assessments, but it was not a cohesive vision. It was a constant search for time, like, 'When am I going to find 10 minutes to make this chart? When can I copy these assessments?' I felt frantic and unprepared."

We have all been there. Let's think about some of the routines we can put in place to avoid the stressful feeling Sue describes. Enter the Meeting with Myself!

This planning routine takes Sue between 60 and 90 minutes per week (she does the heavier lifting of her instructional planning during the school week when she has an extended prep period). By going through this process, Sue is able to be a great teacher *and* do other things that are important to her.

BUILD YOUR MEETING WITH MYSELF CHECKLIST

Having your Meeting with Myself is like building a grocery list. Before you go to the grocery store (or order groceries online!), you have to both clean up *and* prepare. You may need to go through your fridge to figure out what's about to spoil or dig in the back of the freezer to find what's been forgotten. And then you also need to look ahead: What nights do you have enough time to cook? What lunches can be leftovers?

Similarly, as you prepare for the week, you're asking yourself the following: Are there nights you have school events? Some early morning meetings? A big deadline? Enter the Meeting with Myself, to support the creation of your Weekly Worksheet.

 Meeting with Myself: A weekly routine during which you clean up the prior week and prepare for the week ahead.

The Meeting with Myself isn't a concrete tool but rather an agenda through the routine each week of reviewing and updating your Together Tools. Keep in mind your lesson plans should be completed before you start this process. The beauty of this weekly checklist is you will really need to create it only once, with minor updates here and there as you or your environment change. After that, follow and repeat!

I know you have already built a Weekly Worksheet from a previous chapter, and we waited to share this routine until after we introduced ALL of the Together Tools because it wraps them in a neat bow. No doubt you could build a Weekly Worksheet from scratch each week, but following a step-by-step routine ensures it is systematic and nothing is forgotten!

Clean Up

The first section of your Meeting with Myself involves cleaning up the week behind you. No doubt you are left with various odds and ends at the end of a busy teaching week, whether it's a million open tabs on your laptop, some unsent family emails, a messy backpack, or all of the above! Let's take the time to clean things out. Review the following checklist and circle or highlight items that would be helpful to you each week—and then add some of your own!

Clean Up—What steps do you need to take to clean up the week behind you?

☐ Review any student data that affects your time for the following week, for example, pulling students for tutoring

☐ Schedule time to return outstanding phone calls or reply to lingering emails, texts, or voicemails

☐ Review any loose scraps of paper, calendars, memos, or other notices and add the dates and deadlines to your Together Teacher System

☐ Clean out your teacher bag and clean off your teacher workspace

☐ Look at any Meeting Notes for incomplete next steps and transfer them to your Together Teacher System

No doubt you added a few checklist items of your own. Let's shift over to the looking ahead part.

Prepare

Now that you have listed out your Clean Up steps each week, let's continue working on your personalized weekly checklist. Just like getting ready to go to the grocery store, there is probably a set of steps you take each week to prepare for the week ahead. Review the following checklist and see what you can add.

Prepare—What steps do you need to take to prepare for the week ahead? (Reminder: This is helping you build your Weekly Worksheet!)

☐ Name your priorities: What is *most* important, personally and professionally, this week?

☐ Create your schedule by reviewing your Comprehensive Calendar at least three months ahead

☐ Look three months into your Later List to see if there are any projects on which you can make progress

☐ Prep your instructional planning routines—Opening and Closing Routines (more on that in the next section) and prep periods

☐ Review/Process Thought Catchers. Any emails to send or meetings to schedule?

☐ Block time for rest, rejuvenation, socializing, and self-care—or whatever nonwork items matter to you!

At this point, your Weekly Worksheet is likely to be pretty full. You may find that you have very little time left after you have filled in all of this. Remember: things will *never* go exactly according to plan. That is *okay*. We still want to head into each week with a clear view of our time—both professionally and personally—so we can stay in the driver's seat.

> ## POSSIBLE PITFALL: DEFINE THE WORK, DON'T DO THE WORK
>
> One trap we can easily fall into is DOING the work when we meet with ourselves, rather than simply defining the work. Although it can feel easy and rewarding to start plowing through those emails or grading all those essays, remember you are creating time and space to DO that work the following week. This is all about ensuring you spend your time in the ways that matter most the following week.

READER REFLECTION:

- ■ **What is the Meeting with Myself?**
- ■ **How can it help me?**

Now let's take a closer look at various Meeting with Myself agendas from a few of our favorite Together Teachers. We'll see how they clean up the week that came before and prepare for the next one.

TOGETHER TEACHER MEETING WITH MYSELF EXAMPLE CHECKLISTS

Every teacher's approach to a Meeting with Myself is different, but all of the examples outline the steps each teacher takes to plan for the week ahead, to achieve that vision they outlined in the first part of this chapter. Why bother to put it in writing? Well, on a Friday afternoon, the last thing I feel like doing is Meeting with Myself, so I need to make an airtight agenda.

Public Prep Meeting with Myself Example

The example in Figure 6.1 is simply listed in the back of a notebook. This teacher, from Public Prep in New York City, can refer to it each week as they proceed through their Meeting with Myself. Let's look at what makes this simple model so awesome.

Sample: Meeting with Myself

NOTES weekly Meeting

★ Clean Up:
- Electronic Files → off desktop → File lessons & downloaded files
- Emails → Record all dates, file accordingly
- Papers that need to file or discard
- Ensure all remaining work papers are organized
  - graded → to grade → missing work
- Clean up desk
- Revisit personal goals → achieved? ✓
  - working? +
  - nothing? ⚑

★ Prepare:
- Create new weekly worksheet
  - are items complete? ✓ No? Add!
  - look at calendar to add new tasks or deadlines
  - Review priorities
- Review lesson plans & make copies
- Make time for family/friends calls
- Priorities are flagged
- Time to prep food

Figure 6.1 Public Prep Meeting with Myself Example

There are a few juicy nuggets in here you may want to add to your own Meeting with Myself agenda.

■ Clean up the digital files. Yes, yes, yes!

■ Make time for family and friends calls. Love this!

■ Name the priorities for the week!

All of this is leading this teacher to build their Weekly Worksheet!

 Reader Reflection: What can you borrow from this Meeting with Myself checklist?

Anna's Meeting with Myself

In Figure 6.2, you'll see how Anna asks herself questions to structure her Meeting.

I love the personal touches in this model, such as "wash coffee mug and pot." #guilty And my favorite feature of this model is how Anna is asking herself particular questions and planning the weekend work. Knowing exactly what you have to do over the weekend is a lot better than facing a huge backpack of unknowns.

End of Week Self-Meeting

Clean up!
- ☐ Clean desk
- ☐ File papers
- ☐ Clean up art supplies
- ☐ Wash coffee mug and pot

Prepare!
- ☐ Weekly calendar
- ☐ Weekly sheet
- ☐ Daily sheet
- ☐ Dept. meeting agenda (bi-weekly)
- ☐ Weekly lesson-planning meeting agenda
    - ☐ Scott
    - ☐ Shawn and Damen

Did I?
- ☐ Enter next week's lesson plans? -----------------------Yes -or -No
    - ☐ No, but I have time right now.
    - ☐ No, I will need to do it over the weekend.

- ☐ Enter this week's grades?--------------------------------Yes -or -No
    - ☐ No, but I have time right now.
    - ☐ No, I will need to do it over the weekend.

- ☐ Get all materials ready for Monday's lesson?------Yes -or -No
    - ☐ No, I need to do it now!
    - ☐ No, but I have prep time on Monday!
    - ☐ No, I will need to come in a bit early or make a weekend sample!

NOTES/THOUGHTS:

Figure 6.2   Anna's End of Week Self-Meeting

Reader Reflection: What do you want to borrow from Anna's checklist?

Let's peek at one more.

Cloi's Weekly Meeting Agenda

Figure 6.3 presents Cloi's Weekly Meeting with Myself Agenda. Note that her "Arc" is her Together Teacher System; it is a really cool discbound notebook you can purchase at Staples.

Cloi's final item on her Meeting with Myself checklist Clean-up is the all-important "Clean up email inbox." Although we discuss this more in a future chapter, emails and texts are often a big way we build relationships with families and students, so we want to keep on

---

Ms. Craig's Weekly Meeting Agenda

<u>Clean Up</u>
- Clean up electronic files.
    - Sort downloaded or unfiled documents into folders.
    - Get files off of the desktop!
- Clean up email inbox.
    - Go through inbox to ensure all emails have been read and responded to.
    - Ensure that all dates and deadlines from emails have been recorded on Comprehensive Calendar.
    - Delete any spam or unnecessary emails.

<u>Prepare</u>
- Update Google Calendar
    - Review previous week's calendar for complete/incomplete tasks
    - Adjust new calendar based on incomplete tasks from previous week.
    - Use comprehensive calendar to add any deadlines or meetings for this week to Google Calendar
    - Use later list to add any priority items to this week's to do list.
    - Review thought catcher for any items that can/should happen this week, and add them to calendar.
- Review and Reflect on Week Ahead
    - Review this week's calendar created as a whole, day by day
    - Add any additional to-dos that come to mind
    - Ensure priorities for each day are clear

Figure 6.3 Cloi's Weekly Meeting Agenda

top of the communications. Cloi is also thoughtfully reflecting on the prior week's Weekly Worksheet and transferring items over.

 Reader Reflection: What steps does Cloi take that could help you?

Whatever the content of your Meeting with Myself Agenda, you will want to store it in a place where you can review it every week. Many teachers include the checklist within their Together Teacher System, but the most important part is you use it each week to prepare yourself for the upcoming week.

 Reader Reflection: How will you keep your Meeting with Myself agenda?

- ■ Handwrite it and keep it _____
- ■ Type it and store it _____
- ■ Post it visually and hang it _____
- ■ Insert into a digital calendar appointment
- ■ Other: _____

I bet you're wondering when you should do this and how long it should take. Great questions! Grab your Meeting with Myself checklist and your Weekly Worksheet, and buckle up!

LOGISTICS OF MEETING WITH YOURSELF: YOUR WHEN, WHERE, AND WHAT TO BRING

Now that you have determined WHAT you are going to do when you Meet with Yourself, we want to make sure you've secured a good when and where for making this happen.

 FAQ: How long will the Meeting with Myself take you?

For most of us, this weekly planning process takes about 30–60 minutes, depending on how much work we need to process from the previous week.

WHEN, WHERE, AND WHAT TO BRING TO YOUR MEETING WITH MYSELF

When Should You Meet with Yourself?

Ideally, you hold your Meeting with Myself on either Thursday or Friday, in preparation for the following week. Sometimes it can be nearly impossible to evaluate what's ahead after an exhausting workweek. If you cannot map out your next week on Friday during school, the next best time is over the weekend. However, I have heard from *multiple* teachers who work on weekends that establishing what must be accomplished over the weekend *prior* to Saturday reduces the feeling of being overwhelmed. Do not hold your Meeting with Myself on Sunday night or Monday morning, tempting as it may be!

> "I do my Meeting with Myself on Fridays at 3 p.m. It is honestly one of my favorite times of the week. I chose Fridays because my school is empty and quiet, and I'm not thinking about what I need to plan for tomorrow morning. I can really be focused on what I want to accomplish next week. Heading into the weekend, I feel really good. Before having this routine, I was spending thirty minutes on Monday morning making a To-Do list that I couldn't even find on Wednesday!" – Tess H., a middle school ELA teacher
>
> "I get ready for my week on Sunday morning with a friend. We actually go out for pancakes at IHOP! I bring my Weekly Worksheet, Comprehensive Calendar, and Later List. I go through everything and update it all in my laptop. Then I comb through my email and record any new deadlines or appointments." – Brendan C., a special educator

Where Should You Meet with Yourself? Some Together Teachers conduct their Meeting with Myself at school, others at a coffee shop, and others at home on the couch. In COVID-19, you may only have the choice of holding the Meeting at home. Whatever location you choose, you want to make sure you can spread out your materials, remain relatively uninterrupted, and access a printer.

What to Bring to Your Meeting with Myself?

Every teacher needs different materials for their meetings. Consider the checklist below your starter kit. Check or highlight what you may want to bring to your own Meeting with Myself.

- Computer and printer
- Recycle bin or shredder
- Together Teacher System, including your Comprehensive Calendar, Later List, Thought Catchers, and a fresh Weekly Worksheet
- Any data you need to review, such as objective mastery, attendance, or homework completion
- Any loose papers that may have come in that week from any direction
- Unit and lesson plans

 Reader Reflection: Plan your Meeting with Myself.

When will you schedule your Meeting with Yourself?
Where will you hold your Meeting with Yourself?
What will you bring to your Meeting with Yourself?

See you there!

At this point, many teachers begin to think that I'm some kind of robot who simply generates To-Do lists but never has an ounce of fun. In fact, it's just the opposite! If you don't plan time for yourself, you will find yourself always half working and half not working, worrying about all the stuff you need to do rather than enjoying time in which you're truly relaxed. Have you ever noticed how much more efficient you are during the school day when you know you have an evening event and cannot drag your grading home with you? Although it may feel challenging to spend this kind of time preparing in this level of detail, it pays off to have a clear view of your week—to know when it is busy and when it is light; to know what you have to accomplish now and what is coming up later. With a clear point of view about how you want to use your time, you will be so much less prone to distractions and "emergencies."

Now that we have a way to plan for the WEEK, let's peek into some ways to open and close a day. These routines may be no more than 10 to 15 minutes each, but having them ingrained will save you countless minutes that you may otherwise have spent inefficiently.

DAILY ROUTINES: MAKING THE MOST OF OPENING AND CLOSING THE DAY

Similar to the ingrained morning and evening rituals you likely conduct at home—guzzle coffee, take shower, pack lunch, eat breakfast, brush teeth—you also need clear rituals for those times at school. Each day when you arrive at school—whether you are teaching in the building or remotely—there is a set of things you must do to prepare, and each day before you leave, there is a set of things you must do to close out. Our objective is to standardize these actions and eliminate all guesswork so that you can accomplish these necessary tasks in a way that most positively benefits you and your classroom. It also lets you own your schedule rather than reacting to the crises of the day. And when you head into school with a clear plan for how you will use your prep, you will find you are more likely to be protective of the time.

Opening Routines

Many of us already conduct an informal set of rituals when we arrive at school each morning. We check email, say hi to our colleagues, write lesson aims on the board, ensure that all copies are in place, and so on. And most of us had to shift our Opening Routines—whether intentionally or unintentionally—during the pandemic. Regardless of WHAT you are doing when you open, it helps to have it laid out.

Much of our Opening Routine depends on how our school is run. It also depends on our own energy, the availability of classrooms, and other personal obligations. For example, if the copier is routinely broken, making photocopies *should not* be part of your Opening Routine. But if you frequently receive email updates that require action, checking email *should* be a part of your Opening Routine. Your school may also have specific requirements, such as submitting attendance or administering reading tests during off hours, that affect when you can do what. In my third year of teaching, an after-school program run by other instructors limited my access to my classroom after school and forced me to do lesson planning at the incredibly early hour at which I decided to arrive at work. There is no one right way to have an Opening Routine; it is just important that you have one that is clear to you.

Let's peek at a few ways Together Teachers have baked Opening Routines right into their Weekly Worksheets.

Cloi's Opening and Closing Routines

I love the little self-care reminders in Cloi's Opening Routine. . . I mean FILL.UP.THE. WATER.BOTTLE. Right?!

Cloi smartly combined self-care items and classroom work into her Opening and Closing Routines. Ultimately, this will help her remain present and build relationships with her students—because she is not running through the little things in her head!

Let's check out one more model (Figure 6.4) . . .

Ms. Craig's Week January 4, 2016
My Week- 18

		M	T	W	R	F	Weekend
Mtgs/Deadlines		5pm-Mon. Mat. 19	5pm-T/W Materials 19	5pm-R/F Materials 19 6:30pm BodyPump	5pm=Syll & SWYKQ 20	Weekly Mtg. 9:15	Sat: Zumba Sun: Church
To-Do		File Papers PhD Board PhD Bands	Scholar of the Week	Grades Syll/ SWYKQ - Wk 20 Gather GR Books GR Extras	Read Aloud- Wk 20 Reading Comp- Wk 20 Distribute Materials Set up GR	Finish Grading Sort GR Books	Anchor Charts Week's Materials Left Over Grades

Opening Routine	Closing Routine	Priorities
lunch in fridge	arrange desks, clean room M T W R F	Read Aloud Plans- 18
fill water bottle	update board & objectives M T W R F	Read Aloud Anthology 18
comp, charger, water bottle, snack to room	redo color chart & bathroom sticks M T W R F	
set up morning meeting pwrpt	sharpen/pass out pencils M T W R F	
get teacher folder & clipboard	empty turn-in bins & review work M T W R F	
go to staff morning meeting	set up materials for next day M T W R F	
	Kickboard & DREAM Blocks Tracker M T W R F	
	complete to-dos from WW M T W R F	

Lesson Plans	Materials to Prepare	Copies to Send
Reading Syllabus- Week 19	Reading Comp Week 19	Reading Syllabus (4) Week
Read Aloud Plans- Week 18	Guided Reading Materials- 18/19	Read Aloud Plans (4) Week M/T R/F
Read Aloud Plans Week 19	Read Aloud Anthology- 18/19	Read Aloud Anthology (4) Week I M/T R/F
Reading Syllabus- Week 20		Reading Comp Materials (104) Week M/T R/F
		Guided Reading Plans (5) Week 18, 19
		Reading A-Z Books -Week 18, 19
		GR Extras- Week 18, 19

Home/Personal	To-Do	
	-update PhD board	new years preppie and proud acitivity
	-get phD bands	check crayon bags
	SST Proces for Javoni, Jai'Dynn	data pages for binder
	-IEP meeting tracker	
	-scholar info binder	
	-update classroom boards	
	-hallway bulletin board	
	-extra work for Leah, Ryan, Honesty, Ethan	

Weekly Goal: _Scholar Engagement with Engaging Lessons_

Figure 6.4   Cloi's Opening and Closing Routines

George's Opening and Closing Routines

George W., a teacher in New Orleans, has his Opening Routine set (Figure 6.5)!

George has his Opening Routine ready to go, and his Closing Routine varies based on what is happening after school that day.

Although it might feel mundane to list the Opening Routine in your Weekly Worksheet, this practice allows your brain to go on autopilot at the start of the day. George is incredibly purposeful with how he uses the morning hours to get work done and be ready for the day of instruction. I want you to be similarly purposeful and carry the same level of focus heading into your school day. Although it might seem silly to write down everything you want to accomplish in a 20-minute period, I promise that this will ultimately help prevent you from taking more work home! Pull up your Weekly Worksheet and add in your Opening and Closing Routines!

Nilda's morning. "I arrive at 6:15 a.m. and I always start by rereading that day's lesson plans. This is necessary because I plan a week in advance, so I occasionally forget details. On Monday I print out all lessons for the week and put all lesson plans in my Together Teacher System. As I'm making coffee, I highlight stuff to remember and write additional questions to ask within the lesson. After that, I look at email one quick time to see if there is anything that will affect the day, like a student absence."

Anna's morning. "I arrive at 6:40 a.m., say hi to other teachers, and then go straight to set up my desk area. I pull out my Together Teacher System, turn on my laptop, review my Comprehensive Calendar (I keep a higher-level view in my Weekly Worksheet, and room locations for meetings in Outlook), and generally make sure I know what I'm doing that day. I've been trying to leave my computer at school, so I usually have between 5 and 10 emails to take care of and respond to. I do have a fair amount of time in the morning, so I try to get work done. I try and tackle a project, such as something big with attendance or guided reading. If I do the heavier lifting in the morning, I get more done and faster. I learned the hard way that if I save the bigger projects for the afternoon, they take much longer."

Example Opening Routines

Morning Person	Non-Morning person
• Arrive at school, coffee in hand, say hi to other early arrivers.	• Arrive at school, stagger to coffee machine, grunt to other early arrivers.
• Sign in, put lunch in refrigerator, turn on classroom lights, put on soft music.	• Hope there is something good served in the cafeteria for lunch.
• Return garbage cans tipped over on your desk by custodian to their proper location.	• Double-check that all lesson materials and copies are laid out for the day.
• Double-check that all lesson materials and copies are laid out for the day.	• Greet students at the door.
• Set out any materials needed for any early-arrival student jobs, such as papers to hand out, homework to return.	
• Scan email for anything urgent; leave the rest for later.	
• Review your Weekly Worksheet for what you outlined to accomplish for your Opening Routine.	
➢ Make progress on aims of unit plan	
➢ Create end-of-unit assessment	
➢ Grade half of the reading journal responses	
• Greet students at door.	

READER REFLECTION: PLAN YOUR OPENING ROUTINE.

■ How much time do you realistically have for your Opening Routine?

■ Given that, list the elements of your planned Opening Routine.

1

2

3

4

5

George
Planning Routines

Routine	Monday	Tuesday	Wednesday	Thursday	Friday
Before School (7:00-7:45)	o Set up o Pencils Sharpened o HW Set Out o Morning Work o Anchor Charts AM STAFF MEETING!	o Set up o Pencils Sharpened o HW Set Out o Morning Work o Anchor Charts	o Set up o Pencils Sharpened o HW Set Out o Morning Work o Anchor Charts	o Set up o Pencils Sharpened o HW Set Out o Morning Work o Anchor Charts (AM TEAM MEETING!) *Prepare Shout outs!*	o Set up o Pencils Sharpened o HW Set Out o Morning Work o Anchor Charts
Prep 1 (8:35-9:20)	~~Plan Readers Workshop~~ *Pre-conference*	Plan Readers Workshop	Plan Do Nows for Readers Workshop	Grade Exit Slips	Enter Grades
Prep 2 (10:50-11:20)	Write back to ~~students in~~ Reading Journals. *Post-Conference*	Write back to students in Reading Journals.	Write back to students in Reading Journals.	Write back to students in Reading Journals.	Write back to students in Reading Journals.
After School (4:00-5:00)	Weekly Copies ✓ HW ✓ Words Packet o Morning Work o Wed. Assessments	Read Team Behavior Meeting Sarah RW Planning Meeting	Staff PD	Red Team Planning Meeting	Weekly Reflection Meeting

- Plan Guided Reading
- Complete GR binder
    Borderlands 2

Buy Trail Mix for Friday Celebration!

Figure 6.5   George's Planning Routines

Now that you have nailed and documented how you want to open your days, let's shift to their endings. How are you closing your days?

Closing Routines

Whew. Your students are all safely out the door after a good day of learning. If you are lucky, your classroom is in relatively good physical shape after the madness of the instructional day, or if teaching online, your tabs are closed out and you feel good about what you accomplished today. What next? If you are like many teachers, your energy is hitting a low. On the way to the soda machine you pop into a colleague's room so you can debrief with each other about the day. This reminds you of a question you had for your coteacher, so you go back to your classroom to see if he is still there. He has left already, so you open your email and start drafting a message to him. Arg—20 new messages! It's too stressful to review them all now. You close down your computer and wander around the classroom—picking up a few stray pieces of paper, erasing the lesson objectives on the board, and before long an entire hour has flown by. Drat! Now you have to grade all of your exit tickets at home.

So much for relaxing after dinner! Why does this keep happening?! You give up, throw the exit tickets in your bag, glance at the board and think, "I *should* write up my lesson objectives for tomorrow and check my copies," but ultimately you decide to call it a day and save those tasks for the morning.

Now, this is very, very normal, and it is amazing how much time can pass when we stay after school, feel like we are working, but in fact are getting little done of importance or impact. We might as well just go home and take a nap. However, if you take the time to get very clear about what specifically you want to accomplish each afternoon, you will find yourself speeding more efficiently through your work, feeling less prone to distractions, and getting out the door at an earlier hour. A Closing Routine is simply a standard list of things you try to accomplish before you leave school every day.

Example Closing Routines

More after school time	Less after school time
• Take a deep breath, refill water bottle, quickly check in with my colleague to decompress. • Check email and take note of any deadlines that have come my way, answer any short emails, and block time to deal with longer emails. • Review reading and math exit tickets quickly and jot down any reteaching points. • Answer five reading response journals. • Clean out the inbox on my desk and note any To-Dos, file any papers, throw away as much as possible. • Distribute homework assignments to my students' individualized mailboxes. • Erase dry-erase board. • Write next day's teaching objectives and agenda on my Anchor Board. • Review next day's lesson plans and double-check that all teaching materials are available. • Note any parent phone calls to make from home that evening.	• Write and post aims for tomorrow. • Post math meeting information. • Post morning message. • Vacuum carpet.

READER REFLECTION: PLAN YOUR CLOSING ROUTINES.

■ **How much time do you realistically have for your Closing Routine?**

■ **Given that, list the elements of your planned Closing Routine.**

1

2

3

4

5

■ **How will you keep your Opening and Closing Routines front and center?**

TURBO TOGETHERNESS

The process of establishing routines is beneficial whether you are in your first year of teaching or your fifteenth. Having clear and established routines allows you to plan for what is predictable (in a world that often is *not* predictable!) rather than worry about *when* we will fit things in and to make the most of the limited amount of personal and professional "free" time we have. Although it does take some additional time (anywhere from 10 to 20 minutes each day, depending on your Morning and Closing Routines, and at least 60 minutes weekly), that time will pay you back with the ability to get more done and feel less stress.

☐ Create a Meeting with Myself Checklist

☐ Design Opening and Closing Routines

"My Meeting with Myself takes place on Sunday afternoon. This allows me to have enough time to do anything I may have forgotten I need to do for Monday. It also allows me to enjoy my weekend and still be prepared for the week. I like to send any pending emails or make any phone calls at this time as well. I usually try to synthesize and get rid of anything I can from my Thought Catcher. I can see the scope of the upcoming week and the following week."

– Jacqueline F., a teacher in Baltimore

MAINTENANCE MOVES

Try planning and completing each of the routines outlined in this chapter for two weeks. Then complete the following reflection on your own, or use it to talk with a colleague about where you might make tweaks, changes, and improvements.

	What are the benefits I've seen of this routine?	What are the barriers to completing this routine?	What adjustments can I consider making to get more benefits and face fewer barriers?
Meeting with Myself			
Opening Routine			
Closing Routine			

PART 2

Together Your Space, Stuff, and Students

CHAPTER 7

Tidy and Together Up Your Teacher Workspace

SETTING THE SCENE

I remember emptying my pockets at the end of a school day and finding a note that Terrell had written me asking to make up a math quiz, a small slip of paper the school librarian had left in my mailbox informing me of a schedule change, a note a parent handed to me at dismissal asking about additional independent reading for her child, and three confiscated Pokemon cards! And that was only in my *pockets*! Never mind the permission slips collected for the upcoming class trip, the math exit tickets from the past four days, the notes from my professional development (PD) session last Friday, and copies of next week's social studies test—all stashed in various folders around my classroom.

I'd bet all of these are also sitting somewhere in the vicinity of *your* desk, which, last time you checked, was buried under paper. Let's say you teach sixth-grade math—four sections each with 25 kids per section. You collect exit tickets every day and send home homework every night. Your papers for math instruction alone may number *over a thousand* each week. In addition, you probably have notes from parents, materials from a PD session that you meant to review, and a new character-education curriculum that just landed in your mailbox. And as you move around school each day, slips of paper are handed over to you "for review ASAP."

IN THIS CHAPTER, YOU WILL LEARN TO:

■ Set up your desk and instructional resources to build a focused workspace

■ Sort your incoming and outgoing papers to access materials as efficiently as possible

■ Transport your materials between school and home and back again

■ File your digital and hard-copy teaching tools for easy future reference

 Reader Reflection: Take stock of your space! Rate your current practice.

Area	Rating 3 = Rocking It 2 = Needs a Little Help! 1 = Needs a Lot of Help!
My Teacher Workspace (aka the desk) allows me to focus on my actual work, take care of myself, and stay inspired.	
My active papers are sorted efficiently so that I can move quickly to drop items at the office, hand out papers, etc.	
I have a strong system for transporting materials between school and home.	
I can easily locate my digital and hard-copy materials for past lessons, units, tests, etc.	
My Teaching Station (where my instructional materials are) allow for effective instruction.	
I can efficiently find common reference materials at a moment's notice, for example, family phone numbers, key dates, etc.	

We recommend looking at what areas need the most help and jumping to those particular sections in the chapter.

This chapter will help you deal with the daily paper avalanche in a systematic way by teaching you ways to arrange your Teacher Workspace, efficiently transport papers between home and school, organize your lesson plans and materials, and easily locate those PD materials you "carefully" tucked away last year. Let's start with your Teacher Workspace!

TOGETHER UP THAT WORKSPACE

Although we don't have much personal space as teachers, it's likely you at least have a desk, table, or corner that functions as your home base throughout your teaching day. This may also be where you sit to grade, plan lessons, or enter data into your computer. Your Teacher Workspace is where you sit down and concentrate on lesson planning and other important work. For some of you this may be a U-shaped table in the corner of your room, and for others it may be part of a table in a teacher workroom. The following sections outline various ways to keep your paper, projects, and materials in order in your Teacher Workspace so you can be as efficient and productive as possible.

Let's look at two cool samples. Keep in mind we are not going for Pinterest perfect here. Our aim is a functional workspace where you can get your work done and store some stuff! (But if you personally want to Pinterest it up, well, then go for it!)

Teacher Desk at Valence College Prep

The workspace shown in Figure 7.1 is built into the back of a classroom at Valence College Prep in Queens. I mean a floating shelf?! Wow! Let's take apart a few things that make this awesome.

Figure 7.1   Teacher Desk at Valence College Prep

This Together Teacher has:

- Tools to sort and label incoming and outcoming papers
- Cups to rein in the pens and markets
- Spots for office supplies, such as Post-its, tape, and staplers
- Photos of family and friends
- Gifts from current and former students

Greta's Teaching Station

In addition to your actual Teacher Workspace, you may find you want or need an actual Teaching Station. Let's peer into Greta G.'s space in Portland, Maine (Figure 7.2). More things hanging on walls. Command Strips are the best things ever invented!

Figure 7.2   Greta's Teaching Station

Greta said, "I found I needed teaching at my fingertips. So, I have:

- My clipboard with student tracking rosters

- A stand-up file organizer for student handouts organized by day

- Sentimental mugs filled with pens, pencils, highlighters, grown-up scissors

- A ceramic bowl a student made for me with paper clips and binder clips

- A drawer organizer, which holds other supplies I need at my fingertips that are small and I didn't want to look junky—staples, index cards, white-out, etc.

- Basic supplies such as a stapler and tape dispenser, ream of paper, and a treasure box of student pencils

- Wall hanger held with Command hooks that holds frequently needed files

This area contains things that are practical and things that bring me joy."

Now that we have our overall Teacher Workspace and Teaching Stations set up, let's get a little deeper into some helpful elements to include. We will establish an inbox for paper comings and goings, create a kudos board, and set up some self-care!

1. Break Up the Inbox

Many of us may already have an "action bin" or inbox, but we may not use it as smartly or systematically as we wish we could. In theory this is a silver basket on your desk that always looks perfectly neat and holds just two or three papers to be dealt with. But let's be real: most people's inboxes are full of stuff they don't know what to do with. They just sit there collecting piles of junk that you actually never refer to, except for the random rifle-through when trying to locate something critical—resulting in more time annoyingly wasted.

As a result, our inboxes become a massive hodgepodge of a million different To-Dos. When you glance at the stack, you cannot quickly tell what is a five-minute form to sign and what is hours of five-paragraph essays to grade. By creating more specific categories, you can more efficiently process the massive amount of papers handed to you on a daily basis. The next section describes a way to deal with your incoming and outgoing papers more intentionally. At first, all of these mailboxes may seem overly complicated, but once they are set up, they empower students, who know where to put their late notes and permission slips (and therefore aren't interrupting lessons to ask nonacademic questions), and they liberate you from spending your precious prep time sorting through piles. We will start with a few photos of broken-up inboxes (Figure 7.3 and Figure 7.4) and you can choose what works best for you!

Simple Broken-Up Inbox

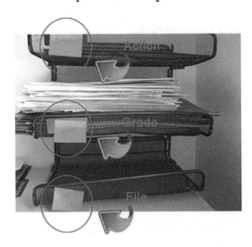

Figure 7.3   Example Inbox

Complex Hanging Inbox

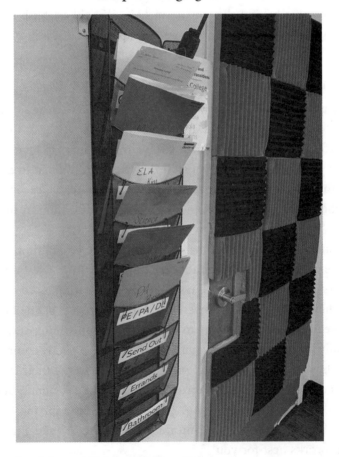

Figure 7.4   Hanging Inbox at Valence College Prep

Whether you select something simple or complex, let's walk through what goes into each bin.

Action. This bin is for stuff that does not fit *any* of the following categories, such as a flyer you need to read about a conference, a calendar with testing preparation, and handouts from that day's meeting. You need to be careful that items do not get "stuck" in here, by sorting through it daily during your Daily Closing Routine or in your Meeting with Myself (discussed in Chapter 6).

Grade. This bin should hold any work that you need to grade—either at school or at home. The papers that enter this bin can be graded quickly, such as homework, simple exit tickets, or classroom work. You may glance through these papers during a prep period, mark them with a check or check-plus, then record them in your grade book and place them in the "Return" bin. Or you may transport them home and then return them the next day. Of course it goes without saying that each set of papers should be paper-clipped together!

Return. This bin is for papers you have graded that need to be returned to students. You may end up emptying out your "Suitcase" (described later in the chapter) and putting your papers in there.

Office. This bin is for anything you need to take to the office or central hub of your school, such as a behavior referral form or a completed Individualized Education Plan (IEP).

Copy. This bin is for anything you need to copy (or if you are so lucky, have copied for you). After making the copies, move the papers to the bins in or near your Teaching Station, where you keep papers to distribute before or during class.

File. This bin is for anything that needs to be filed, such as notes from a PD session, a new insurance form you found in your mailbox, or information about an upcoming report card night. Depending on how you keep your student files, there may be pieces of student work or notes you want to keep on each student. For example, if you wanted to keep all end-of-unit math assessments for each kid, you would file them here until they got transferred (again, hopefully as a student job) into your student files.

 FAQ: What about the papers people hand me all day long?!

When I was teaching, I devised a way to carefully collect the slips of paper that came my way during the day so that I could follow up on or process them. This would include papers collected out of my teacher mailbox when on a trip to the office or the resource room. As you get pieces of paper throughout the day, toss them in the "moving" inbox in the back of your Together Teacher System, if you are a paper-based person. This could simply be a manila folder to "catch things"! If you are a digital person, you may carry a folder or a clipboard and deal with the items digitally during your Meeting with Myself.

The trick here is that you can't forget about them! Each day set aside time to go through the papers and note any deadlines and so on—and then *throw them away*. This practice would be part of your Daily Closing Routine or Meeting with Myself.

Reader Reflection: What are your next steps to break up your inbox?

2. Get Your Self-Care On

Many teachers like to keep personal supplies near their Teacher Workspace, in a special drawer or bin. I find it helpful to stock up on the following items at the beginning of the school year:

■ Granola bars and other healthy nonperishable snacks for low blood sugar moments (or so you can go to the gym right after school!). Many teachers I know keep instant oatmeal, canned soups, and a few other items handy for when they forget their lunch at home or need a hefty after-school snack to carry them through an evening event.

■ A few bottles of water for when you don't have time to fill yours between classes.

■ Aspirin or Tylenol for headaches (being careful that this medication is not accessible to students).

■ A spare pair of comfortable shoes, and Band-Aids for blisters on your feet.

■ Breath mints, Life Savers, or gum.

READER REFLECTION:

■ **What self-care supplies do you need at your desk?**

■ **Are there any you can purchase in bulk?**

3. Keep Your Inspiration High!

Many of us naturally create some kind of kudos or motivational board on which to hang nice notes from students, pictures of friends and families, and key mementos from class trips. Although this certainly isn't essential, it is pleasant to take a deep breath after a long day and reread a note from a former student thanking you for the time you sent a multiplication CD to her home to get extra practice during the summer. Almost twenty years later I still treasure my own letter from Joyce Green.

Reader Reflection: Where and how will you set up a Kudos board?

FAQ: Must I even have a desk?

Another option is to go deskless or create a mobile cart, as in Figure 7.5. Some Together Teachers choose not to have a desk at all!

"I don't have a desk. Having a teacher desk has shown me that I will create clutter if given the extra space. So I have one small table where I keep my essentials: a stash of purple grading pens, a desk organizer that has three compartments, and a basket for notebooks that are collected for the day."

—Tess

Valence College Prep Mobile Cart

Figure 7.5   Mobile Cart at Valence College Prep

TOGETHER TRANSPORT: MOVING MATERIALS BETWEEN SPACES

It is no secret that most teachers take work home at night and on the weekends. To do this well, you have to have a clear system for what to take home, how to transport it, and then how to get it back where it belongs the next morning. I think of this as preparing for a short trip. You probably have some things that always stay packed, like your toiletries, and then you have some things you add for the specific time or location, like a bathing suit if you're going to the beach. Let's think about going back and forth between home and school in the same way. There are some things you always keep in your teaching bag, such as colored pens for grading, lesson plans, and so on. Then there are different things you have to pack for each trip.

Meghan's Traveling Instructional Crate

Let's take a peek at Meghan's traveling crate (Figure 7.6). Inside, Meghan carries:

- Lesson plans by reading level
- A word work wall
- Ziploc bags of leveled books and supporting vocabulary cards
- Whiteboards
- Post-its and markers

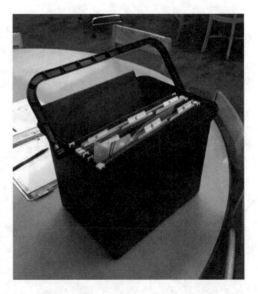

Figure 7.6　Meghan's Instructional Crate

I recommend purchasing a five- or seven-pocket accordion file and setting up tabs to match your teacher inbox so you can easily transfer manila folders between your Workspace and your backpack. It is helpful to have the papers in folders and an accordion file because student work can get damaged very easily when shoved into your bag.

- ■ **Action.** This tab is for stuff you have to do things with, but you don't yet know what!

- ■ **Grade.** This tab is where you would put any clipped papers to take home to grade. After you finish grading them, move them to the Return tab.

- ■ **Return.** This tab is where you transfer already-graded work to return to your students.

- ■ **Office.** This tab is for any papers that need to be returned to the office.

- ■ **Copy.** If you are lesson planning or creating any materials at home, this tab is where you would put the materials you need to copy.

- ■ **File.** You may find a paper in your tote bag about an upcoming PD session and this is where you want to file it for the future.

Now of course, any kind of traveling paper system could easily become a dumping ground. Let's add cleaning this out—and our bags—as a step in our Meeting with Myself each week.

 Reader Reflection: What materials do you need in order to maximize efficiency as you transport work between school and home?

CONTAIN THE INSTRUCTIONAL CHAOS. MEAN, MATERIALS

As teachers, we have SO many bits of stuff to make our lessons go around. I mean, between materials, curriculum manuals, manipulatives, and more, it can become easy to drown in the cacophony of instructional resources. In this section, we will take a quick peek at some of the higher leverage areas that will assist our Togetherness, such as creating professional libraries, digital material storage, and actual physical materials. The gist of this entire section is find things a home, label them, and return them. But if you want more detail, read on.

Create a Professional Library

Many of us are lucky enough to have borrowed, purchased, or been provided with multiple books and pamphlets to support our instructional planning. The key here is actually *finding* and using them when we need them. That wonderful instructional math book you purchased does you no good just sitting on a shelf somewhere. You will want to organize these resources to be as useful as possible and keep them where you do the bulk of your planning work. If you do most of your planning at school, it is helpful to have a bookshelf near your Teacher Workspace. If you do most of your planning at home, you may want to keep your resources in one location at home.

Most teachers choose to organize their instructional books by topic or content area. For example, if you are an elementary school teacher with responsibility for all subjects, you may designate a portion of your bookshelf for math resources and other sections for spelling, science, and so on. If you are a secondary teacher, you may organize your resources by class periods or content units.

READER REFLECTION:

- Where are all of your professional resources currently?

- Where should you situate them to be most useful to you while you plan?

- Are there any that you are no longer using or that are available online?

- Where do all of your workshop, PD, and graduate school materials currently exist?

- Are there any ways to organize them to make them more useful to you?

Organize Your Lesson Plans Electronically

Of course, you can search your hard drive or Google Drive when you want to pull up some lesson materials, but we all know how that goes. You should be able to reuse some of your materials each year, so let's make it easy to find and edit them! Similar to the previous sections in this chapter, we will show you a few samples and share some criteria. Then you can adapt to your context and make it your own.

Laura's Folder Hierarchy

Laura is incredibly intentional about her digital folder structure; (Figure 7.7) let's check it out!

After each unit, Laura carefully labels the PowerPoints and other materials. You can see by using the conventions U1.01, etc., she can keep her files in order of the class—and save time in the future!

Meghan's Google Drive

Meghan (Figure 7.8) is similarly intentional about her Google Drive organization!

File Edit View Tools Help			
Organize ▼ Include in library ▼ Share with ▼ New folder			
Name	Date modified	Type	
⭐ Favorites			
📥 Downloads			
📰 Recent Places			
☁ Google DriveFS			
Classroom Resources	1/13/2020 12:30 PM	File folder	
Content Team	1/16/2020 12:42 PM	File folder	
Summer School	9/5/2019 8:46 PM	File folder	
🖥 Desktop	Unit 1 Exploration & Colonization	9/5/2019 8:58 PM	File folder
📚 Libraries	Unit 2 American Revolution	9/5/2019 8:35 PM	File folder
📄 Documents	Unit 3 Constitution	9/5/2019 8:38 PM	File folder
🎵 Music	Unit 4 Early Republic & Jackson	1/16/2020 8:33 AM	File folder
🖼 Pictures	Unit 5 Industrialization, Manifest Destiny, ...	1/16/2020 6:44 AM	File folder
🎬 Videos	Unit 6 Civil War and Reconstruction	9/5/2019 8:39 PM	File folder
	Unit 7 STAAR & IA4 Prep	9/5/2019 8:39 PM	File folder

File Edit View Tools Help			
Organize ▼ Include in library ▼ Share with ▼ New folder			
Name	Date modified	Type	
⭐ Favorites			
📥 Downloads	U1.00 Welcome!	8/15/2018 5:45 AM	Microsc
📰 Recent Places	U1.01 Analyzing Documents using HAPPY	8/15/2018 5:45 AM	Microsc
☁ Google DriveFS	U1.01 Welcome!	7/24/2019 2:40 PM	Microsc
	U1.02 Reasons for European Exploration	8/15/2018 5:45 AM	Microsc
🖥 Desktop	U1.03 European Empires	8/22/2019 6:13 AM	Microsc
📚 Libraries	U1.04 Triangular Trade	8/23/2019 8:47 AM	Microsc
📄 Documents	U1.05 TEA Strategy	8/17/2019 9:26 AM	Microsc
🎵 Music	U1.06 Jamestown & Plymouth	8/23/2019 8:39 AM	Microsc
🖼 Pictures	U1.07 13 Colonies	8/27/2019 7:03 AM	Microsc
🎬 Videos	U1.08 13 Colonial Regions	8/27/2019 7:24 AM	Microsc
👤 Laura Burrow	U1.09 Religion in the Colonies 2019	8/29/2019 6:20 AM	Microsc
	U1.09 Religion in the Colonies	8/23/2018 8:35 AM	Microsc
💻 Computer	U1.10 Reasons for Colonial Self Governm...	8/30/2019 8:45 AM	Microsc
🌐 Network	U1.11 Enlightenment Ideas	8/28/2018 11:13 AM	Microsc
🎛 Control Panel	U1.12 Mayflower Compact	9/4/2019 6:13 AM	Microsc
🎛 All Control Pane	U1.13 Colonial Government	9/5/2019 8:17 AM	Microsc
🎨 Appearance and	U1.14 DBQ Essay Structure	9/11/2019 9:45 AM	Microsc
🕐 Clock, Languag	U1.15 Analyzing Documents	9/4/2018 7:03 AM	Microsc
🕒 Ease of Access	U1.16 Station Review	9/6/2019 8:34 AM	Microsc
🖧 Hardware and S	U1.17 DBQ Essay Final	9/6/2018 7:57 AM	Microsc
🌐 Network and Int	U1.18 CUA	9/7/2018 8:54 AM	Microsc
📦 Programs			
🔒 System and Sec			

Figure 7.7 Laura's Electronic Folders

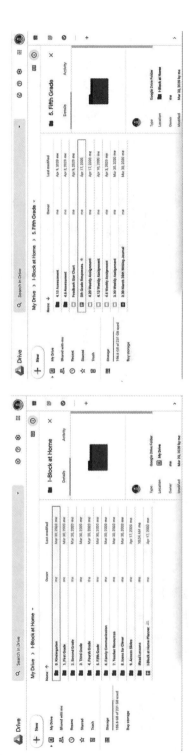

Figure 7.8 Meghan's Google Drive

If we go deeper, let's peek at Meghan's fifth-grade folder. She lists each assignment labeled by date.

Given how much work we put into creating really great lessons and units, we want to be able to use them, share them, and perfect them. Both Laura and Meghan have clear, simple, and thoughtful systems for organizing their digital materials.

Doing so requires an intentional filing system, so here is a basic summary of a simple approach.

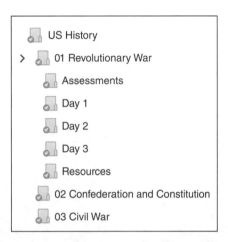

□ On your computer, create a file folder for each section or class you teach. For example, if you are a secondary teacher, the folder would be called US History. If you are an elementary school teacher with different subjects to teach, you may have a Math folder and a Writing folder.

□ Within each folder, include a subfolder for the unit name—in this case, Revolutionary War.

□ Inside that subfolder, create further subfolders for each day of the lesson, such as Day One, Day Two, Day Three, Assessments, and Resources.

□ The folder for each day would house a lesson plan, homework assignments, in-class handouts, supporting PowerPoint materials, and exit tickets.

READER REFLECTION:

■ **What electronic folders, files, or labels do you need to adjust?**

■ **How will you name your documents consistently?**

Clean Out the Cupboards! Organizing the ACTUAL Materials

Of course, this could be an entire book, and again, we are not going for Pinterest perfect here. We want our actual class materials to be efficiently located and well taken care of, so we don't waste our precious time tracking things down. Let's peek at a few examples! And if you need more models, definitely look on Pinterest or for all the other great books out there on classroom arrangement and procedures.

Nadia's Book Bins

Nadia A., an elementary educator in Austin, carefully organizes her class library with labels for each category (Figure 7.9).

Figure 7.9 Nadia's Book Bins

Veronica's Unit Labels

Veronica U., a pre-K teacher in Washington, DC, uses the old-fashioned laminated label method (Figure 7.10) to distinguish between types of books.

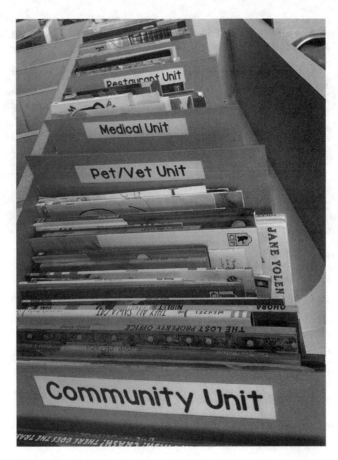

Figure 7.10   Veronica's Unit Labels

Veronica's Unit Bins

If you have a lot of stuff—such as art supplies, science materials, or thematic unit manipulatives—you may want to group them in bins, (Figure 7.11) like Veronica!

Figure 7.11   Veronica's Unit Storage

However you choose to organize your instructional materials, and whether you are lucky enough to have actual cabinets or shelves, we will want to follow the same simple process.

■ Stockpile anything you see that can be used for storage. Think used Amazon boxes, clear tubs, and so on.

■ Group similar items together.

■ Label the outside of the boxes or tubs. If you are not the label-maker type, masking tape and a Sharpie work just fine!

■ If handling individual items, such as calculators, give each item a number or barcode.

■ Stack or store them.

■ Bonus points for making a Table of Contents for your Cupboards.

    Reader Reflection: What are your next steps to clean out your cupboards?

NEW TEACHER ALERT

New teachers: trust me. When you go to teach the Revolutionary War unit next year, you will be so grateful to have everything in one place. The few seconds it takes to clearly name a document or put away all of the materials in a clear plastic tub will make all the difference in years to come. The reason I suggest organizing your instructional files by unit rather than by the date you previously taught the lesson is that this way makes them easier to relocate in the future. You may find that next year it makes sense to change the order of instruction or you may want to share your materials with a colleague.

FINDING WHAT YOU NEED WHEN YOU NEED IT

As hard as we try to be electronic and clutter-free, we still need to have certain pieces of reference information in hard-copy form at our fingertips. Depending on how frequently you refer to these pieces, you may want to keep some of them in a section of your Together Teacher System. Other pieces may be in individual manila folders in your filing cabinet or in hanging file crates so that you can find them quickly. Let's discuss both options.

At Your Fingertips Stuff!

Most teachers need to have a few key pieces of information ready at a moment's notice. Your clipboard will get cluttered if all of this information sits on it, so I recommend making a tab in your Together Teacher system—or a digital folder—and inserting it here. In the next section, I will recommend some possible items you may need at your fingertips throughout the teaching day.

- **Student information.** It is helpful to have frequently needed student information such as bus lists, after-school tutoring rosters, and reading levels listed in one place to easily reference during the day.

- **Family contact information.** Even though your students' family contact information is likely kept in a centralized database or on your own hard drive, it is helpful to have a printed version of all family phone numbers in your Together Teacher binder. You will be grateful. Plus, you are unlikely to enter eighty-something student phone numbers into your mobile phone. You may also use Google Voice, Class Dojo, or other piece of software to maintain all of those parent phone numbers.

■ **Colleague list and phone numbers.** Although it's likely you have the phone numbers of your closest colleagues, it's less likely that you have time to enter contact information for the entire staff. However, there will be times when you will want to have these phone numbers accessible—to call about a student, a snow day, or a missing homework assignment. Colleagues' and students' phone numbers may also come in handy when you are on a field trip and don't have access to a central database.

READER REFLECTION:

■ **What materials do you need at your fingertips?**

■ **Where should you put them so they are easily accessible (filing cabinet in labeled manila folders, hanging file crate, and so on)?**

Reference Information (aka "I Don't Need It Right Now, But I Might Later!")

Most teachers find there is a set of material they need to reference regularly, but not necessarily carry around at all times. Usually these are organized in a specific binder or filing cabinet. I have found it useful to keep a stack of hanging file folders, manila file folders, file folder labels, and a Sharpie marker all near a file cabinet area. There are many schools of thought regarding best ways to organize file cabinets, but I have generally found that the more specific the file names, the better, and that grouping like items with like items will help with searching for the correct materials. Each of us has different levels of paperwork to file. Don't worry about organizing it perfectly at first. If you cannot scan the paper and file it electronically, just get in the habit of dumping papers you may need to reference in the future into a labeled file folder in your cabinet or crate. Once individual files start to accumulate and you see categories emerge, then you can take the time to organize it more clearly and group manila folders in a hanging file folder. For now, just get those papers out of your inbox!

Some folders I have seen teachers create include the following:

■ **Testing Information**

Some teachers like to have information about how state test questions are formatted or specific skills their students need to master.

■ **State and District Standards**

To ensure lesson alignment with standards, teachers find it helpful to have their standards easily accessible.

■ **Professional Development Ideas**

This is where you would put flyers or other information relevant to interesting professional development ideas.

■ **Administrative Information**

This folder may contain information about benefits, retirement options, life insurance, and fingerprinting information.

READER REFLECTION:

■ **What materials do you need to reference regularly?**

■ **Where should you put them so they are easily accessible (filing cabinet in labeled manila folders, hanging file crate, and so on)?**

CARRY IT WITH YOU

You will likely find you need to take notes or write things down while teaching! Whether lesson adjustments or parents to call, most teachers feel a bit lost without a clipboard. But as I mentioned earlier, because our clipboards *hold* everything we need—from lesson plans to To-Do lists, notes *on* students and notes *from* students, behavior trackers and mastery trackers, state standards to reading levels—they become very full very quickly and quickly transform into a messy jumble of stuff, some of which requires action and some that just needs an occasional reference.

First step, let's purge! Go get your clipboard (or your equivalent folders and notebooks) and take a look at what they hold. Anything outdated? Stuff to copy? Bring to the office?

Now that you've given your clipboard a cold, hard look, let's talk about what should be on there and how it should be arranged. Let's take a gander at how Lindsey N., a first-grade teacher in Providence, uses clipboards (Figure 7.12) to keep her lesson plans and academic observation charts on hand.

Lindsey's Lesson Plans

Lesson plans are usually the first thing we refer to each day. Most Together Teachers like to have them on the top of their clipboard so they can refer to them while teaching. For

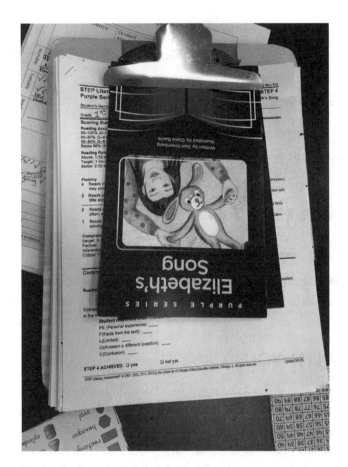

Figure 7.12   Lindsey's Clipboard—With Lesson Plans

example, if you have carefully planned higher-order thinking questions to ask while you read a history text, you will want your lesson plans easily accessible. Another trick many teachers use is to binder-clip their lesson plans to the front or back of their Together Teacher System.

Lindsey's Academic Observation Charts

Academic observations, like those shown in Figure 7.13, are the backbone of our teaching practice. Heads up: properly recording these observations is my obsession. As a frequent teacher observer, I die a little inside when I see folks teaching *without* a handy way to capture data to inform both their short- and long-term planning.

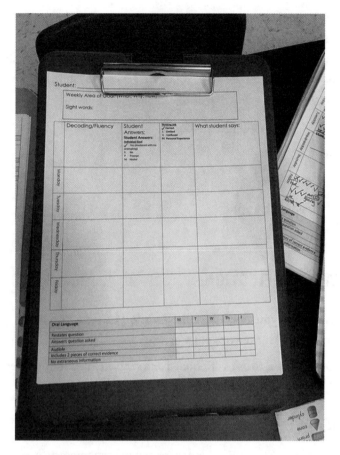

Figure 7.13 Lindsey's Clipboard—With Academic Observation Charts

Behavioral Data Logs

As teachers, we are constant collectors of data, and (at least for the time being) most of the data is on paper. As a teacher I was never empty handed. On my clipboard at all times were places to track informal instructional observations, behavior additions and deductions, participation points, and much more.

Behavioral data may include participation, positive and negative behavior, and any other behaviors you are monitoring. To track voluntary class participation, many Together Teachers keep a seating chart on their clipboard. Putting tick marks on this sheet is much more efficient than scanning a grade book for names listed in alphabetical order. During the Meeting with Myself, you can count up participation points and enter them into your grade book.

Homework Tracking Log

Homework tracking really depends on whether you are grading for effort, for completion, or for accuracy—or for some combination of these. At the very least you will want to know that everyone completed the homework. If you cannot grade all pieces of homework every day, you'll need a system for at least getting to it sometimes.

Now that we have discussed various instructional materials that Together Teachers put on their clipboards (or after a tab in their Together Teacher System), it is your turn to think about what you need to carry while teaching.

Basic Clipboard Materials Include:

☐ Lesson Plans

☐ Student Mastery Charts

☐ Student Participation Tracking

☐ Homework Tracking

READER REFLECTION:

■ **What do you need to carry while you teach? Lesson plans? Behavior trackers? Homework logs?**

■ **Do you want to use a clipboard or a section in your Together Teacher System?**

TURBO TOGETHERNESS

As we mentioned at the start of this chapter, paper management is a *beast* and having the right information at your fingertips takes a lot of planning. Hopefully we have walked through almost every piece of paper you encounter as a teacher and have designated a place to put it so that you can get everything done, capture real-time data and To-Dos, and have reference materials easily available.

☐ Set up your desk to create a more focused workspace.

☐ Create a system to manage your ingoing and outgoing papers.

☐ Identify how you will transport your materials between school and home and back again.

☐ Create and name folders (digital or hard copy) to store your teaching tools for future reference.

☐ Create a system for what you'll need with you when you teach: clipboard, instruction materials, etc.

☐ Identify what materials you'll need to reference on an ongoing basis and create a system for storing them.

Marin reflects back on her teaching career: "As I went into my second year of teaching, I discovered something amazing—the paper clip. No longer were student papers spread out all over my desk, the guided reading table, and student desks. No longer did I need to 'clean up' by making crisscrossing stacks of different worksheets and tests to correct. No longer was student work squashed in the bottom of my backpack with my snacks and leaky water bottle. Sounds obvious, right? It was such a simple thing, but it helped me *so* much. Not just with paper, but with my overall sense of being as a teacher. Paper clips meant more organization, which meant a cleaner classroom, which meant a calmer me, which meant calmer kids, which meant I could manage, which meant I could *teach*."

MAINTENANCE MOVES

After a month of making your adjustments to Tidy and Together Up Your Workspace, let's retake that self-assessment.

Area	Rating 3 = Rocking It 2 = Needs a Little Help! 1 = Needs a Lot of Help!
My Teacher Workspace (aka the desk) allows me to focus on my actual work, take care of myself, and stay inspired.	
My active papers are sorted efficiently so that I can move quickly to drop items at the office, hand out papers, etc.	
I have a strong system for transporting materials between school and home.	
I can easily locate my digital and hard-copy materials for past lessons, units, tests, etc.	
My Teaching Station (where my instructional materials are) allows for effective instruction.	
I can efficiently find common reference materials at a moment's notice, for example, family phone numbers, key dates, etc.	

Together Tour:

Angela Mu

Angela Mu teaches Introduction to Arts to students in grades 5–8 in Elmhurst, New York.

What is your favorite office supply you use in your classroom? Why?

I have quite a few MAGNETIC clips. I even stock some extras in my drawer to be prepared to use them!

What is your most used organizational tool to keep YOURSELF Together?

My Weekly Planner created on Google Sheets is my GPS and kind of my BFF! It is what I refer to constantly to keep me on track and on task sometimes over 20 times throughout the day. Links to meetings, lesson planning blocks, and when to complete observations for my department are all listed there.

How do you re-Together yourself when unexpected things pop up?

The schedule of a school is one where you must expect the unexpected to come up. First I need a mental reset where I'll take a few minutes to take some breaths and drink a yummy beverage—peach green tea is my go-to! Then I jump over to my Weekly Planner to readjust my schedule, identify my priorities, and reach out to the people that need to be informed of shifts that are occurring.

What is a time you had to adjust your Together practice and why?

I am currently adjusting my Togetherness practices since this is the first year we have a hybrid model due to the pandemic. This changed the logistics of routines and created some additional tasks to be added.

What is your top Together Trick to share with other teachers?

Use a countdown timer if you need an extra boost to complete a task you're not too excited about. Trying to beat the clock is one way I motivate myself to stay focused on it.

What is your favorite teaching snack?

My favorite teaching snack is apple cinnamon mini rice crisps!

Why does Togetherness matter to you?

Togetherness allows me to stay organized and helps me create a better work–life balance.

CHAPTER 8

The Inbox, the Texts, the Messages: Tame the Communications Chaos

SETTING THE SCENE

Consider, for a moment, a recent email you received from your principal or a parent. Oh, yes, you know the one I'm talking about—that email you opened, read, tried to make sense of, and then closed. Typically, we check our email quickly between classes, become overwhelmed by what we find in our inboxes, log out to suppress the anxiety, and fail to capture any important action steps or deadlines. By the time we log back in, a new swarm of emails has landed, making older messages not marked "new" as good as gone.

Communications are particularly challenging for us as teachers because we are not in front of our computers most of the day. We have limited time to process and respond to the important information that is being shuttled back and forth electronically across our schools. For many of us, email is an enormous time-suck. It can easily become the default activity whenever we have a free 5 or 10 minutes. The problem with compulsive email checking is that it doesn't give us time to actually *deal with* the message, so we end up raising our stress levels without any satisfaction of completion.

IN THIS CHAPTER, YOU WILL LEARN TO:

■ Create simple and efficient systems for responding to and filing email

■ Determine format and standards for writing clear emails.

■ Design regular routines for reviewing and acting upon forms of communication

■ Balance multiple incoming sources of information, such as texts, Slack, etc.

In this chapter, we will focus on habits that Together Teachers use to effectively manage all of the communication that comes from so many directions. In the first edition of this book, we focused this entire chapter on email. But fast forward almost ten years, and we now have a proliferation of ways people communicate. Add in the pandemic, and we have at least four more. Between Google Classroom, Slack, GChat, Canvas, Class Dojo, texts, GroupMe, Zoom, Microsoft Teams, and individual district platforms, information management has become, well, unmanageable.

   Reader Reflection: Self-assessment

Statement	Self-Assessment Score (1 to 5) (1=Not even close) (5=Got this down!)
I have a disciplined routine for checking and responding to email and other communications.	
I regularly reduce my inbox to fewer than 20 emails per week.	
When writing emails, I format them to ensure they are recipient-friendly.	
My colleagues, families, and students consider me responsive.	
I have a simple and effective filing system for managing my email; it is easy to find what I need.	

Name one strength and one gap in your current communications management system

Strength: _____

Area for growth: _____

■ If you are looking for support with organization and management of your inbox, start with the section titled Set Up for Success.

■ If your gaps/next steps are related to building better routines for checking and responding to email, begin with Establish Communications Routines or. . .Stop Checking Constantly!

■ If your gaps/next steps revolve around writing better emails, go to the section titled Write to Be Heard, or Stop Sending Open-Ended Emails!

Email Is Not the Enemy, But . . .

Email is not the enemy, but when it is abused, neglected, or not cared for properly, it can become out of control. *Out of control* means that your inbox is full of hidden To-Dos not accounted for in your Together Teacher System, thereby causing you tremendous stress and increasing the likelihood of missing something important. Why does this matter? It matters because most of us spend too much time scrolling through our inbox, rereading messages, and figuring out what we need to do with them, rather than systematically deciding how to deal with each email once and for all. Keep in mind that each school has its own unique communication culture, so you may have to adapt some of the ideas to work in your own context. We're assuming you work in a school where email is used as a regular communication tool between teachers, teachers and parents, and teachers and administrators. And email is certainly helpful for SOME things but not everything. The following is a quick chart that shares our beliefs.

Email is GREAT for. . .	Email is NOT so great for. . .
Nonurgent questions	Student emergencies
Distributing information to a large group	Controversial topics
Coordinating logistics	Anything that could spur lots of
Sharing documents	questions or back-and-forth replies
Asking clear questions of specific people	and exchanges
Following up to summarize a decision, meeting, or conversation	

After reviewing the previous chart, consider how well your school is doing in managing communications efficiently and effectively. Even if you are handy-dandy at being masterfully responsive, you may have a role to play in your school's culture overall. Let's focus on ourselves first, though, shall we?

SET UP FOR SUCCESS

Our goal here is to get our inbox as tidy as possible. To be clear, this does not mean you are answering every single message every day. Rather, you will answer quick questions and note when you need to block out time for longer replies on your Weekly Worksheet or Comprehensive Calendar. We will take a few small steps to create a simpler, more efficient structure for your inboxes.

 Reader Reflection: Checklist time! Use the following checklist to clean up your inbox so we can start your transformation with a clean slate:

☐ **Limit your total number of email accounts.** Aim for as few accounts as possible, so you don't waste your time searching for information in one place or another. For most teachers, this means:

■ a school account,

■ a personal account, and

■ one account for "junk" email, to use when you need to give an address to a shopping website.

☐ **Unsubscribe from any junk or updates you don't read.**

☐ **Synch your phone.** Set your phone options up so that emails you delete never appear in your inbox. This ensures that you don't have to reread the same old email over and over. Once you read an email on your phone and write a reply, you should delete it so you never have to read it again. The double read takes way too much time in your already busy day.

☐ **Direct your family and friends to where you want them to go.** Tell them which email account you prefer they use. For most of us, this is a case in which separation of the professional and personal is actually helpful. This way, you can avoid your

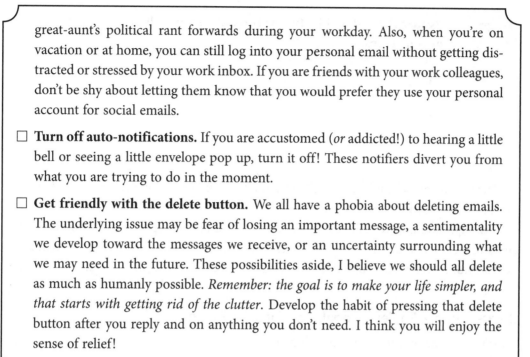

great-aunt's political rant forwards during your workday. Also, when you're on vacation or at home, you can still log into your personal email without getting distracted or stressed by your work inbox. If you are friends with your work colleagues, don't be shy about letting them know that you would prefer they use your personal account for social emails.

☐ **Turn off auto-notifications.** If you are accustomed (*or* addicted!) to hearing a little bell or seeing a little envelope pop up, turn it off! These notifiers divert you from what you are trying to do in the moment.

☐ **Get friendly with the delete button.** We all have a phobia about deleting emails. The underlying issue may be fear of losing an important message, a sentimentality we develop toward the messages we receive, or an uncertainty surrounding what we may need in the future. These possibilities aside, I believe we should all delete as much as humanly possible. *Remember: the goal is to make your life simpler, and that starts with getting rid of the clutter.* Develop the habit of pressing that delete button after you reply and on anything you don't need. I think you will enjoy the sense of relief!

A drastic approach—Declare email bankruptcy. If you are not sure where to start, you may need to use your one and only get-out-of-jail-free card and declare email bankruptcy. This involves deleting *every* message in your inbox. You can do a quick search on YouTube and find instructions on email bankruptcy! You may want to alert your colleagues in advance, and you should remember that you can declare bankruptcy only one time! It's scary, but you can do it. Close your eyes, take a deep breath, highlight, and drag your deleted messages into the trash. There—you *did* it! Get used to this feeling and purge your inbox regularly with using the methods that follow in this chapter. Caroline L., a teacher in Providence, notes, "Two years ago, my school leader sat next to me and forced me to delete everything. Truly, I have not looked back. I stole his folders. I have an Action Items folder (if it's not important enough to go there, I reply right away). I try to make sure emails are logistical, so I try to avoid communicating planning stuff via email. I check email once a day."

Reader Reflection: List two or three steps you will take to regain control of your inbox:

1

2

3

Great! Now go schedule the work time for these in your Comprehensive Calendar or Weekly Worksheet!

Although I do not want people to go crazy setting up a complex system for email filing and storage, there are some options that can make your inbox easier to get through. In the next section, I'll share best practices for filing and referencing information in your inboxes.

Create Simple Folders, Labels, or Tags for Filing

I don't recommend setting up fancy filing systems, because they are too time consuming to maintain. These days, searching is faster than filing, and your inbox should not function as a storage cabinet. Constant scrolling to figure out what you have to do is an inefficient use of your time. I recommend setting up just a few labels, folders, or tags.

Jesse's Before and After Inbox

Let's peek at a simple filing system in Figure 8.1.

As you can see, Jesse sets up very simple folders and numbers them with broad headings. A summary of his system follows.

1. **Processed:** If you have a deleting phobia, this is where all other emails that do not require action can be housed.

2. **Upcoming Meetings:** Drag and drop any emails about meeting agendas, notes, and next steps here.

3. **Projects:** An email can be saved to the projects folder if it contains material you need to reference for a project you are actively working on or if you anticipate needing the information in the future.

4. **Reference:** This is where you'll keep emails about instructional matters, passwords, dress code, or other policy/administrative issues.

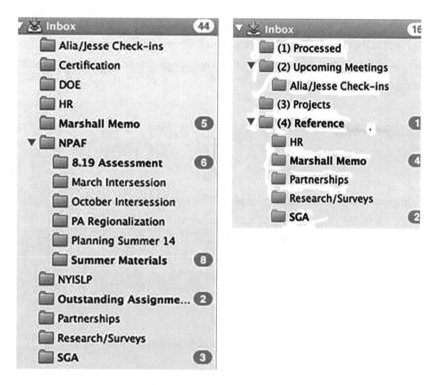

Figure 8.1   Jesse's Inbox: Before & After

Your email folders organize themselves alphabetically by default. You can override this function with a few quick tricks.

■ Put a number in front of each folder. For example, if you want the Upcoming Meetings folder to come first, then name that folder 1–Upcoming Meetings.

■ If you want to group particular folders, give them similar first names (see Figure 8.2). For example, if you want all of your instructional emails grouped together, you may label them "Instructional—Math" and then "Instructional—Reading."

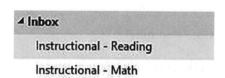

Figure 8.2   Folders for Instructional Emails

After this, respond to what's left. This is the hardest step, when it comes down to it, because you'll actually have to do more than click on a few buttons. But once you get this far, you'll have a lot fewer messages, and that alone may give you motivation to start working through the messages that remain.

TECH TIP:

If your Comprehensive Calendar or Weekly Worksheet is digital, you can simply drag the email into the calendar onto the day you want to deal with it, or into the digital task functions of both Outlook and Google.

READER REFLECTION:

List the current email folders, tags, or labels you plan to delete.

1

2

3

List the new email folder, tags, or labels you plan to create.

1

2

3

Now that you've got this new folder and label plan in place, head to your inbox and go make it happen!

Reader Reflection: Pop quiz!

What would you do with each of the following emails that have landed in your inbox? You are reviewing at 11:00 a.m., right before lunch duty.

The email you receive:	What you'll do/How you'll respond/ Where it will go:*
An update from your assistant principal that names the students who are *not* riding the bus today.	
An email from your grade-level leader confirming that she can meet with a parent on Tuesday.	
An urgent email from the office staff asking if you can call a parent ASAP about a "bathroom incident."	
A lengthy email from your academic coach giving feedback on your literature lesson plans.	
An email from your after-school coordinator laying out the process for finding additional work time for students in the afternoon.	

* Answers found at the end of the chapter.

Of course, all of the folders or labels in the world won't help us if we check incessantly, so let's address that next.

 FAQ: What about texts, Slack, GroupMe, and other notifications?

Welp, times have changed! There are a LOT more methods of communication than email these days. So, what do you do about the constant incoming stream of chatter?

■ Create a folder on your phone for all the real-time communications, so they are in one easy-to-reference place

- Commit to reviewing the folder every few hours and do not go anywhere else on your phone such as. . . ahem, Instagram. #togethertruth
- Keep your Weekly Worksheet handy to jot down any action steps

ESTABLISH COMMUNICATIONS ROUTINES OR . . . STOP CHECKING CONSTANTLY!

Now that we've tackled structural issues like inbox setup and folder downsizing, let's get a little more personal. Let's talk about ways to curb our own information addiction and be more purposeful about when we actually "do" email. It will help to start by reading about Verana and examining her own email habits and then reflecting on our own!

READER REFLECTION: UNDERLINE/CIRCLE

<u>Underline</u> habits you already have in place; circle new habits you may want to try.

Verana receives A LOT of email. However, like most of us, she doesn't have much "extra" time in her day and certainly didn't get into this line of work to answer email all day! That said, her colleagues and families count on her to be responsive. Let's look at a day in her life and see how she deals with this challenge.

7:15–7:30 a.m. After arriving at work, Verana does a quick scan of her email on her laptop while drinking a cup of coffee, mass deletes anything she won't need, and answers three urgent, short questions from folks on her agreed-upon VIP/rapid response-needed list: one from an operations director (so she doesn't hold up his process), one from a principal with an instructional question, and another from a colleague about the unit plan they are designing together. Her colleagues have flagged these emails as QQs (or Quick Questions) to signal that these require only "yes/no" answers. She flags/stars three other emails that will require longer responses and turns these emails into Tasks for her Weekly Worksheet. Everything else has to wait. She turns her attention toward one of her priorities—setting up her student stations.

10:00–10:30 a.m. During a designated email work block already booked in her calendar during her prep period, Verana again scans her total inbox on her laptop, trashes anything unnecessary, and files a few items into folders. For example, another teacher on her grade-level team shared the rubrics he is using on an upcoming writing assignment and asked for her input to ensure alignment. Verana stores this with her other curriculum planning materials in her Projects folder. She checks her calendar and schedules a time to carefully review and respond. She can pull up those materials when she needs them, but they're out of her inbox until then.

12:30–12:45 p.m. It's lunchtime! Verana scans her email on her phone. She receives a very long email that is unclear on what she needs to do next, so she forwards it back to the sender and asks him to bullet out his specific questions. A few emails from school distribution lists have gone directly to folders set aside for school communications. Otherwise, Verana scans, trashes, files a few things in her Processed folder, and then replies to any leftover emails from earlier in the day.

5:00–6:00 p.m. Students are gone for the day. This is when a lot of people call or email her! Before responding to these immediate requests, Verana tackles those three emails from the morning that required longer responses. Then, she tries to find the colleague who emailed her with assessment questions, so she can discuss in person. Too complicated for email! She also notes in her calendar a few emails she needs to tackle that evening at home—hoping to keep these to a minimum. After that, she works through her inbox starting with the emails that came in YESTERDAY, not the stuff from today!

READER REFLECTION:

- **What is one thing you are doing well in managing your email?**
- **What is one small thing you could change about your email routines that would have a big impact?**

Why Email Is Hard to Resist

Reducing the frequency with which you check your email takes an *incredibly* high amount of discipline. I'm a moderately disciplined person myself and it's *all I can do* not to check my iPhone right now as I write this paragraph. Why do we all struggle with this? I think there are a few reasons.

Reason 1: Focusing is *hard*. It is incredibly hard to focus these days with so much coming at us from all directions. At any given moment you may have an incoming text from a parent, an urgent email from your assistant principal—and your mom leaving you three voice mails about your grandparents' 50th wedding anniversary. Answering emails is one way we *feel* accomplished—sometimes without actually moving much of value forward.

Reason 2: Email *feels* like a nifty little present. We all secretly hope that what may appear in our inboxes is actually more *interesting* than what we are doing right at this moment. One of my favorite teacher trainers in the country says, "Each email feels like it could be some sort of little, neatly wrapped gift—waiting there for you in bold font, teasing you with possibility. How could you *not* open it?"

Reason 3: Being proactive is much harder than being reactive. Reacting is easier than acting. Replying is always easier because you get to think less. You can just *do. Oh, someone needs something from me? Let me help them. I am so useful and important.* It is *much* easier to reply to an email from your grade-level chair about a student discipline issue than it is to think about how to crack the nut with your struggling readers.

So, given all of these temptations and reasons to be glued to our inboxes, how do we fight this habit? The first way is to have designated times that you check email, rather than half-heartedly checking it all day long.

Routines for Checking

How often to check email often depends on the culture and practices of your school, but most teachers can get away with checking two to three times per day. Most teachers check email first thing in the morning, at some point in the middle of the day, and again at the end of the day. The pandemic may have shifted some of these habits, and things may also require adjusting when we change roles or environments.

If your school uses email frequently to communicate about urgent issues	If your school regularly sends emails containing important information and deadlines but does not use email for urgent issues	If your school uses email irregularly
Try to check email briefly every few hours. Write down any action steps, file anything that needs to be referenced later, and delete anything you do not need to read again. Do not just scan and close. You will be doing double work later.	Choose one to three times per day to read email, and deal with it using the strategies listed in the next section.	Choose once per day to read and reply. • Tier your customer service. Make a list of who gets high-priority responses. For example, your principal or parents with urgent questions may get immediate replies. • Weekly cleanout as part of Meeting with Myself. Each week you will ensure there are no unanswered or unresolved emails.

You will note that *none* of these options say to check email between every class and at every prep period. This will result only in raising your blood pressure. By proactively electing times of day to review and deal with your email (or to delay responses that take more time), you'll move through your inbox much more efficiently.

Think about when it will make the most sense for you to check your email. Nadia, a teacher in Austin, notes, "I have worked to consolidate my email. I read through it, identify the action step, and reply with *Got it*. I hate clutter. If I see an email that isn't time sensitive, I'll deal with it later in the week."

 Reader Reflection: When will you schedule your email checks? Create a schedule for yourself in the following table.

I will check my email at the following times:	For how long?	On which device?
Check #1—		
Check #2—		
Check #3—		
Check #4—		

I will **not** check my email at the following times:

Now go schedule your email checking times in your Comprehensive Calendar or on your Weekly Worksheet!

Responding Efficiently

Now that we have discussed *when* to check email, let's discuss *how* to check email. As you read, the teachers mentioned in this chapter try to touch each email only one time—and resist looking at email all day long as a distraction. I've found that most of us need structured choices to help us check email only once. One of my favorite blogs, Productive Flourishing (http://www.productiveflourishing.com), describes a method called STAR that will help you deal with the email deluge.

What to do with your email? The STAR-D method

■ **S**can your inbox for senders and subjects. This step gives you a higher perspective on what's in your inbox: you have to know where you're starting from and where you're going.

■ **T**rash everything that's not relevant, useful, or something you want or need. You may see 60% of the messages in your inbox disappear at this one step alone.

■ **A**rchive means "archive relevant reference information." A lot of messages just contain information that you want to keep but don't need any specific action from you at this time. Archiving them clears them from your attention, and this may account for 20% to 30% of the messages in your inbox.

■ **R**espond. This is an easy one.

■ **D**efer. This means the email will take too much time, and it needs to be dealt with later. This can be dangerous territory if you forget to check your deferral mechanism, so use it wisely. Most email clients have mechanisms, such as Boomerang, that allow you to send emails back to yourself on a certain date.

 Reader Reflection: What is your email deferral method? (e.g. flag, star, write in a To-Do list)

Deferral Methods	
Google	**Outlook**
Boomerang back to yourself	Delay delivery
Star the email	Drag to calendar
Priority-sorted inbox	Flag
Drag to Tasks	

Now that we have reviewed how to structure your inbox and plan your routines, let's dive into how we actually communicate.

FAQ: This sounds great, but there is no way I can get my school on board with using email like this. My team leader/principal/coach expects me to be glued to the screen every second!

The email beast cannot be conquered alone. If you like these ideas and think they could help your school tame email (or at least use it more wisely), here are a few ways to start:

- If your culture allows it, have a courageous conversation with your school leaders about the impact being glued to your phone has on your ability to build relationships with students.

- Tell your grade-level team or department what you have been reading about, what you're noticing is challenging, and share this chapter with them.

- Ask them if they would be willing to try a simple set of Communication Agreements. We'll discuss these later in the chapter.

- Use the Communications Audit (found on our website) to gather data. Things could be better—or worse—than you think.

CREATE SCHOOLWIDE COMMUNICATION AGREEMENTS

Many schools have revisited their approach to communications in light of the pandemic, thus attempting to articulate expectations that have previously been unspoken. Figure 8.3 shows how Arthur Ashe School in New Orleans lays out their communication agreements.

School Communication Agreements

I appreciate many things about Arthur Ashe's agreements, including:

1. Clarity of when you use various forms of communications

2. Naming respect for the recipient and writing accordingly.

3. Cutting countless responses. Fewer emails!

4. Delineating between what can be in-person/video call versus text versus email.

 Reader Reflection: Does your school need Communication Agreements? What is the top challenge you hope to address?

20-21 STAFF COMMUNICATION NORMS

"To effectively communicate, we must realize that we are all different in the way we perceive the world and use this understanding as a guide to our communication with others."- Anthony Robbins

During these unprecedented times, how we communicate and what we communicate will be crucial to our health as a school and team; therefore establishing a clear communication plan will be crucial. With that being said, please see the communication plan below and familiarize yourself as this is how we will interact as a team moving forward.

Form of Communication	Purpose or Typical Use
Person to Person (or Google Hangout)	1:1 meetings, Grade-level meetings, Team Huddles, Difficult Conversations or ugent student concerns
Text	Use for quick responses, shoutouts, or immediate needs, ie. Operational Needs, Send-Outs (Behavior Assistance other than fighting/crisis)
Phone Call	Use this for urgent matter (such as a crisis) and/or something that will take 3-5 minutes to discuss/resolve
Email	Use to follow-up on in-person conversations or meetings, 2nd Way to call off (after speaking with your supervisor; see Sick Day Protocol)

Email Norms:
- ★ We use our Firstline Schools email for all official school business. We adhere to the FLS Handbook when emailing about students (refer to the FLS Handbook about student privacy).
- ★ General Rules for using emails (adapted from MCD and TED's Chris Anderson)
    - ○ Respect Recipients' Time- This is the fundamental rule. As the message sender, the onus is on YOU to minimize the time your email will take to process. Even if it means taking more time at your end before sending. **We respond to all emails within 24 hours.**
    - ○ Make Subject Lines and Content Clearer- Start with a subject line that clearly labels the topic. Use crisp, muddle-free sentences. If the email has to be longer than five sentences, make sure the first provides the basic reason for writing. Avoid strange fonts and colours. We will use the following codes in our subject lines: **QQ- quick question, ACTION- This item requires an action from the receiver, Follow-Up-item requires follow-up, reminder or FYI**
    - ○ Slash Surplus cc's- CC's are like mating bunnies. For every recipient you add, you are dramatically multiplying total response time. Not to be done lightly! When there are multiple recipients, please don't default to 'Reply All'. Maybe you only need to cc a couple of people on the original thread. Or none.
    - ○ Cut Contentless Responses- You don't need to reply to every email, especially not those that are themselves clear responses. An email saying "Thanks for your note. I'm in." does not need you to reply "Great." That just cost someone another 30 seconds.

Figure 8.3   Arthur Ashe's Communication Norms

WRITE TO BE HEARD, OR STOP SENDING OPEN-ENDED EMAILS!

I have frequently seen how the problem with email and other communications—too many or lack of clarity—lies with the author of the message rather than its already overburdened recipients. Many of us unintentionally use email as an opportunity to revisit our college creative writing skills, rather than viewing it as a tool to help us complete our work more efficiently. Emails should be warm, brief, and clear. It sounds silly but a clearly written email can make all the difference, because it will spur equally clear (and fewer) follow-up items.

Let's read an effective email (Figure 8.4). What do you notice?

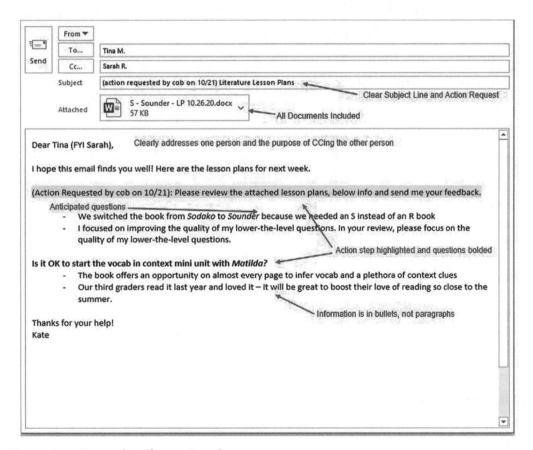

Figure 8.4   Example Effective Email

Elements of an Effective Email

- **Actions requested are at the beginning of the email.** All your reader really cares about is what he or she needs to do and by when.

- **Context.** There is a clear context for the teacher's ask, which is offered *after* the actions requested.

- **Specificity.** The teacher names what time is meant by "close of business" and exactly where the forms are to be turned in.

- **Clarity.** A resource is provided for additional information.

- **A clear subject line** includes the topic and the Response-Requested-By date.

- **Good use of spaces, bullets, and other signposts** helps the reader determine what's most important. If you really want to get clear replies to your questions, bullet them.

- **Do the heavy lifting for the recipient.** Propose possible solutions or responses.

Dangers of Unclear Messages	
If it's written without a clear deadline. . .	You'll receive a less thoughtful ASAP reply or none at all
If you embed questions throughout rather than clearly list or bullet. . .	You and others will spend more time reading and replying
If information is missing. . .	You and others will spend more time playing email ping-pong as you shoot messages back and forth

Clean Up Those Subject Lines

I am a bit of a zealot on clear subject lines. They create and clarify the level of priority for your audience. When subject lines are not clear or when they create unnecessary urgency, we get glued to our inboxes and feel compelled to respond to everything the second it hits. To combat this, we can use some simple tags to help clarify the nature of the email for our reader. The following table contains a few samples of subject lines that are commonly used in schools with strong communication systems.

Sample Email Subject Lines and Examples

Type of Subject Line	Definition	Example
FYI	This stands for *For Your Information,* meaning the reader should be kept in the loop on the email's subject but *does not have to respond.*	**Subject Line: FYI: Victoria's Mom has been contacted** Dear Jenny, I contacted Victoria's mom about the missing homework, and she is on top of it moving forward. Maia
Action Requested by X Date	When you request that someone else do something but you do not need a reply.	**Subject Line: Parent Phone Calls [Action Requested between 10/7–10/17]** Dear Grade Team, As we discussed in this week's meeting, please make at least five positive parent phone calls between 10/7 and 10/17 and record them in the Google document. Thanks, Jenny
Response Requested by X Date	You are expecting a reply from your respondent. Your school or team should establish norms for response times so you can be clear on what is expected of you. Some schools set up an agreement that you should allow three to four days for messages that require a 30-minute or more reply.	**Subject Line: Best Approach to Student Holiday Celebration [Response Requested by 11/17]** Dear Grade Team, As you know, it is time to determine our collective approach to student holidays in our grade. We have three options: 1. Class potluck 2. A small Secret Santa exchange within classrooms 3. No celebration but a thematic unit Please let me know your choice or alternative suggestion by November 17. Thanks, Jenny

(Continued)

Type of Subject Line	Definition	Example
QQ	This stands for *Quick Question*. Consider it reserved for items that are *truly* quick questions, meaning that the receiver can give a yes or no answer. The general expectation here is 12 to 24 hours of response time.	**Subject Line: QQ: "Gloria's Way"?** Jenny, Do you have the book *Gloria's Way*? Maia
Urgent	Use this one wisely. This means you need a reply in less than 24 hours, and you should follow up with a phone call to signal your urgency. If you feel yourself compelled into the world of red exclamation points, remember that most people with whom you work are *not* in front of their computer all day; therefore, a phone call or text *may* be more appropriate.	**Subject Line: URGENT/IMPT: Terrell's missing permission slip** Dear Jenny, Terrell forgot his permission slip for today's trip. Can you please have the office call his family as soon as possible? Maia

Now, you don't want to start just using these subject lines without discussing them with your department, grade level, or school community. That would not go over very well! This is great stuff to include in your school's Communication Agreements, like the previous example.

> ### Tech Tip:
>
> Take full advantage of Outlook and Google to create email templates for standard questions. For example, let's say you get lots of questions from guardians about passwords! Wouldn't it be great to have a plug 'n' play template ready to go?

Format Your Emails to Get Better Replies

It sounds simple but the way you format your emails can be a help or hindrance to your reader. Although it may feel overly formal at first, remember the goals are to help you get a reply and help you get what you need to move forward.

Reader Reflection: Edit it!
Read the following email from a teacher to her colleagues:

Hey Team,

Thanks so much for your input at today's grade-level meeting. I wanted to recap our next steps. Can you all review and let me know if they look right to you? Candace, you agreed to ask Michelle if we can adjust the time of our Funtastic Friday. When will you have an answer? Frost, you said you'd buy the food. Thanks for having that ready the Thursday before the Funtastic Friday. Amanda, you said you would get prizes for games. When will you have that info?

Thanks so much!

Kate

Reader Reflection: List three ways to improve this email:

- ■ **Rewrite this email in the space below:**
- ■ **What elements of an effective email did you incorporate?**

EMAIL: USE IT, DON'T ABUSE IT!

In our current digital world (and the pandemic has multiplied this 10 times over), we can find ourselves using email for almost everything at all times of day: urgent issues, missives about our complaints, quick questions, complicated student issues, funny videos, tricky parent situations, and so on. Although email is always convenient, it is not always appropriate.

Common Email Offenses

Now that you will ask yourself "Do I need to send this?" before hitting the Send button, let's talk about when it is appropriate to use email and when it is not. The four most common email offenses that all of us commit are listed in the following table.

Four Common Email Offenses

Using email in an emergency	Some schools create email urgency addictions for both the teachers and the administrators by using email in emergency situations. If you have to run to check your email every hour, you can't focus on teaching. *Email is not for emergencies*. Set up different protocols in your school for emergencies, preferably using phone, texting, walkie-talkie, or an old-fashioned note sent by student messenger to the principal.
Using email to resolve conflicts or disagreements	I have a personal rule on this one: If I find myself irritated by an email, I have to wait at least 24 hours to reply. Just avoid this. You know why. Nothing good ever happens. Set up a time to speak in person. Avoid starting email wars. If you receive an email that may be laden with emotions, resist the urge to reply. Pick up the phone or have a meeting to discuss the issue.
Using email to deal with complex issues	Complex issues (e.g. overhauling your team's approach to writing instruction) usually involve multiple people and lots of nuance, neither of which lend themselves well to email. Given the scope of the topic (and likely strong opinions!), save complex issues for department meetings.

Using email to give unsolicited feedback or to try to initiate major change	Change is good. Change from teachers is especially good. But writing an email to your principal that is incredibly long-winded and replete with big issues and new ideas will end up being very time-consuming for you—and cumbersome for your principal to respond to. It's unlikely you'll get a thoughtful reply. Schedule a meeting instead.

READER REFLECTION: LOOK IN THE MIRROR

■ **What's one email offense you are sometimes guilty of?**

■ **What's one change you can commit to making?**

Now what we have established that email is not always the answer for complexity, let's look at ways we CAN actually handle issues of more depth. The next section shares ideas to keep conversations moving.

FAQ: What if my boss abuses email?

We get it. Your coach, principal, district, or colleagues may not abide by this chapter. Perhaps urgent news is delivered via email daily. Perhaps it feels like you need to be constantly glued to your messages. And then this sets the tone for everyone else. We hear you. Here are a few ideas if you face this predicament.

■ Urgent messages constantly delivered via email? Plan a quick scan each hour looking for stuff from the urgent sender. Or consider creating filters to grab these emails quickly.

■ Tricky news shared for input within a message? See if you can schedule a meeting to thoughtfully communicate your thoughts in person.

■ Huge paragraphs that are tough to decipher constantly land in your inbox? Set aside extra time in your Weekly Worksheet to decode the actual asks. If you have a strong relationship, you could even offer some assistance in the form of drafting the emails or setting up a clear outline! Be prepared to pitch in!

Communicate Differently: Moving Beyond Email

Here is a list of ideas for when you can use email to *start* communication on an issue, even if you may need to ultimately resolve it through some other means.

Options to Move Beyond Email

Propose solutions. Earlier we discussed the common error often made via email in which the sender throws out too many questions at one time. Instead, be the person who offers solutions to the challenge you've just posed. By proposing ideas, you give people something to respond to so they don't have to come up with the answers all by themselves. This will ease the load on them and increase the chance that they will respond. You will be amazed at how much more quickly things get resolved.	"Hi everyone—With our grade-level field trip coming up on May 12, let's figure out how we want to handle permission slips. A few options: 1. Work together to create, then handle distribution/collection/tracking in homeroom 2. Divide and conquer tasks (one of us creates + distributes, one collects, one handles calling families with reminders) 3. Have students turn them in to office; we divvy them up and track through shared Google doc Please let me know your preferred option by end of day on Friday, and we'll get started at our grade-level meeting next Tuesday."
Create daily huddles. If you find yourself obsessively emailing your coteacher (despite being in the same room!) or dashing off a missive to your grade-level chair at the end of every day, consider adding a "daily huddle" to your calendar. You may find that meeting in person for a few minutes each day is all you need to discuss items that would constitute 5 to 10 separate emails.	For example, "Hi 11th-grade team—Here is the agenda for our huddle tomorrow morning at 7:15 in Room 212: 1. Check in (2 min) 2. Field trip planning (10 min) 3. Next steps + closing (5 min) See you then!"

Shut down the email chains. You've all experienced it: the back and forth that adds person after person to a largely irrelevant email chain. When you review all of the messages in full, you notice that each person involved has raised a different issue (And what about this behavior issue? And while we are at it, should this student go on the field trip? And what about this incentive system overall?). Nothing moves forward, and the only thing created is confusion. Instead, step in and offer a concrete next step. You do not have to be the official leader of the team or grade to suggest this. Trust me, people will appreciate this necessary intervention.

For example, "Hey, all, I'm so glad we have so many opinions on this important issue. I think it makes sense for us to gather for 15 minutes tomorrow to try and resolve this. If this works, can we each bring our ideas for solving this, and can everyone be free at 4 p.m.? Just reply to me directly and we will meet in Ms. Anderson's room."

FAQ: What about texting? Many teachers and schools use texting—or other fast-acting messaging services—throughout the day. If you CAN deal with it in the moment, please do! But if you are distracted all day by incoming messages, consider marking off certain times to check and act on them, just as you will for email.

TURBO TOGETHERNESS

Email organization is one of those things we tend to put off until a rainy day when we magically have a time to file the six thousand messages that have accumulated in the past few years. Sorry; that day is not coming.

Instead, here's a checklist you can use NOW to get started on taming your inbox:

☐ To stage the initial intervention, review the list of structural suggestions in the Set Up for Success section.

☐ Limit your total number of email accounts.

- ☐ Unsubscribe to any junk or updates you don't bother to read.
- ☐ Get your phone and computer inboxes synchronized.
- ☐ Direct your family and friends to where you want them to go.
- ☐ Turn off the auto-notifications.
- ☐ Get friendly with the delete button.
- ☐ Declare email bankruptcy if needed.
- ☐ Set up simple filing systems and get your emails filed.
  - ☐ Processed
  - ☐ Upcoming meetings
  - ☐ Projects
  - ☐ Reference
- ☐ Select times of day to answer emails and block them into your schedule on your Weekly Worksheet.
- ☐ Use the STAR-D method to go through your emails with a clear purpose.
  - ☐ **Scan**
  - ☐ **Trash**
  - ☐ **Archive**
  - ☐ **Respond**
  - ☐ **Defer**
- ☐ Establish clear writing habits.
- ☐ Decide if email is the best way to communicate the information.

MAINTENANCE MOVES

Once you have tried all of these strategies for at least a month, consider gathering data about how it is going. Here is a nifty table to gather up some of details about incoming and outgoing communications. You could complete it as a whole grade level or department—or even whole school team—and work to create some simple communication agreements.

	Day 1	Day 2	Day 3	Day 4
EMAIL	How many work-related emails did I SEND by end of day?			
	Sort by SENT messages. Did I send any groups or individuals more than five messages? If so, who?			
	How many work-related emails did I RECEIVE by end of day?			
	Did any individuals send me more than five messages? List them!			
	Select five randomly received emails. How well were they written? 3 = easy to reply 1 = really hard to reply	Example: Email from grade-level lead regarding next week's field trip. Kind of a random paragraph. Rating = 1. **1.** **2.** **3.** **4.**			

(*Continued*)

	Day 1	Day 2	Day 3	Day 4
EMAIL	How many TIMES did you check your email per day? *Feel free to use hash marks if you are writing by hand.*			
	How many hours/minutes did you spend replying to email? *End of day total is fine.*			
	Review messages at end of each day. Select **A.** at least one RECEIVED and **B.** one SENT email that should not have been sent, and state why.	**A.** Received an email from coteacher that could have waited for our 1:1 as it was not an urgent matter. **B.** Sent an email to VP that could have waited for professional development.		

TEXTS	How many work-related texts did I RECEIVE?				
	How many work-related texts did I SEND?				
PHONE CALLS	How many work-related phone calls did I RECEIVE?				
	How many work-related phone calls did I MAKE?				
	Other daily reflections?				

* Email Quiz Answer Key:

1. A daily email update from your assistant principal that names the students who are *not* riding the bus: Quickly copy onto your bus list (kept in your Together Teacher System as a frequently referenced document) the names of three students who are not going on the bus. Then delete the email.

2. A reply email from your grade-level leader stating she can meet with a parent on Tuesday: Reply quickly to confirm the room location and enter the information into your Comprehensive Calendar *or* send the grade-level leader a meeting invite with the room details. File the email in the Meetings folder.

3. An urgent email from the office staff asking if you can call a parent ASAP about a "bathroom incident": Write this down in the schedule portion of your Weekly Worksheet for the next "free time" you have and include the parent's phone number. Reply to the office staff immediately to let them know you will follow up, and delete the email.

4. A lengthy email from your academic coach giving feedback on your literature lesson plans: Leave the email in your inbox until you revise the plans after school that day. Advanced answer: File in the Projects folder in a subfolder called Lesson Plan Feedback. Return to the feedback the next day when you have a Time Block for updating your plans. This Time Block in your schedule will trigger you to return to the information, so that's right, you guessed it, go ahead and delete that email!

5. An email from your after-school coordinator laying out the process for finding additional work time for students in the afternoon: File in the Projects folder in a subfolder called After School. Put a note in the Next Week section of your Weekly Worksheet and build this into your schedule for the following week.

CHAPTER 9

Papers, Supplies, and Assignments: Support Student Togetherness

SETTING THE SCENE

How quickly student papers, those wonderful collections of student learning, become the bane of our existence. They're everywhere—sitting on teacher desks, in student desks, in teacher tote bags, in student backpacks; they litter the hallway, get shoved into lockers, and bust out of binders, seeming to multiply at every minute! I thought long and hard about including this chapter or not, but after spending an afternoon in New Orleans with a group of post-high school students juggling schoolwork and internships, I remain increasingly convinced teachers have a big role to play in helping students use their time well. The shift to student-at-home during the pandemic also cast a bright light on the need to help students set up their space and manage their time, just as we do as teachers.

IN THIS CHAPTER, YOU WILL LEARN TO:

■ Share long-term calendars and daily To-Dos for students to self-manage

■ Consider key aspects of your classroom, such as student papers and student space

■ Set up your classroom and expectations to support Student Togetherness

An article from Harvard University describes all of these skills like this: "Being able to focus, hold, and work with information in mind, filter distractions, and switch gears is like having an air traffic control system at a busy airport to manage the arrivals and departures of dozens of planes on multiple runways. In the brain, this air traffic control mechanism is called executive function." Schools and teachers play a huge role in helping students learn these skills, which in turn, will help them prepare for life! No one wants to be late to a wedding, delayed on a college assignment, or worse.

 Reader Reflection: Student togetherness self-assessment

Rate each area on a scale of 0–3. Zero means you have not yet thought about it; 3 means you are 100% there.

My classroom materials and methods model organization to my students.	I set expectations for Student Togetherness through clear diagrams and models.	I clearly communicate our short- and long-term classroom assignments.	I teach and support Student Togetherness through explicit instruction.

As you rate yourself, feel free to jump around to sections of this chapter that will support Student Togetherness the most. Let's get started with the easiest section—giving our students a sense of what is coming in our classrooms.

DISPLAYING CLASS SCHEDULES AND SYLLABI

We want to get our students thinking ahead so they can learn to plan and anticipate—skills they will need in college and beyond. In this section, we will review several simple ways to ensure we are helping our students plan their own long-term activities—whether simply thinking ahead to recess or planning to complete a long-term assignment.

Post Daily Class Activities

At the elementary level, it can be helpful to lay out the full day schedule for your students to see, like Nadia does in Figure 9.1. Students can easily follow along with the flow of the day, prepare their materials for the upcoming classes, and mentally get ready for fun breaks!

Figure 9.1   Nadia's Daily Schedule for Students

Teachers of younger grades may find a simple outline of the plan for the day is an effective way to communicate with students. Secondary teachers may want to give their students a longer-term view of assignments, readings, and other coursework.

Share Weekly Class Schedules Digitally

Because we couldn't use our whiteboards during the pandemic, we had to get used to posting agendas and sharing schedules in different ways. Figure 9.2 shows how Jessica S., a second-grade teacher in Charlotte, shared the weekly Zoom overview with her students.

Jessica's class could refer to just one place to see what instruction was live, when they had independent work time, and when they'd connect with other teachers. I like this model because it was one place to peek for the entire schedule with all links right there!

Mrs. Secondi's HOMEROOM Schedule				
	MONDAY	**TUESDAY**	**WEDNESDAY**	**THURSDAY**
8:30 - 9:00	**Morning Meeting** with Ms. Secondi			
9:00 - 10:20	**Block 1 LIVE** -- Instruction & Work Time with Ms. Secondi (Language Arts)			
10:20 - 10:30	**Break** (bathroom/snack)			
10:30 - 11:00	Connect LIVE **Art**	Connect LIVE **Media**	Connect LIVE **Technology**	Connect LIVE **Music**
11:00 - 12:00	**Block 2 LIVE** -- Instruction & Work Time with Ms. Sisley (Science/Social Studies)			
12:00 - 12:30	**Lunch**			
12:30 - 1:00	**Recess**			
1:00 - 1:30	**Independent Work Time (assignments are posted in Canvas)**			
1:30 - 1:55	**Block 2 LIVE (continued)** -- Instruction & Work Time with Ms. Sisley (Science/Social Studies)			
2:00 - 3:20	**Block 3 LIVE** -- Instruction & Work Time with Ms. Alexander (Math			
3:20 - 3:30	**Mrs. Secondi's Office Hours** -- Need Help with any of your work? Come see me during this time.			

Figure 9.2 Jessica's Virtual Learning Daily Schedule

Reader Reflection: How are you sharing schedules with your students?

For those of you instructing older students, you may find it helpful to articulate your plans for the semester with a clear class expectation and a syllabus. Let's peek at a few more examples.

Julia's Syllabus

Julia Z, a high school teacher in California, shares this nifty infographic (Figure 9.3) she shares with her students to outline the class.

It is helpful that Julia takes the time to spell out a few things very clearly:

■ Materials needed each day

■ General outline of daily schedule

■ And bonus points for laying out "How to Succeed"

Kate's Class Expectations

Kate B., a high school teacher in Denver, gives her students a clear vision of the entire semester (Figure 9.4).

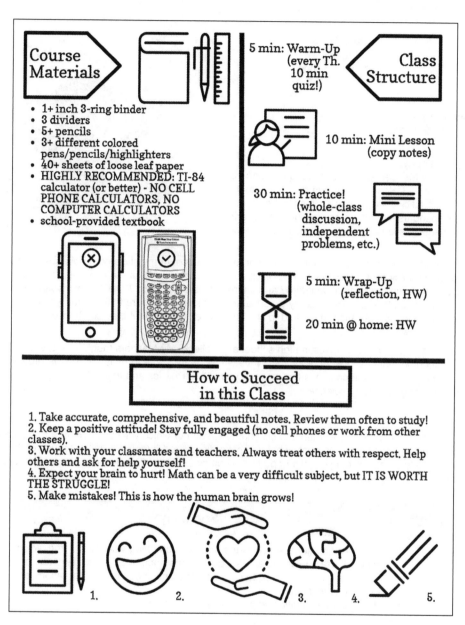

Figure 9.3 Julia's Algebra I Syllabus

Posted Class Assignments

Although it can be hard to think super far into the future, we do our students a disservice if we don't project forward for them. Forecasting into the future helps students plan backwards to meet important deadlines, carve out time for what they need and want to do, and prepare for the unexpected. Figure 9.5 shows an entire grade-level staff committed to posting their assignments in a single Google calendar for their students.

2020-2021
Physics
North High School

Remind group:
Text @*** to *****

My Philosophy:
Welcome to Ms. Berger's Physics class at North High
School. I am a lifelong learner and my goal is to make
science as fascinating for you as it is for me. As a result,
we will spend as much time as possible on exploring and
experimenting, even when we are in the virtual world.

The most important thing to me is that each and every student in my classroom believes that they
can become a scientist if they want. With Black adults making up 9% of the STEM (science, technology, engineering and math) workforce and Latinx adults making up 7% of the workforce (Pew
Research Center, 2018), I take it as my personal responsibility to ensure that all students in my
classroom have the education they need to choose a career in STEM if they so choose.

One more thing: I HATED Physics in high school and college. My teachers taught in a dry way that
was all about formulas and word problems. While we will learn some formulas and solve problems,
my goal for the end of the course is that each of you LOVE Physics and enjoy the process of learning by exploring and doing science.

Content:
The Physics curriculum is broken up into six chapters, each of which will culminate in a demonstration of learning that asks you to apply what you have discovered during the unit. Because of the
unpredictability of this school year, we hope to thoroughly learn the first four units, and will extend
into magnetism and waves if we are able.

Unit Title	Summary
Energy	Students first get a sense of the basics of graphing velocity vs. time, which they will use as evidence to support claims about energy transfers and conversions. They are asked to consider differences between observations and inferences and apply these ideas in multiple experiments.
Force	Students build force explanations for motion, ultimately establishing and formalizing Newton's Laws of motion. Students evaluate the effect of multiple forces and formalize ideas about net force. Ultimately, students collect evidence about force pairs and evaluate the strength of forces during collisions involving objects of different masses and use this evidence to establish Newton's Third Law of motion.

Figure 9.4 Kate's Physics Syllabus

Unit Title	Summary
Gravitation	In this chapter, students learn about orbits, projectiles, gravity, and friction. Friction. They will explore the difference between mass and weight, and make predictions and evaluate data to determine how different objects act in the presence of different gravitational fields.
Charge	Students learn about static electricity and current electricity throughout the unit, eventually creating a visual model of how electricity works. The big concepts students develop throughout this chapter include models for charging insulators, charging conductors, and current electricity.
Magnetism	Students create a model for magnetism that can explain many different observations involving magnets, thus providing an example of how models are proposed, tested, and modified based on evidence. This experience provides the opportunity for students to engage in the scientific practice of developing and using models and engaging in argument from evidence.
Waves	Students learn how sound travels from a source to a listener. They then compare properties of sound and light to begin to develop a wave model of light and to compare and contrast models for light and sound. Students learn about the differences between two different models of light energy.

Required Materials (bring to class every day):
- Composition book (pick up at school on 8/28 or 8/29)
- Pencils
- Colored pencils or pens (at least five colors)
- Graphing calculator (can be checked out from school)
- Chromebook and charger

Grading Policy:
To promote equity, I implement restorative justice discipline policies, learn culturally responsive instructional strategies, and expand the classes' repertoire of assignments and assessments to address the different ways students learn. By continuing to use century-old grading practices, I would inadvertently perpetuate achievement and opportunity gaps. Grading practices in which teachers choose to award or subtract points in a grade for students' behaviors are just as susceptible to misinterpretation and implicit bias as these disciplinary practices (Downey & Pribesh, 2004). With this mindset, I would be remiss if I left my grading system virtually unchanged.

At North High School and in DPS, our curriculum is built around the Next Generation Science Standards (NGSS). The NGSS are broken into Disciplinary Core Ideas and Science and Engineering Practices. Within each area there are specific standards students must meet. These three areas and their accompanying standards become the grading criteria for our course.

Grade Calculation:
Product (projects, tests, presentations, lab reports): 80%
    Disciplinary Core Ideas (DCI): 40%
    Science and Engineering Practices (SEP): 40%
Process (classwork and participation): 20%

Figure 9.4   *(Continued)*

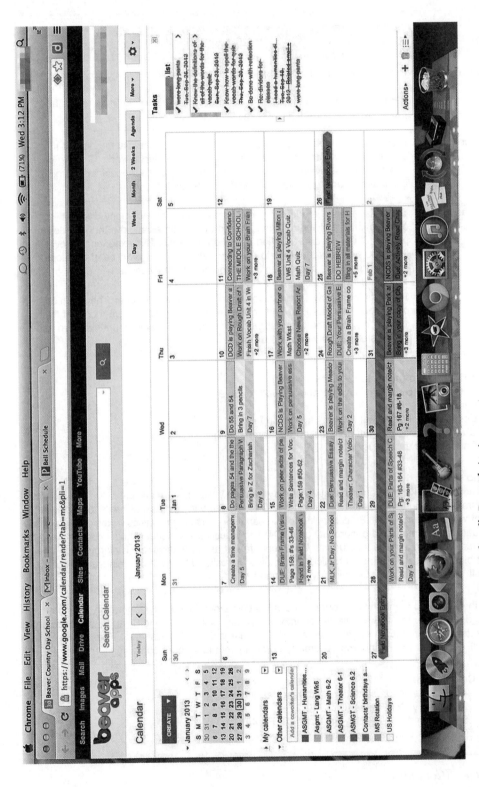

Figure 9.5 Beaver County Day School's Posted Assignments

You can even get very specific, as this weekly view of Google Classroom shows. Imagine a high school student simply opening this view of Google calendar (Figure 9.6) and seeing all of their assignments at once! No planner even needed. Of course, you have to train students to review it regularly, but we can do this!

Whether you purchase or make planners, post a classroom calendar on your wall, publish a syllabus on Canvas, or set up a calendar on your classroom website, giving your students a glimpse of upcoming assignments, holidays, and schoolwide events will help them ensure they are spending their time on what matters.

READER REFLECTION:

■ **How are you forecasting, modeling, and publishing assignment expectations for your students?**

■ **What's one action step you can borrow from the preceding examples?**

Now that we've discussed how schools and teachers can help their students, let's shift to tools students can use to keep themselves Together.

Figure 9.6   Student View of Google Classroom

TOGETHER STUDENT TOOLS CREATED BY SCHOOLS

Getting students, even from as young as preschool, to think about their time, will provide them with agency and support their overall development. From three-year-olds creating Play Plans as part of the Tools of the Mind curriculum to high school students maintaining a Google calendar of extracurriculars, we can all support students with time management. This section will discuss student planners, class calendars, and other methods for supporting students in planning their own time. We want to help them think of time as a commodity to spend on things we need and want to do. Just like with our stuff, the tools are cool but the habits matter more.

MIDDLE SCHOOL STUDENTS TELL ME HOW THEY STAY ORGANIZED

- **Delaying gratification and/or rewards.** Several of the students talked about taking a limited amount of TV or screen time after school and then doing homework. Many specifically named how long they allowed themselves to "play" before getting to work.

- **Hiding or removing phones.** All cited their smartphones as huge distractions when doing homework. Most realized they just had to put them away.

- **Keeping aware of energy levels.** They know that getting enough sleep is very important, and all started their homework in time to get to bed at a reasonable hour.

- **Determining the right environment.** Most of the students I talked with said they tried to get as much homework as possible finished during extra minutes of time during the school day. All of them said they retreated to quiet-ish places in their homes to complete their work, which often required negotiating shared space with siblings.

- **Fueling their bodies.** Many of the students also participated on athletic teams, and they all talked about the importance of good snacks and full and healthy meals.

Whole School Planners

If you are looking for a uniform approach to handle student planning, see if your school or grade level can create a consistent student planner.

Figure 9.7 is an example from Great Oaks Charter School in Newark of how teachers support student use of planners by ensuring students record their assignments.

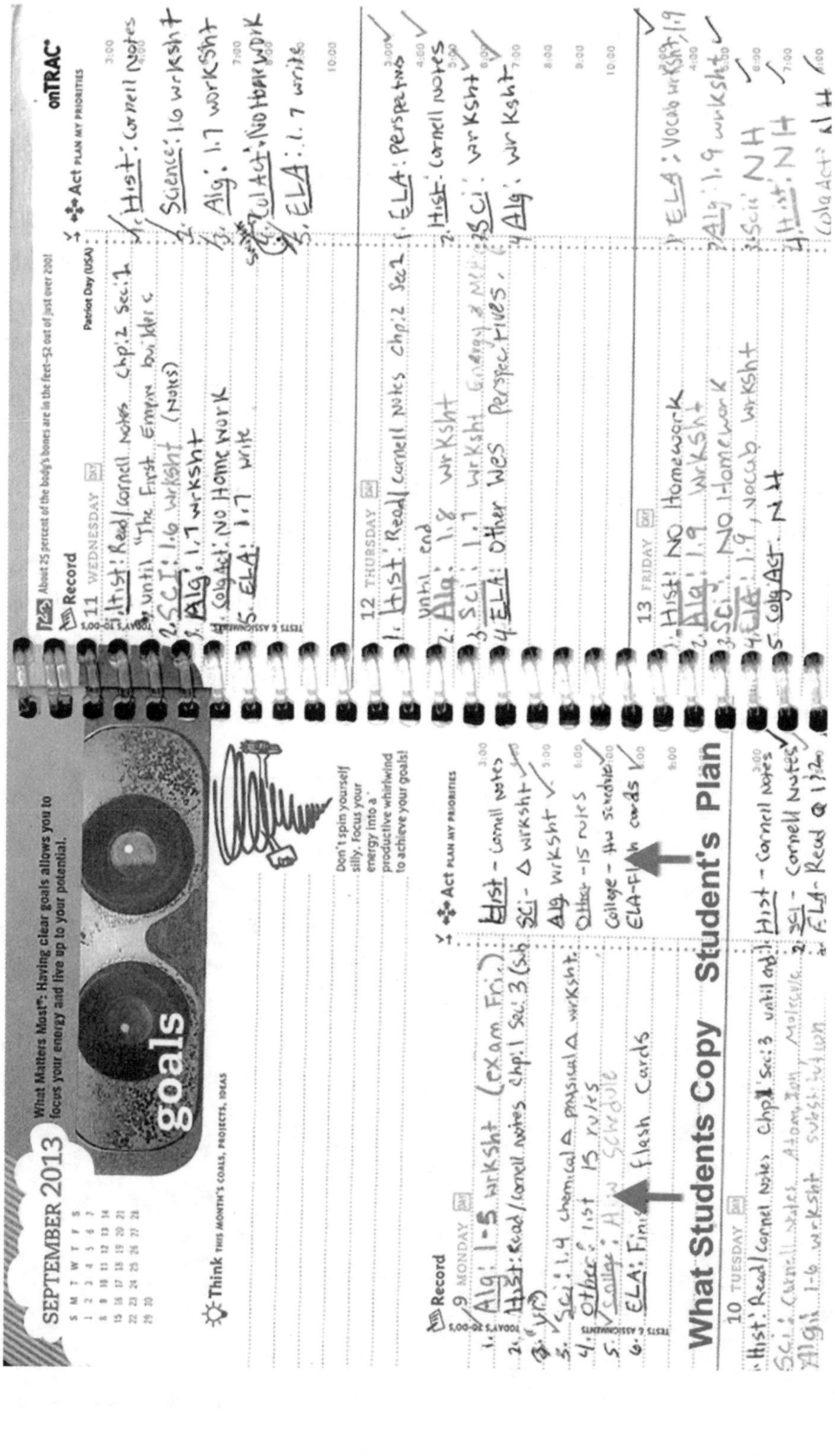

Figure 9.7   Student Planner at Great Oaks Charter School

Valence College Prep School-Created Planners

Similarly, Valence College Prep created their own student planners by subject area. (Figure 9.8) Teachers post what to record each day, and then students make a scheduled plan for when they'll complete the work.

Gem College Prep's Weekly Worksheets for Students

And if you don't like any of the commercial planners out there, you can always make your own. Gem College Prep, in Idaho, created their own tool (Figure 9.9). Sonya L., their director of curriculum, assessment, and professional development, says, "We now use this basic template K–12 with modifications depending on grade level. Teacher teams across the network complete the weekly scholar agendas before pushing them out for scholars to own as they go into their week. We have found that teachers, scholars, and parents love this new resource! Not only does it help scholars stay organized, but it also builds student ownership of their learning, academic accountability, and college-ready competencies like time management and goal setting!!"

Sonya adds, "When we pivoted to online learning last spring, we were challenged by how to organize assignments, lessons, and independent work expectations. We wanted to develop a framework that allowed students to take ownership of their learning while still feeling supported by their teachers. These digital planners [Figure 9.10] are pushed out weekly to each scholar via Canvas. Students then add to and edit their own planner, check off items as they complete them, and submit it back to their teacher for review at the end of each week."

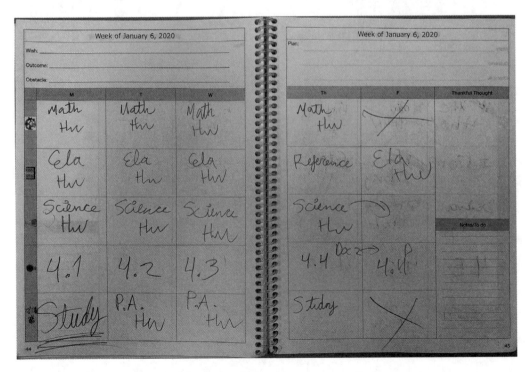

Figure 9.8   Student Planner at Valence College Prep

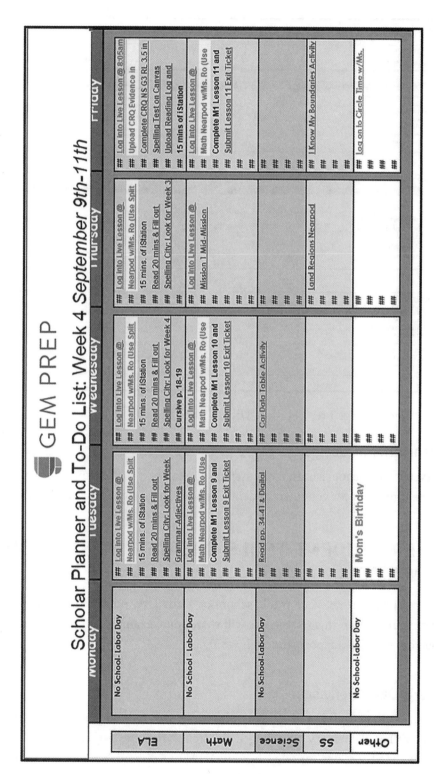

Figure 9.9 Gem College Prep's Student Weekly Worksheet

Gem Prep DIGITAL PLANNER

*All assignments are DUE on the date listed in your course To Do List. All work must be completed. A grade of zero (0)

DATE 8/31/2020

Subject	Assignment	Status	Submitted?
Monday 8/31/2020			
Course	**Assignments from my Canvas To Do List and any other items due this week**		
Math	Khan academy and nearpods		X
Science	monday quiz		X
English	electric boogaloo reading guide		X
History	Nearpods		X
IDLA 1	IDLA Pathways		X
IDLA 2	IDLA Lifetime fitness		X
College Prep	Digital planner		X
NOTES:			
Tuesday 9/1/2020			
Course	**Assignments from my Canvas To Do List and any other items due this week**		
Math	Khan academy and Nearpods		X
Science	Tuesday lab		X
English	Electric boogaloo worksheet		X
History	some more nearpods		X
IDLA 1	IDLA Pathways		X
IDLA 2	IDLA Lifetime Fittness		X
College Prep	Digital planner		X
NOTES:			
Wednesday 9/2/2020			
Course	**Assignments from my Canvas To Do List and any other items due this week**		
Math	Khan academy		X
Science	Tuesday lab extra time		X
English	Electric boogaloo worksheet		X
History	Nearpods		X
IDLA 1	IDLA pathways		X
IDLA 2	IDLA lifetime fittness		X
College Prep	Digital planner		X
NOTES: GPA Check: 3.75			

Figure 9.10 Gem College Prep's Student Digital Planner

Post Assignments in Google

Of course, even if your school isn't into one system, you can take matters into your own hands and just create something for your own students. Let's peek into some options about this next.

TOGETHER STUDENT TOOLS CREATED BY STUDENTS AND FAMILIES

Sometimes, you just can't get your whole school or grade level on board, or you just need something of your own. In this section, we will share some examples of parent and student created Together Tools to support student learning.

Christopher's Daily Worksheet

Enter Chrystie, an educator and parent who designed individualized planner pages (Figure 9.11) for her elementary school-aged children during the pandemic.

Chrystie included sections for what her kids HAD to do and WANTED to do. How's that for a life lesson?! She reports that "It's helping us as parents because we don't have to say 'no' to something they want to do. They are slowly understanding that time is a limited

Christopher's Daily Worksheet:
Complete before your morning meeting!

Week of: Sep 7

My day at a glance: Friday 9/11/2020 (Day & Date)

Today my goal is: to try my best on the Easy dom test

Today I am excited about: finishing school today!

My schedule today:

9:00 – 9:15 Homeroom	
9:15 – 10:45 ELA Block	
11:00 – 11:30 Social Studies	
11:30 – 12:00 Lunch	
12:00 – 12:30 Recess/PE	
12:30 – 2:00 Math Block	
2:00 – 2:45 Intervention	
3:00 – 3:30 Science	

Things I WANT to do today:	Things I HAVE to do today:
• Play with nieghbors • Play with my legos • Play soccer game	• Do Kumon • school

Before School I will:	After School I will:
• Follow what my mom says	• Do evening journal • play with legos

Complete before your evening journal!

Best thing that happened today: _____

_____

If I were to describe today using an emoji, it would be: _____ because: _____

_____

Tomorrow I am looking forward to: _____

_____

Figure 9.11 Christopher's Daily Worksheet

commodity and they can't do everything. I like that I don't have to micromanage their schedules and it's one less thing for me to worry about. I'm hopeful some of these skills will carry on into adulthood!"

MJ's Notebook-Based/Color-Coded To-Do List

MJ, a fourth grader based in Houston, created her own color-coded To-Do list for the day in her notebook (Figure 9.12). During the pandemic, she managed herself while her parents worked full time, right down to packing her dance bag for class every day!

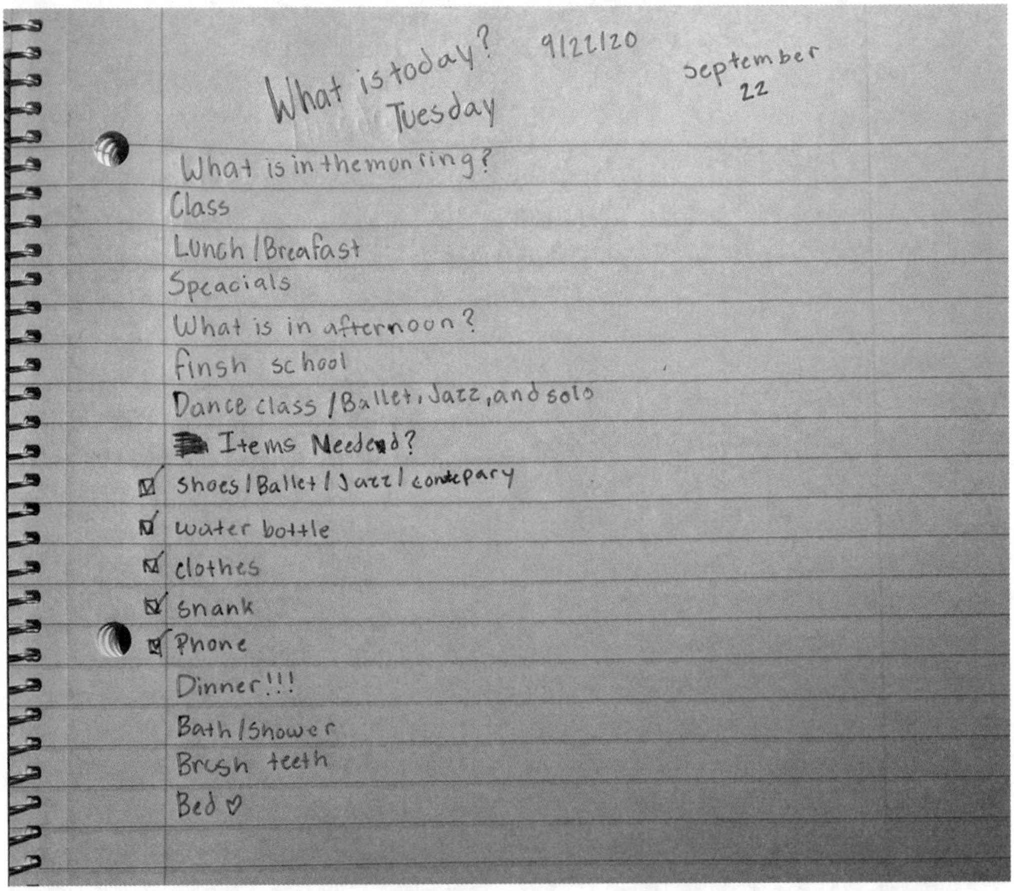

Figure 9.12   MJ's To-Do List

MJ says this helps her see what is coming up throughout the day! MJ uses gold for her school day activities, purple for her dance class needs, and blue for evening routines at home.

Brayden's Google Classroom Calendar

Brayden, a ninth grader in Providence, uses features in Google Classroom (Figure 9.13) to track his assignments. Brayden explains that it is easier to use the platforms the school already has in place—Google—rather than build his own system.

READER REFLECTION:

- **How do you currently help students record their tasks and plan their time?**
- **What is your next step in teaching Student Togetherness?**

Now that we have tackled a bit of student TIME, let's take a gander at student space and stuff.

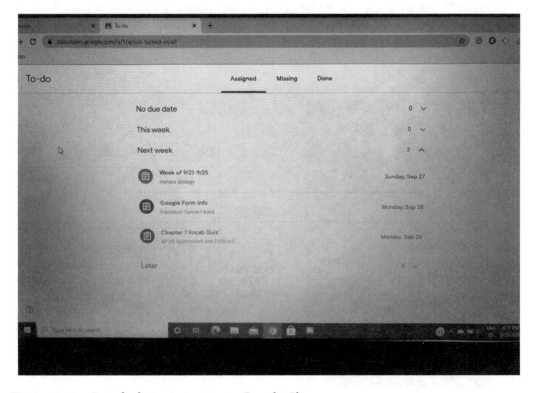

Figure 9.13   Brayden's Assignments in Google Classroom

SUPPORT STUDENT SPACE SET-UP

Most teachers have an immediate reaction when I ask them about the state of their students' desks—a reaction that usually ends with a sigh. Many families became intimately aware of their children's space habits during the pandemic. Just like adults, students need to be taught why it is important to be organized AND exactly how to do it. In this section you will read about how to set expectations for desks, lockers, backpacks, and binders. You will also learn various ways that Together Teachers set and reinforce these expectations.

Tame the Exploding Desk!

A desk diagram can show students exactly how to arrange their folders and textbooks. For example, I had my fifth graders keep their morning materials on the left and afternoon materials on the right. Many teachers, like Dan S., describe and diagram exactly what should be on students' desks during each lesson. Kevin L. shows us expectations (Figure 9.14) for how all of the K–4 students at his school should organize their space.

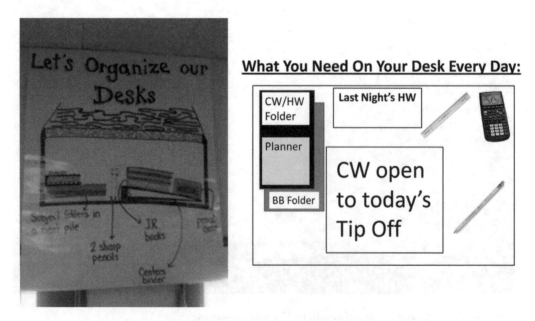

Figure 9.14 Kevin (left) and Dan (right) Set Expectations for Student Desks

READER REFLECTION:

■ **List your expectations for student desks:**

   ■ Inside:

   ■ On Top:

■ **How can you make these even more clear to students?**

Desktop Set-Up

Desks don't always have a ton of space for students to spread out, especially if they switch classrooms. Valence College Prep gets creative with storing student materials during instructional time. Take a peek in Figure 9.15!

Valence College Prep's Under Desk Storage

These H-rubber bands go a long, long way. Add a student water bottle, an organized binder, and tennis balls to save the floors (and our ears!), and students have a steady workspace ready for them.

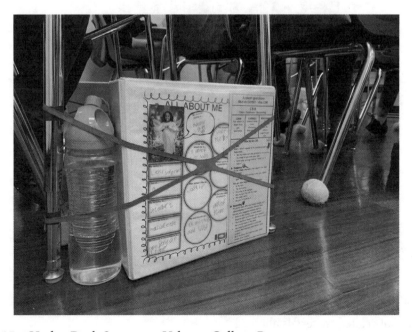

Figure 9.15   Under-Desk Storage at Valence College Prep

Grab a Seat Sack

Some schools or teachers purchase Seat Sacks for their students (see Recommended Resources at www.thetogethergroup.com) to neatly store all of their materials so that books, papers, and supplies do not get lost in the depths of desks and backpacks. Look at the photo of a Seat Sack in Figure 9.16 and notice how carefully they are set up within the classroom.

Of course, just setting up the Seat Sacks and giving them to students is not enough. Together Teachers let students know what to put in their sacks and when. Here are Anna's expectations, which help ensure that the Seat Sacks don't become dumping grounds for crumpled papers and lunch wrappers!

Figure 9.16   Seat Sacks at AF Brownsville

Expectations for Student Seat Sacks

■ Only school-related materials allowed

■ No food or clothing

■ All notebooks, folders, and so on must be horizontal in the Seat Sack—if vertical, things can get knocked out

■ Every couple of weeks, "Deskarina," a mysterious fairylike creature who floats around the school at night doing desk inspections, visits the classroom and places treats on the desks of those scholars with neat and tidy seat sacks.

Now that we have considered our space, do we dare go there. . . PAPER?!

Avoid the Student Paper Avalanche!

Many teachers foster student organization by giving explicit directions on how to keep folders and binders in order. This section describes some ways Together Teachers train and support their students in maintaining these kinds of classroom materials.

An elementary school teacher can be specific about the layout of students' homework folders by clearly designating the right-hand pocket for items going home and the left-hand pocket for completed items to return to school (Figure 9.17). If you teach students to transfer papers from one side to the other, and also share this system with parents, your students' folders will avoid becoming overstuffed paper traps.

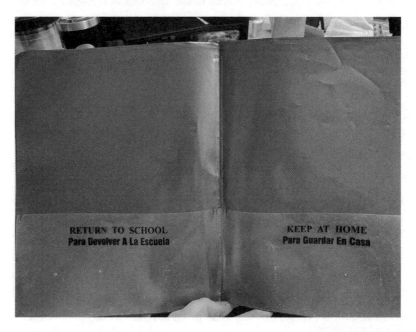

Figure 9.17 Leah's Take-Home Folder for Students

KIPP Austin's Take-Home Folder

Binders

Similarly, you can set expectations for student binders by helping them create tabs for homework, classwork, lab reports, and tests. In Figure 9.18, Brent M., a high school teacher, shares his explicit expectations and why they matter so much.

Similarly, Michelle K., a teacher in the Bay area, borrows ideas from the AVID program to create binder checks for her secondary students (Figure 9.19).

GET BINDERIZED

"Science is organized knowledge. Wisdom is organized life."
Immanuel Kant (18th Century Existential[1] Philosopher)

In this class I hope to not only make you better scientists, but also, more wise in ways of life. To be successful in this class, you *must* be organized. Hopefully you'll see the benefits of working hard and being organized and will implement a similar system in your other classes.

WHAT YOU NEED
- Binder—must be at least 1.5 inches (3.81 cm) and have 3 rings
- Divider Tabs—you must have 8 sections in your binder. You may purchase 8-tab dividers from Wal-Mart or you may make your (hole punch file folders, tape Stickies to colored paper etc. . .)

SETTING UP YOUR TABS
Your binder will contain all of the work that you do in this class (and *ONLY* this class) over the course of the year. It will be set up into eight basic sections:

1. General Rules / Information
2. Daily Work Organizers and TAKS Practice
3. Notes / Handouts / Homework
4. Quizzes / Tests
5. Demos / Labs / Projects
6. Readings
7. Science Fair
8. Goals / Reflections

BINDER TESTS
To test your organizational skills, we will have binder tests on every other Wednesday. They will be done on PowerPoint and each question will remain on the screen for 30 seconds. Sample questions follow below.

3. According to the lab rubric, how many points is the results section worth?	6. What was the first word on question #10 on Quiz #5?

It is *EXTREMELY* important that you keep an orderly binder for this class, as it will help your grade and will teach you invaluable organizational skills.

Figure 9.18   Brent's Binder Expectations for Students

Michelle says, "Sometimes I pair a well-organized student with someone who is less so to work together during homeroom or independent work time. I also try to check backpacks every week and not let students leave class until everything is put in their binders."

As students get older you can be less explicit about exactly where things go, but I know many high school teachers who give infamous surprise binder quizzes to see if students have indeed held onto all of their lesson notes from the semester.

Notebooks

Cassidy C., a teacher in Texas, asks her students to keep a Table of Contents (Figure 9.20) in their Five Star notebooks so they can find their notes and study materials more easily. By asking her students to maintain this Table of Contents, Cassidy not only teaches science content but also valuable study skills.

Michelle K's Student Binder

Section 1 – Yearlong Information
- Expectations Homework
- You Can Grow Your Intelligence
- Math Syllabus
- Mathematics Expectations and Policies
- Syllabus, Routines and Procedures Scavenger Hunt

Section 2 – Do-Nows
- Do-Now sheet
- Keep your old Do-Nows so we can measure growth

Section 3 – Worksheets
- Any handouts where we are practicing a new math skill

Section 4 – Projects/HW
- Numbers of my life
- Community building reflections

Section 5 – Quizzes
- Vocabulary quizzes
- Multiplication quizzes

Figure 9.19   Michelle's Binder Expectations for Students

Cassidy notes, "I was able to get my school to buy every kid a Five Star notebook. We use it for guided notes, and we have a table of contents that we all keep up with. Today we finished page 58 of notes! We use these notebooks only for class notes. I have a separate packet with Do Firsts and any practice. I've limited their notebooks to just notes so that it's not overwhelming. I have kids come back from high school and tell me that they are still going back to it."

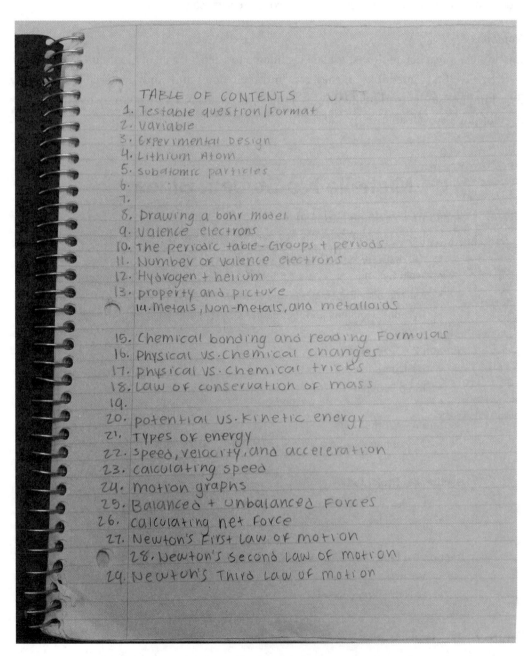

Figure 9.20   Table of Contents from Cassidy's Student Notebooks

READER REFLECTION:

■ **What are your expectations for how your students keep their papers organized?**

■ **Which students would benefit from more explicit instruction in this area?**

■ **What can you do to help them?**

Now that you have made your expectations clear for kids—and yourself!—let's go into how to actually TEACH Togetherness.

TEACHING STUDENTS TOGETHERNESS

Of course, if we hold our students accountable for these expectations, we have to be prepared and Together ourselves. In this section, we look at how teachers model Togetherness, make time for it, and make it fun! By making small moves throughout your teaching day, you can help students gain important life skills of Togetherness.

Cassidy's Strong Start Bulletin Board

We cannot expect our students to magically be excited to copy down assignments, file their work, or organize their Google Drive. As teachers, we want to ensure our space signals our Togetherness expectations. In Figure 9.21, Cassidy signals her expectations through a Strong Start and explicitly signals students could "copy homework into agenda"—and gives students time to do it!

Note the very first step after getting to your seat is to copy down your homework into your agenda, and then where to place your homework and agenda. I love that it is simply part of the beginning of class expectations.

Reader Reflection: How can you build in time for Togetherness within your actual lesson plans?

Dan's Post-Class Planner Expectations

Dan S., a high school teacher in Brooklyn, also builds time into his class for students to focus on Togetherness. Figure 9.22 a visual anchor from his classroom.

I love many things about this model, but a few jump out:

■ Make sure students complete the entire information capture. All means ALL.

■ Ensuring students can read their own handwriting later!

■ And bonus points for having students consider how long assignments take.

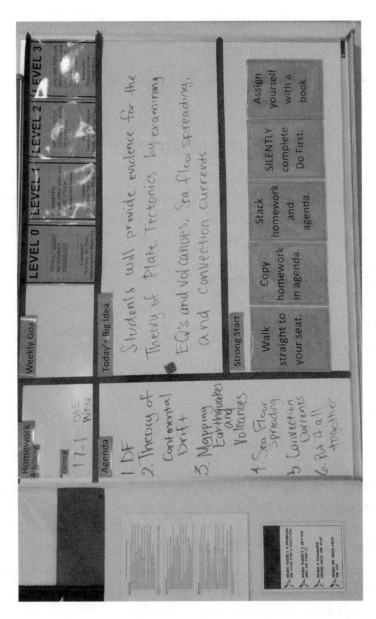

Figure 9.21 Cassidy's Bulletin Board

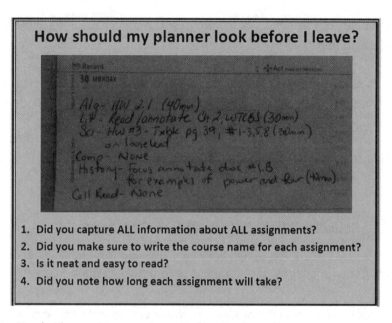

Figure 9.22   Dan's Planner Expectations: Before Students Leave

Dan even gives his students a model for AFTER they complete the work, as seen in Figure 9.23. Remember, although checkmarks may feel intuitive to US, they are not always obvious to our students.

As a mom who recently coached her own fifth grader to write her teacher to ask why she received a C on a writing project, I was especially taken with the second point in the post below. "Did you write down any parts you had trouble with so you can follow up?" This

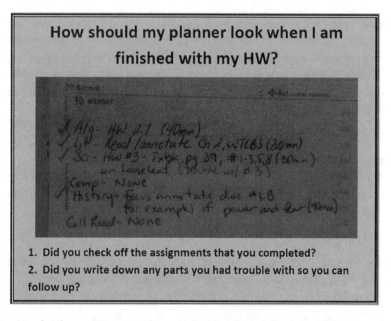

Figure 9.23   Dan's Planner Expectations: After Students Complete Homework

will be a key skill for our students as they progress through challenging subject areas—and even in jobs later in life!

 Reader Reflection: How can you build time at the end of class to ensure students walk out the door ready to be successful?

Now that we've built time into our lessons to help students get it Together, we can also consider whole school options. Warning: I love this example so much! I may get a little excited here.

Crescent City Schools' Whole School Binder Challenge

Here's a fun way to create a grade-level or schoolwide organization challenge: Crescent City School's International Binder Week—complete with Binder Fashion Shows (Figure 9.24).

This week is International Binder Week, which is a very special week when we join with nations around the world to celebrate personal organization! Our students have been furiously organizing their binders, desks and cubbies, and this week students on each team will be showing off their organizational skills!

- Middle school students will be working all week to keep their binders organized. Students will compete in binder fashion shows to see who is the most organized in each homeroom. This year Pierre the Binder Inspecteur will make his second appearance as the host for the Teal Team fashion show. Blue Team let scholars add props to their runway walks! Winners receive: a sash, crown and glory ☺

- Students on the Red Team (grades 3 – 4) will be tidying up their desks! They will have their annual desk fashion show on Wednesday, and on Friday they will be giving out the "Cleanest Classroom Award." Since Wednesdays are Red Team meetings, they have a Desk Fashion Show and have special guests come and judge the cleanliness. The winner of the competition gets a pair of Desk Fairy wings!

- K-1-2 will be highlighting organization of cubbies, folders, and pencil/supply bags...and they are hoping that the Desk Fairy makes an appearance! On Wednesday, K-1-2 scholars will be displaying their excellence in organization during breakfast. The winners will receive a "Most Organized Homeroom" for showing unity in keeping it all together!

In honor of this incredible week, this is a great time for you to organize your own binders, classrooms, bulletin boards, and personal systems! Please feel free to wear your International Binder Week hat from last year any day this week ☺

Figure 9.24 Crescent City Schools' International Binder Week

I mean, an International Binder Week?! I asked Julie, the principal of the school, why she and her staff invested so much time in teaching students—both elementary and secondary—how to be organized. Her awesome replies:

- **Student habits:** We are not only responsible for teaching content, but we also believe in teaching our kids the habits of mind that will enable their future success.

- **Student learning:** For students to really learn, they need to be able to find their homework, review their class notes, and meet deadlines. This all requires being organized.

- **Student independence:** With elementary students managing their own work for the day, I can hear a second grader refer to his weekly plan and say, "I should do my sight words right now because I've already chosen independent reading three times this week!"

Julie and her team also make an effort to make International Binder Week FUN (Figure 9.25). I mean, if you can't have fun with Togetherness... Seriously, it will also help keep students motivated and invested in the outcomes.

Figure 9.25   The Binder Fairy at Crescent City Schools

THAT ONE STUDENT WITH AN EXPLODING BACKPACK

You are probably thinking about that one student of yours whose desk may be a paper explosion, who is very bright but can never find her homework, with the backpack that has papers from six months ago crumpled in the bottom. One of my favorite students of all time—we will call him Kenny—was a total math whiz but his grades suffered because he frequently lost homework, was late turning in essays, and forgot to bring home materials necessary to complete his homework.

To help get him on track, I worked with Kenny to develop a special checkout system: he would be the last person to leave so I could check whether his homework was copied, that he had the right materials to complete his homework, and that his homework folder was clearly arranged for his mother to review. After a few months of intensive support, we were able to dial down, and although Kenny wasn't perfect, his organization (and thus his grades!) improved dramatically.

FAQ: What about missing student work?
Another small way we can help our students master time is to make sure they are responsible for any work they miss due to class absences. Whether you set up an email system, designate a missing work folder for kids to check (Figure 9.26), or employ a student helper, you are creating another method for students to take responsibility for their own work.

Student Togetherness is rarely a standalone subject at school (unless it is folded into advisory or study skills), and we all know how these skills help us as adults. However you choose to define Student Togetherness in your classroom, be sure you are explicit in the articulation and instruction of your expectations. Students are whirlwinds of energy and excitement (isn't that why we got into this work?), and although a few of them come by the "organization" gene naturally, most kids need strong instruction and investment incentives. We've got to let them know why this matters so much! And it all starts with our OWN Togetherness!

Figure 9.26 Cassidy's Missing Work Crate

TURBO TOGETHERNESS

Your students—and maybe even your own children—will benefit from you laying out expectations for Togetherness. And perhaps more important, the opportunity to practice these skills in a supportive environment will really help them thrive. We all know adults who are not organized. They can appear flustered, frustrated, and stressed—and pass this energy on to those around them. Students' self-esteem is built up when they feel a sense achievement at accomplishing their goals, which in turn builds more confidence for the future.

☐ Align as a school or grade level on Togetherness supports and outcomes for students.

☐ Share long-term calendars and daily To-Dos for students to self-manage.

☐ Consider key aspects of your classroom, such as student papers and student space.

Chrystie, an educator and parent featured earlier, reminds us of the lessons that students learn as they practice Togetherness: "I realized early on that my kids are definitely natural "what-ers." They were great at writing lists of things they both wanted and needed to do but not the best at getting everything done. We noticed they were most successful when we gave them a time frame to complete tasks. Shifting responsibility to them to first identify what they want and need to do each week, but then watching them think through WHEN they can fit all that in their schedule has been an eye opener. It has forced them to think through what their actual priorities are and what tradeoff costs exist. It also makes them slow down and realize they can't over commit themselves. They can't do homework, study, go to soccer, play LEGOs, AND hang out with the neighbors all in one day."

MAINTENANCE MOVES

After one month of laying out Togetherness expectations for students, consider following up with a student or family survey on how your Togetherness moves are supporting students.

Questions could include:

■ How often do you and your student review the syllabus, class calendar, or class website?

■ Do you have a daily check-in with your student to check assignments, backpacks, etc.?

Or you could easily gather data around:

■ Percentage of students coming to class prepared with necessary materials

■ Percentage of students turning assignments in on time or early

PART 3

Together
Your Teaching

CHAPTER 10

Plan, Plan, and Plan Some More: Make Lesson Planning Efficient!

SETTING THE SCENE

Lesson planning. Groan. It's at the heart of what we do as teachers. But at the same time, it seems there are never enough hours to get it done, unrealistic expectations about detail or quality, and materials shortages. You probably had to modify your lesson planning process massively during the pandemic and distance learning era (which, at the time of publication, was still ongoing). But even still, lesson planning is often done in teams, receives lots of reviews and input, and requires gathering materials, modifying activities, and, oh wait, actually TEACHING! It's just such an enormous task. Many of us vacillate from phoning it in to memorizing lessons someone else wrote to spending hours deep in an Internet rabbit hole researching exactly how to teach a particular objective. #beenthere Planning can make or break your day with your students—and yourself!

IN THIS CHAPTER, YOU WILL LEARN TO:

- Create a longer-term view of your lesson plans

- Structure your ideal environment, location, time, and materials for lesson plan development

- Efficiently gather, store, and share lesson materials

- Make the most of your required grading software and supplement as needed

I will NOT be helping you write the perfect lesson objective or select just the right unit plan format. But I WILL help you make sure the bulk of your time spent planning is used as efficiently and effectively as possible. Let's jump right into some great examples.

TOGETHER TEACHERS' LONG-TERM PLANNING EXAMPLES

We all have our lesson plans, but many of us also need to step back and see the bigger picture. Let's look at how a few people do that.

Melissa's Weekly Long-Term Sketch

Melissa R., a third-grade teacher in Maryland, adds the Long-Term Sketch shown in Figure 10.1 as a layer on top of her lesson plans to see what is around the bend—especially good to see during a holiday stretch where some instructional weeks are much shorter!

I love that Melissa lays out all of the weeks and that she can adjust to meet student needs. Melissa says, "I created this document to help my team and I prioritize what I would be teaching each week. It helped me to have a week-by-week outline because I could see which concepts repeat themselves, and which did not. I also had a nice visual of the progression of the learning, which helped me pace myself and better differentiate my lessons for my students."

 Reader Reflection: How could laying out your objectives across a period of weeks save you time—and support your students?

Reading

Week 1 Nov. 11-14	Narrative - Poetry • Refer to stanzas when referring to parts of poems. (Whole group) • Compare how events unfold in a narrative story versus a narrative poem. (Whole group) • Distinguish literal from non-literal language, analyze how poets use descriptions of thoughts and feelings. (Small group) • Sequence events in a narrative.
Week 2 Nov. 18-22	Narrative - Poetry • Compare themes and settings of texts by the same author (Whole group) • Refer to parts of poems when speaking or writing about a text. (Whole group/small in group in written response) • Ask and answer questions to demonstrate understanding of a text. (Small group) • Distinguish a personal point of view from that of the narrator. (Small group)
Week 3 Nov. 25-Dec. 2	Narrative - Poetry/Folktales/Legends • Use dramatic terms in reference to parts of a play. (Whole group) • Describe how a character's actions contribute to the sequence of events. (Small group) • *Use sentence level context as a clue to the meaning of the word or phrase.*
Week 4 Dec. 3-Dec. 9	Narrative - Plays/Folktales/Legends • Describe how parts of plays build on earlier sections (Whole group) • Compare the characters and plots of stories written by the same author (Whole group) • Determine a central message and explain how it is conveyed through key details from the text. (Small group)

Figure 10.1   Melissa's Weekly Overview

Source: Melissa R., a third-grade teacher in Maryland

Caroline's Monthly Lesson Plan Overlay—Across a Calendar

In addition to day-by-day lesson plans, you may also benefit from a unit overview laid out across an actual monthly calendar, like Caroline L.'s in Rhode Island (Figure 10.2). She's able to see school holidays and other happenings and make sure homework assignments don't collide. You could even give a copy of something similar to your students or families (more on that in the chapter on Student Togetherness!).

The benefit of this Monthly Overlay is Caroline—and her team—can see how their teaching objectives interact with the overall calendar. Caroline could see MLK day, and she could ensure she had a reading passage to support that holiday. Or she could note that there was less actual instructional time the week of January 27 because there was mock state testing. If you wanted to get REALLY fancy, you could consider adding this stuff straight to your Comprehensive Calendar!

Reader Reflection: How could laying your lesson plans over an actual Monthly Calendar help you?

January

Sunday	Monday	Tuesday	Wednesday	Thursday	Friday	Saturday
			1	2	3	4
5	6	7	8 Unit 4	9	10	11
12	13	14	15 Unit 4	16	17	18
19	20 NO SCHOOL: MLK DAY	21 75 min: Hidden Figures (pp. 1-20) **Teacher/Student Read, Discussion + Literary Notebooks** Paragraph Response	22 **Close Reading Quiz (Wk 21)**	23 75 min: Hidden Figures (pp. 21-end) **Teacher/Student Read, Discussion + Literary Notebooks** Paragraph Response	24 ELA: Reteach + Mystery Passage Beyond MLK Jr. Forgotten Heroes of the Civil Rights Movement Quiz Reteach	25
26 75 min: Bravo! 5 poems (pp. 1-10) **Teacher/Student Read, Discussion + Literary Notebooks** Paragraph Response	27	28 MOCK RICAS #1	29 MOCK RICAS #1	30 75 min: Bravo! 6 poems (pp. 11-22) **Teacher/Student Read, Discussion + Literary Notebooks** Paragraph Response	31 NO ELA MATH MOCK	

Figure 10.2 Caroline's Monthly Plan

Eric's Year-Long Lesson Plan Sketch

Eric N., a high school teacher in Denver, looks very far ahead to map out his year. In his spreadsheet (the first two pages of which you can see in Figure 10.3), he includes the teaching day across the top and the month down the side. Within each day, he writes his instructional objective for each class. This gives him a big-picture view of what he is teaching when—and reminds him of events and holidays.

The benefits of Eric's Year-Long Plan are enormous, including seeing how he can vary instructional strategies since he inserts most lesson plan elements, including Do-Nows and Exit Tickets, into his Year-Long Plan.

 Reader Reflection: What is one step you can take to get a bigger picture view of your lesson planning?

Now that you have landed on a way to calendarize and organize your long-term lesson planning, let's delve into what it takes to write your weekly and daily plans.

YEAR-LONG PLAN

Week		Monday	Tuesday	Wednesday	Thursday	Friday
		8-19	8-20	8-21	8-22	8-23
August	1	First day freshmen Intro to schoolwide/classroom procedures Standards: NA CLO: I can in writing determine the expectations that will help me to succeed as a Viking Scholar. Do Now: Fill out Magic Cards Exit Ticket: 3 strategies for success CFU's: Questioning/ Conferring with students Collaboration: Individual/pairs Supports: Syllabus, Grading Policy (expand in syllabus) Mini Lesson: none	First day all What is Geography Standards: NA CLO: I can in writing describe the topics that I will be learning and how they are interconnected. Do Now . . . Map and Questions Exit: Answer two questions using the lenses CFU's: Conferring during student discussions, monitoring student shares to whole class. Gradual release: I do, We do, interspersed with whole class share outs. Collaboration: pairs Supports: photos, sentence stems	Reading/Writing Preassessment—SLO Measure		Map Components ELG 1A: using map components CLO: I can in writing define and use map components to analyze and read a map. Do Now . . . Map and questions Exit: applying map components. CFU's: questions during presentation, conferring, share outs. Mini lesson: using map components Supports: sentence stems, collaboration

	8-26	8-27	8-28	8-29	8-30
2	Map Components Day 2 CLO: I can in writing analyze and extract information from maps using my knowledge of map components. Do Now: review of map components TS: Schema, monitoring for meaning. Spiraled: map components Mini lesson: modeling the use of map components, I do, we do you do CFU's: after Do Now, after I do, while conferring Exit: questions related to map components. Supports: collaboration, scaffolds sentence stems.	Absolute Location and relative location—site and situation CLO: I can in writing use grid systems to determine a place's absolute location. TS: Solve Problems Spiraled: map components Mini lesson: Finding Lat and Long Exit slip: Practice Lat and Long	Map Component Quiz X Thematic Maps Practice CLO: I can in writing analyze thematic maps using information from keys/legends TS: Schema, Determining Importance Spiraled: map components Mini lesson: What is a theme? Worktime: Powerpoint Using evidence to determine types of thematic maps and purposes. Exit slip: Create a thematic map of your bedroom that includes at least two of the map components	World Tear Maps CLO: I can tactically create a map of the world using my schema of the continents and map components. Do Now: Continent and Ocean Map Review CFU's: Check-ins interspersed while groups complete tear maps. TS: Schema Spiraled: Continents, Latitude and Long, Grid Systems Mini lesson: Mental Map—Relative location Work time: Tear Maps in groups Exit slip: How well did you know the world shapes? Why do we need a mental map?

Figure 10.3 Eric's Year-Long Plan

WHAT IS THE ACTUAL WORK OF LESSON PLANNING?

Lesson planning processes vary from school to school, district to district—and sometimes even classroom to classroom! Our goal is for you to figure out how much work lesson planning actually takes for you in your classroom. At a minimum, most lessons have a clear objective, materials, procedures, group work, and assessment. In some cases, you may find value in "scripting" the questions you want to ask your students.

Throughout the remainder of this chapter, we will work through the Lesson Plan Workload Estimator step by step. Because planning is one of our main job responsibilities, we need to carefully understand our workload, mental capacity, and environment. By detailing each of these dimensions, we can figure out how to actually fit in lesson planning. I hope you end this chapter with a clear sense of your planning workload and new ideas for how to best accomplish the work. We'll also point out ways to plug planning into your Together Tools along the way.

Planning Workload Estimator

To Be Planned	Level of Brainpower Required 3 = major focus brainpower 2 = in between 1 = I can do this in front of the TV with my eyes closed	Materials Required	When/How Long?	Where Do I Need to Be?

Now that you have a sense of the Planning Workload Estimator (say that 10 times fast!), let's get started with what form your lesson plans actually take. For many of us, this is simply a school requirement, but sometimes we may need to supplement along the way.

NEW TEACHER TIP: QUESTIONS TO ASK WHEN FIGURING OUT LESSON PLAN WORKLOAD

- What curriculum is used in each subject?
- What standards are used?
- If a prepackaged curriculum, are all accompanying materials also purchased?
- Do we create any lesson plans from scratch?
- What lesson plan template is used? Is it required?
- Do teachers co-plan and divide work?
- Do we create our own assessments?
- When are lesson plans due?
- Who reviews lesson plans?
- What is the turnaround time for feedback?
- How are lesson plans stored?

Here are a few possible sample outcomes of your lesson planning workload:

- **Example Outcome 1:** You teach elementary school all subjects and there is purchased curriculum for science, social studies, and math. However, the math curriculum needs significant modification. Literacy is all created in house and uses a workshop method.

- **Example Outcome 2:** You teach middle school English language arts (ELA) and you and the other ELA teacher write unit plans for each text, drawing on some preexisting curriculum and Common Core Standards.

- **Example Outcome 3:** You teach high school AP chemistry, physics, and calculus. That's right, three preps. For each subject, there is existing stuff from a former teacher and items you have collected over the years. Generally, you are on your own.

Based on the answers to the questions above, you could have varying workloads that fall across a spectrum.

Reviewing standards and building from scratch	Modifying existing curriculum	Synthesizing or internalizing other curriculum	Tailoring other people's plans

You may find it helpful to segregate your planning work into two types. For example, I may need to focus a lot more to relearn a physics concept versus creating a student handout or exit ticket.

 Reader Reflection: And the workload is . . . Now that you know the answers to the preceding questions, sketch out what you know of your required workload. An example is completed below for you.

To Be Planned	Level of Brainpower Required 3 = major focus brainpower 2 = in between 1 = I can do this in front of the TV with my eyes closed	Materials Required	When/How Long?	Where Do I Need to Be?
Math Lesson Plans (Weekly)	3 because...			

As you can imagine, as you shift grade levels and subject areas—and most definitely schools—you will have to reassess your workload each time.

COPLANNING WITH COLLEAGUES

Coplanning with a content or grade team can be an amazing and huge time saver—or a time-suck—depending on the approach. There are lots of ways of coplanning, including:

- Elementary school teachers who each tackle a content area and share lesson plans
- Grade teams who plan entire units across grades
- Vertically aligned content areas teams who map out years together
- Teachers who help each other each week with making copies, procuring materials, etc.
- Colleagues who help with special events, such as 100s Day or a science fair

Before you dive wholeheartedly into detailed plans for coplanning, let's take a few presteps that could help set you up for success in the long term.

1. Determine if you WANT to coplan or if you HAVE to coplan.
2. Decide purpose for coplanning. Is it to save time? Align on curriculum?
3. Determine roles and responsibilities for coplanning. Who is doing what?
4. Set deadlines for feedback or materials collection.
5. Clarify where and how materials are stored.
6. Debrief how process is working.

Now that you know your workload and the brainpower it requires, you can consider materials required, and when and where it makes sense to do your planning. Doing this assessment is essential because of the time lesson planning takes teachers. No one wants to be up until midnight—or later—creating student handouts for the next day.

MATERIALS NEEDED FOR LESSON PLANNING

In this section, we will identify what materials you need with you during your planning time and how to be as efficient as possible with getting set up for work. The last thing any of us wants to do is settle in at Starbucks and realize we left school without our beloved Everyday Mathematics teachers' manual.

Reader Reflection: It's likely there's a standard set of items you need while lesson planning. Check off which materials you need with you during planning time.

- ☐ Computer or laptop to create lesson plans, handouts, etc.
- ☐ Plan book or templates with required format for planning
- ☐ Various curriculum materials, either for reference or internalization
- ☐ Professional planning materials, such as books, professional development handouts, and so on
- ☐ Student data to determine differentiation, groupings, and mastery of material
- ☐ Last year's lesson plans and notes (more on how to store these easily later)
- ☐ Other: _____

If it helps you, you may want to segregate all of your planning materials into one tub, crate, or tote bag, so you can go into the planning zone with relative ease. If you have one place in your classroom or a teacher office where you can store everything, all the better. In the next two pictures (Figure 10.4 and Figure 10.5), you will see Sue created an actual Lesson Planning Tote Bag with the instructional text and Common Core Standards so she can plan on the fly! And Jessica designed actual tubs with her planning materials so she can move to different locations easily.

Sue's Lesson Planning Bag

Figure 10.4   Sue's Lesson Planning Tote Bag

Jessica's (At Home) Teacher Tubs

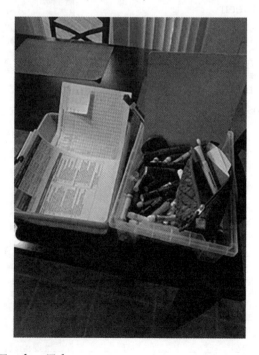

Figure 10.5   Jessica's Teacher Tubs

Don't make planning a "climb to the mountaintop" activity. By breaking the planning process into bite-size pieces and having materials at-the-ready, it can become more efficient—and perhaps more enjoyable!

Tech Tip

You may find it easier to digitize individual hard-copy handouts if there is not a digital copy.

 Reader Reflection: Keep adding to the Lesson Plan Workload Estimator.

Planning Workload Estimator

To Be Planned	Level of Brainpower Required 3 = major focus brainpower 2 = in between 1 = I can do this in front of the TV with my eyes closed	Materials Required	When/How Long?	Where Do I Need to Be?
Math Lesson Plans (Weekly)	*3*	*University of Chicago curriculum Student Assessment Data*		

Now that you know the workload and WHAT materials you need with you while planning, let's think about WHEN and WHERE you want to do your planning. As with all of your routines, this may vary week over week, but it's still helpful to consider what makes the most sense right now. Time is our most limited resources as teachers, and planning is one of the heaviest cognitive lifts we handle. If we don't give it explicit time in our weeks, it will slowly pile up on us. And you got it, it is time to pull out your Weekly Worksheet!

DETERMINE DAY AND TIME TO PLAN

Let's first start with figuring out how much time you actually have on your hands. By the time we factor in sleeping, commuting, ACTUAL teaching, and other fixed time slots, you are likely left with time in pockets: before school, during school (otherwise known as prep periods), after school, and at home on nights and weekends. You did some of this thinking for our Ideal Week exercise in a previous chapter but let's go a little deeper.

It starts with figuring out how much time you actually have. As with any teaching situation, this can vary a lot by school or even by grade level. Possible scenarios:

I'm a morning person and my school is open very, very early. I do not have a team planning situation. No one disturbs me and all of my materials are in my classroom. My prep periods are often taken over with coverages and IEP meetings, so I cannot consistently count on them. I decide to do my heavier brain work of lesson planning on M, T, and W mornings and copies and material gathering for the week on Thursday or Friday during my prep periods. To make the early mornings palatable, I bring special coffee and put on music.

Scenario A

I work on a team of people that swaps lesson plans for subject areas. I am responsible for creating an entire subject area and then internalizing other people's plans. The team likes to plan in the same room so we can swap ideas in real time. I am a night owl. I pick Wednesday nights at a coffee shop to do my planning and the team meets together on Thursday and Fridays. I make copies and gather materials over the weekend.

Scenario B

I am a secondary teacher who has to travel between classrooms to teach various sections of writing. My materials for teaching mostly live on a cart, and all of my instructional resources are at home. I am prone to being interrupted at school, so I block out Saturday mornings for planning time and then make copies and gather materials on Mondays and Tuesdays (for the following week!).

Scenario C

Now that you have considered possible scenarios, let's think about your own plan.

 Reader Reflection: Figure out WHEN to do your Lesson Planning by asking yourself the following questions:

- When do I do my best thinking work?

- When is my brain exhausted?

- Where do I keep most of my planning materials?

- Do I need the Internet when planning?

- Do I have time to work before school?

- Do I LIKE to work before school?

- How much prep time do I have daily?

- How much of that prep time is spoken for by other commitments, for example, duties, meetings, etc.?

- Do I have time to work after school?

- Do I LIKE to work after school?

■ Do I prefer to work at home in the evenings or on weekends? What type of work do I like to do there?

■ Do I owe other people copies of my plans?

 Reader Reflection: Keep adding to the Lesson Plan Workload Estimator and complete the When column.

To Be Planned	Level of Brainpower Required 3 = major focus brainpower 2 = in between 1 = I can do this in front of the TV with my eyes closed	Materials Required	When/How Long?	Where Do I Need to Be?
Math Lesson Plans (Weekly)	3	University of Chicago curriculum Student Assessment Data	I think this is a solid 2 hours.	

Now let's actually figure out what type of work to do when!

Elisa C., in Austin, describes how she breaks down different types of lesson planning based on her location and concentration levels.

- "If I need to read a lesson, I will do that first thing in the morning. I have two free periods. The first free period, I plan all the copies, and second period, I make the copies."

- "We have three second-grade classrooms, and we all use the same copies for math, reading, and writing. We divide the work, and I do all the reading copies."

Emily W., also in Austin, describes a similar breakdown: "My morning prep is when I do anything that requires critical thinking. During my lunch prep that falls after class, I do quick stuff."

 FAQ: How much planning is too much planning?

I LOVED planning as a teacher. I mean LOVED IT. To the exclusion of other important parts of my job. If you think you are spending too much time on planning, there are a few ways to check yourself.

- Ask a coach, colleague, or friend of a similar grade or subject how much time they spend planning

- If this isn't enough, watch someone plan, or coplan with them to see what you can learn.

- Consider that you may be planning too far in advance and will need to make revisions based on student learning.

At this point, you know the WHAT AND WHEN of your lesson planning work (and have inserted them right into your Weekly Worksheet, I hope! If not, go ahead and do it now!). Let's figure out the WHERE.

WHERE SHOULD I LESSON PLAN?

In my ideal world, every school would have a place where teachers could have their own offices, or a quiet shared space, for the intellectual part of teaching. But space is a scarce commodity at most schools. It can be hard to find a quiet place to focus, particularly if you are thinking through new subject matter or analyzing student data.

> Some teachers are able to pull off planning IN the school building. Laura does her planning "In the classroom, lights off, door locked. Phone off."
>
> And in another vein entirely, Cassidy, a mom with a little one at home, says, "I have a young daughter, so knowing that I won't do anything once I get home has forced me to change a lot of things. I stay and work after school from 4:00–5:30 p.m., and use my planning time. On the weekends, I wake up at 6 a.m., 2–2.5 hours before the rest of my family. I had to figure out a new rhythm."

READER REFLECTION:

- Where do I complete my best work?
- Do I like to be in the mix with people or completely alone?
- Do I need the Internet or is it better to be disconnected?
- What kind of workspace do I need? A couch? Desk? Whiteboard?
- What work can be done at school versus at home?
- What keeps me motivated?

Keep in mind that your Where right now won't be your Where forever. You can always swing back to this chapter as your needs change and re-select your Where.

Reader Reflection: Keep adding to the Lesson Plan Workload Estimator and complete the Where column.

To Be Planned	Level of Brainpower Required 3 = major focus brainpower 2 = in between 1 = I can do this in front of the TV with my eyes closed	Materials Required	When/How Long?	Where Do I Need to Be?
Math Lesson Plans (Weekly)	3	University of Chicago curriculum Student Assessment Data	I think this is a solid two hours.	Quiet location. Either my home workspace with the door closed or a coffee shop that has room to spread out.

Next up? How to use your lesson plans while teaching, and where you store them for the current week and beyond.

Well, that was a Together Journey into lesson planning whats, whens, wheres, and hows. Remember, the more you do upfront, the more time you will save later for all of the other parts of your job you love. And hey, a little more sleep to boot!

WHAT ABOUT SUBSTITUTE PLANS?

Inevitably, you will be sick or attending professional development, and you'll need to leave plans for someone else to be with your students. I suggest having a day or two's worth of emergency lesson plans at the ready. I recommend building a binder that includes:

- A welcome letter to the sub
- Roster and seating charts, including the names of two or three extra-helpful students per class
- Nametags for each student
- Classroom rules and procedures
- Scripted lesson plans and copies of handouts for the entire class (preferably all stapled and ready to pass out)
- Extra supplies and a little thank-you gift!
- Handouts for students to write substitute day updates back to you—the teacher—with how things went

TURBO TOGETHERNESS

If you want to jump-start this chapter, you can simply pull up the Planning Workload Estimator Chart and complete each section without reading my surrounding text. My feelings won't be hurt. And here is a handy checklist to get it started.

- ☐ Determine exactly what needs to be planned over the course of a semester.
- ☐ Estimate the amount of cognitive brainpower it takes you.
- ☐ Consider partnering with a colleague or co-teacher.
- ☐ Figure out how long each planning task takes you.
- ☐ Decide the best location to complete your planning.

To Be Planned	Level of Brainpower Required 3 = major focus brainpower 2 = in between 1 = I can do this in front of the TV with my eyes closed	Materials Required	When/How Long?	Where Do I Need to Be?

Tess notes, "After my fourth year of teaching, I made a switch from lesson planning 'anywhere' to strictly planning either at school or in quiet, work-focused spaces (i.e. library, Starbucks). I found that even when I thought I was 100% focused in louder places, I was making small mistakes in my plans and student handouts due to distractions. I've also limited my planning to only during the week. It took me three years to make the executive decision I will NOT bring any work home on the weekends."

MAINTENANCE MOVES

■ **Lesson planning still taking too long?** Track your time for a week and see how long it actually takes you. Better yet, do this with a colleague and compare notes. Bonus points for an experienced colleague.

■ **Distracted and scrambling for materials while planning?** Make a checklist of all curriculum materials you need before you "settle in"! Bonus points for packing a delicious snack.

■ **Procrastinating getting started?** Break each planning task into even smaller chunks on your Weekly Worksheet. For example, instead of saying that you will "write math lesson plans," you may need to make the task even smaller. "Write math exit tickets," "Create anchor charts," "Design Google slides."

■ **Only planning day by day and not seeing where you are going?** Get ahead on a week's worth of plans and place on a Monthly Calendar (it could even overlap with your Comprehensive Calendar!) or move to a Yearlong Plan.

Together Tour:

Eric Nielsen

Eric Nielsen is a high school social studies teacher in Denver, CO.

What is your favorite office supply you use in your classroom? Why?

I love my doc cam. My document camera is probably my most prized go-to. I can model for students annotations and thinking out-louds in reading and the use of evidence. Each day I will model for students the expectations for the work and how to process their thinking in the work. We often will work together, and then once I have completed the mini lesson I can move around the room conferring with students as they work on the assignment.

What is your most used organizational tool to keep YOURSELF Together?

I use a course calendar that follows daily, weekly, and monthly plans. I have assignments linked in this calendar so that each week as I prepare for the weekly lessons, each slide presentation, graphic organizer, evidence, deliverables, etc. is hyperlinked in this calendar.

How do you re-Together yourself when unexpected things pop up?

When I find unexpected things pop up, which they do all the time, I usually reach out to my colleagues for guidance and support if I am under stress. This typically allows me time to communicate and process any additional stressors that may be out of the ordinary.

What is a time you had to adjust your Together practice and why?

During our current remote setting, having to readjust is a daily struggle. I usually prefer having more physical work for students and many of my go-to assignments and organizers are on paper. I have had to transfer everything into digital versions for lessons yet at the same time keep routines that students will recognize once we get back into the classroom.

What is your top Together Trick to share with other teachers?

Do not forget self-care during this current school year. This reminder is so vital to your mental and physical health.

What is your favorite teaching snack?

Mixed nuts is my go-to.

Why does Togetherness matter to you?

I need to stay focused and on track. When I get off task or behind, I am not 100% available for my students and my family; I stress, I lose sleep. Staying Together is so important in teaching as it is so easy to get off track, to get distracted, and to lose sight of our own needs. Staying Together allows me to stay on track when unexpected things arise.

CHAPTER 11

Grading, Assessing, and More!

SETTING THE SCENE

So. I remember when I learned that spelling was a subject that required a report card grade. THE NIGHT BEFORE report cards were due. Note to self: Ask for what district report cards look like IN ADVANCE. You are not me. Thank goodness. But many of us still find ourselves drowning in grading, and we want to find a better way.

IN THIS CHAPTER, YOU WILL LEARN TO:

■ Determine what exactly you are assessing and why

■ Get clear on your process for monitoring in-class progress

■ Figure out when and where you grade

■ Share grades with families

Whether you are new to the profession or 30 years in, we can agree that grading is something most of us dread. But with some planning, efficiency tweaks, and old-fashioned hacks, we can go from getting bogged down in paper to using grading as a way to inform our actual teaching, communicate with students and families, and celebrate progress. Let's get to it.

 Reader Reflection: How does your current assessment process work for you and your students/families?

■ **How much time would I ideally spend with assessing student work?**

■ **How much time do I actually spend?**

■ **What is my system for communicating grades with students? When and where do I do this?**

■ **What is my process for communicating grades with families? When and where do I do this?**

DETERMINE WHAT YOU ARE GRADING AND WHY

This is not an instructional text. I won't get into the details of what you should grade, or even how. But as you carefully design objectives and plan lessons, you'll want to make sure you are clear with yourself, your students, and your families about what will be graded and how they'll receive feedback. For example:

■ Some lessons may require detailed exit ticket grading, whereas others may just get a scan

■ Daily reading logs may have just a fraction of them taken home each night

■ Long-form nonfiction persuasive essays may need detailed comments in each student's Google Doc

■ The morning Do-Nows may be peer graded

Remember, all grading is feedback! You'll want to think about the purpose of each type of grading you do before you dive in. Or else you end up with two giant tote bags of papers dragged home every weekend. #guilty Similar to planning, assessing student work is one of the primary activities of teachers—and the one that often elicits the biggest groan. By knowing your priorities within grading student assignments, making the process incredibly efficient, and communicating with students regularly, you can use your grading to actually inform your teaching—and not stay up late with a stack of essays. Mindy R., a teacher in Providence, reminds us of her process: "I look at data from reading quizzes every week and think about the one or two things I want to go after. It might be that, one week, I'm really focused on grading thesis statements."

Reader Reflection: Throughout this chapter, we will work through our Grading Workload Estimator. Our goal here is to consider what we grade, how often, how much time it takes, where you want to be physically located, and how you return it to students and families. Let's peek at the Estimator in the next image.

We will pop in a common item to grade—Math Exit Tickets. But go ahead and look through all of your lesson and unit plans and list the items you regularly assess in the first column and the frequency of review in the second column.

Grading Capacity Estimator Machine

All the Assessments	Frequency of Review	Collection Method	Level of Brainpower Required 3 = major focus brainpower 2 = in between 1 = I can do this in front of the TV with my eyes closed	When and Where I Will Grade the Assessment	How Is It Returned?
Math Exit Tickets	Daily				

Now that you know WHAT you plan on assessing and how often, and maybe you've already even built grading time into your Weekly Worksheet (see how this all fits Together!?), let's use the Estimator to break things down even more. For example, if it is just daily Exit Tickets, I may need to block only 5–10 minutes a day to scan them to figure out what to reteach. But if I'm grading essays or a unit test, I may need to block out two or three hours in a quiet space.

Let's look at various ways to collect artifacts for assessment.

USE OF CLASSROOM VOLUNTEERS

If you are fortunate enough to host an occasional classroom volunteer or intern, you know there's nothing worse than spending more time explaining and delegating tasks than it takes to actually do them yourself. Or worse—having nothing for them to do. Consider setting up a volunteer bin, like Cloi did (Figure 11.1), with some easy skill activities, such as stapling, returning papers, or collating each week during your Meeting with Myself. Then you have it ready to go! With a teaching assistant or some other type of trained help, you can build their support into your lesson planning so they can support small groups or prepare materials. I keenly remember my first volunteer gig in my daughter's second-grade classroom; her teacher knew I had elementary instruction experience, and so she handed me reading folders, highlighted passages, and a question and answer key. I got myself right to work helping with a nonfiction lesson!

Figure 11.1   Cloi's Volunteer Drawers

DETERMINE HOW YOU COLLECT STUDENT WORK

Nowadays there are many more ways to collect materials than 20 years ago when I was a teacher with paperclipped stacks of papers in folders. Sure, some of the stuff may still come in the old-fashioned way, but who wants to deal with a messy Google Drive of essay submissions! Not me!

Let's go back to what you plan on grading and how you plan to collect it. This can actually take a lot of time, but with a few thoughtful pre-moves, creative collection can actually make grading more efficient.

TIPS AND TRICKS FOR COLLECTING PHYSICAL STUDENT WORK

■ Be clear how the responses should be written. For example, show your work in a particular box, but write your answer down the right-hand side of the paper.

■ Plan which sections of the papers you will grade at a time. It may be more efficient to grade all of the page 1 multiple choice before going into all of the essays.

■ Number your students (at beginning of the year), and teach them to write their student numbers on the upper right-hand corner of their papers

■ Use student helpers to collect, alphabetize, and paper clip—bonus points for a Post-it Note to a friend who didn't turn in the assignment!

■ Using grouping and color-coding if you have lots of students. For example, all journals graded on Tuesdays are red, all journals graded on Wednesdays are blue, etc.

■ Return work to cubbies or pockets to save time

Ultimately, what we care about is not Pinterest perfect paper pockets, but that we are as efficient as possible with our grading collection and sorting so we can get some time back for the actual thoughtful review of the work. Knowing the full picture of the workload is the only way to get a handle on this. Let's peek at a few examples to get our juices flowing.

Valence College Prep's Student Work Files

In this classroom at Valence College Prep (Figure 11.2), simple crates are used for student work.

Figure 11.2   Student Work Files at Valence College Prep

Emily's Paper Collection System

When you're collecting hard-copy items, it helps to have them easily grouped to grab and go. Figure 11.3 shows how Emily M., a teacher in Denver, could easily calendar a day to grade work completed by the purple group, the pink group, and so on (see Figure 11.3). This also makes it easy for students to turn in materials to the proper location.

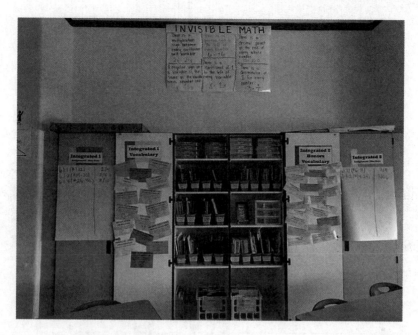

Figure 11.3 Emily's Paper Storage

But how about the digital side? Many of us got a crash course in how to collect work digitally during the pandemic.

Collecting Digital Work

Of course, many of us now receive student work electronically. Gone are the days of the purple flair pen. It can take a bit of time to get into the groove with digital student feedback. Michelle G., an elementary educator in Maryland, describes how she approaches work submitted electronically: "I use SpeedGrader in Canvas and copy and paste feedback from one student to another if the errors show similar misunderstandings. At times, I create a bank of 'feedback statements' that I will tweak to personalize to each student. If verbal feedback is best, I record my statements using the upload media tool in Canvas SpeedGrader."

Now is a good time to revisit each of your lesson plans and make sure you understand WHAT you are collecting, HOW you are collecting it, and how you PLAN to grade it. Ultimately, grading takes us time, so we want to be disciplined in what we grade and how we collect it!

Reader Reflection: Let's keep moving on our Grading Workload Estimator! For each item you grade, list your collection method.

All the Assessments	Frequency of Review	Collection Method	Level of Brainpower Required 3 = major focus brainpower 2 = in between 1 = I can do this in front of the TV with my eyes closed	When and Where I Will Grade the Assessment	How Is It Returned?
Math Exit Tickets	Daily	Students submit via Google Forms			

Now the rubber meets the road: tracking student progress along the way, and using it to inform your feedback and future lesson delivery. Your school may have already designed grading systems for you, in which case, skip the next section OR read on to see how you might supplement or tweak these.

GETTING EFFICIENT WITH THE ACTUAL GRADING

The number one piece of advice we hear from experienced teachers is prioritize what you are actually grading and why. But once you have that narrowed down, there are still a few tidbits of efficiency that can assist us.

Format Your Assessments for Quick Grading

Jeff V.'s example shows a Student Number on the upper right (quick for alphabetizing!) and an answer key that allows him a fast scan down the right-hand side of the page

Figure 11.4   Jeff's Assessment—With Answer Key!

(see Figure 11.4). The time spent formatting during your planning time (block it in your Weekly Worksheet) will save time on the back end!

Create a Key for Common Corrections

No doubt, you will start to see some similar patterns for common corrections. Don't write out the correction for each student each time. That will never get us to sleep at night. Consider creating a key or chart, like the photo seen in Figure 11.5 from DC Prep. Or create a document to pass out to students once you identify trends in their work. For example, if your whole class is struggling with a particular math problem-solving method, perhaps you create a handout annotating that method, share it with the whole class, and ask everyone to fix their own work.

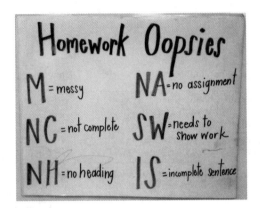

Figure 11.5   Homework Key at DC Prep

Hire Some Student Coaches

One teacher shared this idea on my blog a few years back: "In my fifth-grade class, we are doing a self-paced curriculum for math this year using Schoology. Once a student finishes a unit, they become a 'peer coach' for that unit. Peer coaches have various responsibilities, including, as the title would suggest, coaching other students who are still working in that unit. We also have a 'Peer Coach of the Day' each day who is in charge of grading student work. They LOVE it—they get to sit at a special table, equipped with answer keys, and check other students' work. If anything is incorrect, they hand it back to the student immediately to fix. At the end of class, I know any work that has been turned in receives full credit, since nothing gets turned in until it is completely correct. Students take ownership of their work, and I'm freed up to work with struggling students!"

Of course, with any student helper method, be sure you are following your school's particular policies and procedures. Some schools allow and support these methods; others do not, depending on the type of assessment.

 Reader Reflection: How can you make your grading more efficient?

KEEPING UP WITH STUDENT PROGRESS

Even when you are not taking formal grades, you will want a way to track ongoing observations so you can tailor your lessons accordingly. These observations inform how you spend your time, like if you want to tutor a child at recess or rework a lesson plan. In this section, you will see a few ways teachers do this regularly, both on paper and digitally.

Nadia's Progress Monitoring

Nadia keeps a tracker (Figure 11.6) on her clipboard throughout her teaching day and makes laps around the classroom to see who is learning the objectives.

My takeaway from Nadia's system is its overall simplicity and quick targeting of students according to need. We are always trying to make the most of our time for ourselves—and our students!

Let's peek at a second example of progress monitoring.

Math Group 1

Group 1	Lap Name:	Lap Name:	Lap Name:	Lap Name: End Product
David* (table)				
Eliza* (table)				
Henry*				
Miranda*				
James				
Alberto*				
Kayleigh				
Jessica				
John				
Katherine				
Natalia				
Madelyn				
Ezekiel				

Figure 11.6 Nadia's Progress Monitoring Chart

Date:							
Lesson Objective:							
	STEP Level	Main Purpose	Gist	Evidence	Complete Sentences	Text Features	Notes
Jessica	Pre						
Anna	Pre						
Joaquin	1						
Susanna	1						
Alex	1						
Jennifer	2						
Elizabeth	2						
Richard	3						
Amanda	3						
Daniel	3						
Heidi	4						
Frank	4						
Cristel	5						

Figure 11.7   Elisa's Student Mastery Tracker

Elisa's Student Mastery Chart

Figure 11.7 is a digital model from Elisa, a teacher in Austin. Elisa's system is super focused on the priorities of her lesson. At a glance, she is able to see where her students are currently and quickly check off if they are learning the targets of her lesson. Creating a quick tracker like this ensures you stay focused avoid time spent redlining essays for material you have not yet taught!

Elisa says, "When we are in reading class, I have a packet for the whole week, the date and the lesson and the questions they need to answer. Whenever we finish reading, I go over questions with them and discuss possible answers. As they are answering, I'm marking stuff off to see what I need to reteach and why." Again, love the simplicity here; we always want the most efficient methods possible for you to gauge the success of your lessons.

Let's look at one more model from a secondary teacher.

Emily's Objectives Tracker

Emily built the spreadsheet shown in Figure 11.8 with her department. Although it is complex at first glance, Emily shares her rationale: "The key thing I wanted to learn from Exit Tickets was, 'Which students do I need to focus on tomorrow?'" And with 150 students, that can be tricky to figure out each day! Welp, spreadsheets to the rescue!

Test Question	1	2	3	4	5	6	7	8	9	10
Topic	Writing equation from a graph	Table / Graph / Equation from Scenario	Draw graph, write equation	Error analysis	Slope from points	Slope from a table	Slope from a table	Unit conversion	Unit conversion	Evaluate expression
Aligned ET	2.1.2	SLO Quiz		2.2.3 Q1	2.1.4 Q1	2.1.4 Q2	2.2.2	2.2.4	2.2.4	Checkpoint
Period 1 Smith Average	58.33%	64.15%	39.25%	61.29%	27.19%	58.76%	49.24%	44.19%	34.25%	72.11%
Period 2 Smith Average	13.64%	47.26%	31.27%	38.19%	59.27%	48.19%	67.76%	74.18%	27.18%	79.21%
Period 4 Smith Average	26.32%	43.53%	47.15%	41.37%	67.25%	18.71%	79.19%	49.17%	29.45%	64.33%
Period 3 Gonzalez Average	36.84%	31.29%	28.75%	39.22%	71.11%	41.22%	66.75%	53.15%	31.47%	58.52%
Period 4 Gonzalez Average	33.33%	58.75%	68.15%	51.11%	41.34%	54.29%	48.91%	57.28%	38.29%	72.36%
Period 6 Gonzalez Average	31.25%	21.25%	57.27%	36.04%	33.71%	64.23%	28.71%	34.62%	48.15%	68.52%
Period 1 McAllister Average	49.17%	61.25%	36.79%	18.95%	62.88%	61.28%	14.32%	18.47%	57.21%	67.81%
Period 2 McAllister Average	54.75%	53.14%	24.81%	58.14%	65.17%	31.24%	19.75%	50.87%	62.15%	60.39%
Period 3 McAllister Average	33.64%	37.15%	51.25%	41.26%	71.36%	43.28%	23.41%	61.27%	51.01%	72.29%
Period 5 McAllister Average	36.71%	41.24%	43.24%	63.66%	73.14%	24.51%	18.71%	45.19%	49.81%	46.25%
Period 6 McAllister Average	44.15%	21.27%	64.81%	52.11%	48.79%	40.21%	27.72%	71.11%	19.21%	71.53%
Overall Average	38.01%	43.66%	44.79%	45.58%	56.47%	44.17%	40.41%	50.86%	40.74%	66.67%

Figure 11.8   Emily's Grade-Level Objectives Tracker

Emily supports this spreadsheet with a larger system that helps her answer her question even more efficiently.

■ Emily uses Google Forms to create daily exit tickets

■ The Google Form responses automatically populate to her spreadsheet

Emily says this took her grading from 60 minutes a day to closer to 3 to 5 minutes—and she can better target which students need more assistance! Faster AND smarter!

Emily, Elisa, and Nadia each take time to group students according to mastery level, and then pay close attention to how each one is doing with the given objectives. This also helps with not having to grade everything and being strategic in what and how you grade—which ultimately saves everyone time!

 Reader Reflection: How do you monitor progress with your students? What are you doing as you walk around during class—whether you're online or in person?

New Teacher Alert: If you're not yet familiar with or have not yet been trained on your school or district's grading software, make sure you find a way to do it soon. The more practice you get, the more useful the tool will be and the more efficiently you'll learn to use it! It will be no fun to figure out how to enter everything the week before report cards are due!

SELECTING A GRADEBOOK OR GRADING SOFTWARE

Gone are the days of handwriting grades into some green and white boxes and then averaging them with a calculator! Most school systems have adopted software that makes it easier to enter grades, weigh percentages, and share with students and families.

Gradebooks we have seen:

- Illuminate
- Schoology
- PowerSchool
- Other options

What if you don't find the gradebook used by your school to be helpful? You can always create a Google Sheet to enter your own grades, comments, and ongoing data. You can use this in addition to your mandated system to gather better information for your students.

 Reader Reflection: Do you need to supplement your school's grading system? If so, how?

WHEN AND WHERE ARE YOU GRADING?

And now we've come full circle. We're back to the Weekly Worksheet. You've probably already blocked off time for grading, but let's get really strategic about it. This is mostly a matter of personal preference, though some schools require grades turned in at a certain time or location. Some teachers prefer a "shoving a turkey sandwich in mouth while I go" approach, whereas others save up grading in huge batches to sit down to at the just right time and place. Some of the materials will be based on personal preference (hello, purple Flair pens), and other materials may have a district required component. For example, if your school uses Illuminate, you may need an Internet connection when entering grades. If you grade a lot using Google Forms or Docs, you will also need Internet connection. If you are cozying up with a pen and paper, you may wish for soft music and lighting.

Option 1: Grade in Small Batches Whenever You Can

Many teachers we interviewed like to grade constantly, so the work doesn't pile up into a huge stack. Tess says, "Grading can be really hard to fit in, but our school commitment to grades is a minimum of two grades entered per week into our progress monitoring platform. My personal goal is three grades per week. I made this goal because teaching 100 kids daily means I can't be communicating to families consistently. At least through grades, students are getting consistent feedback as to how they are doing. My coteacher and I also split the grading between the two of us, which helps a lot."

If this is your preference, you will want to make sure:

- Materials are at the ready, such as organized digital files or paperclipped stacks of work and answer keys

- Any highlighters, pens, or stickers are handy for writing feedback to students

Sue takes us through her Grading Bag (Figure 11.9): "The contents of the bag are just what I need to do the task, but not enough to distract me. I always keep the stack of student work small; no more than three or four different assignments for about 50 students. Anything more is not a small task, and I also only put 'easy' grading into this bag. This work is meant to be accomplished in 20–30 minutes."

Figure 11.9   Sue's Student Work Tote Bag

If you select this approach, you may want to make a Sue-type tote bag. Before long, you'll find yourself grading right before a staff meeting, in the dentist's chair, or when you're waiting for the bus. This approach works well for the grading that requires less deep thought. However, if this isn't your preference or you're grading long history essays, you'll find you'll also need bigger chunks of higher-energy time and focus.

Option 2: Grade in Batches

Another approach could be to grade in weekly batches, segmenting out certain types of grading per day—based on student needs and your own environment. For example, you might review Reading Logs on Mondays, first drafts on Tuesdays, and quizzes every Thursday. And guess what, we can put those To-Dos right into our Weekly Worksheets.

Lindsey says, "Math has the most data coming from it. Thursdays are my day to look at **goal cards.** [Figure 11.10] Every student has a goal card, a specific reading skill, they struggle to read the word correctly, I will look for chunks in a word."

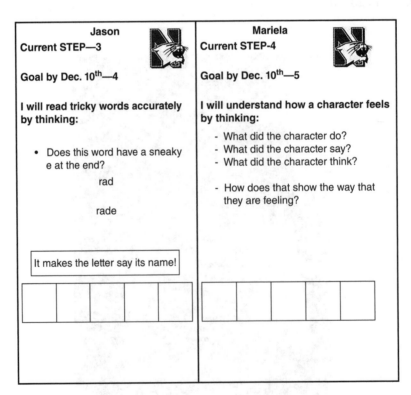

Figure 11.10 Lindsey's Student Goal Cards

Laura sets up a similar structure: "Students turn in homework on a Monday, I grade and enter it on Tuesdays, and Fridays they take their quiz and I grade it in the moment." The benefit of grading in cycles is the predictability. In Laura's case, she knows she always needs to use her prep period on Tuesdays for grading, and can therefore schedule meetings and activities on other days. This method can also work well if your school is reasonably together with similar days for assessments, and so on.

Option 3: Grade in Big Chunks Less Often

In some cases, you may need extended time to review student work in great detail. Glenda G., a first-grade teacher, describes, "I take all of my grading home. If I am doing it at school quickly, I am not looking at work well. Every other weekend, I spend a lot of time grading." If this is the case, you will want to look at your Weekly Worksheet and figure out when and where this can happen. It could be:

- In your classroom with the door closed and soft music on
- At a library or coffee shop (think treats!)
- At your home in a comfy spot
- With a group of teachers out and about somewhere

If this is your preference, again, consider the materials you will want nearby for efficiency. Do you need:

- Internet access to input grades or write comments?
- Any materials to mark up student work?
- Access to food, snacks, restroom, or headphones?

Regardless of your preference—or even if you're still figuring out what your preference actually is—grading can get the better of you if you don't have a clear plan for the what, how, and when and where of it. Try an approach for a month and then evaluate how it's going.

 Reader Reflection: Continue filling in your Grading Capacity Chart, this time noting the level of brainpower required and the when and where.

All the Assessments	Frequency of Review	Collection Method	Level of Brain-power Required 3 = major focus brainpower 2 = in between 1 – I can do this in front of the TV with my eyes closed	When and Where I Will Grade the Assessment	How Is It Returned?
Math Exit Tickets	Daily	Students submit via Google Classroom.	1.5	Each day right after the lesson, so I can adjust for the next day. I need to have access to my lesson plans.	

Now enter your realistic grading time in your Weekly Worksheet! This is important because grading takes up a significant portion of our time as teachers, and it is helpful to define in advance when and where you are grading. This can let you communicate with a spouse about weekend work time, or pick a day to come early or stay late at school.

 FAQ: Can I use a volunteer to help with grading? As always, check with your district's privacy policies! But if you have an intern, parent volunteer, or high school student and a stack of multiple-choice grading to complete, you can definitely get some assistance. Be sure to also ask your helper to organize things in the order you'll need to enter grades easily.

OK. Now that you've done all this grading, let's not forget to build a process to actually review and analyze the data to make it useful!

OUT-OF-THE-BLUE POSITIVE PRAISE

Of course, we parents all want to hear about how our kiddos are doing a great job, and it's so lovely to receive a positive phone call, text, or email. Many teachers aim to send two or three positive forms of communication each week. And, of course, if this time is built into your Weekly Worksheet or Meeting with Myself, then it is that much easier to make it happen.

In training thousands of teachers over the past few decades, positive student contact comes up over and over as something we all want to do more of for our kids. Because writing, calling, or texting your students will likely never feel urgent, it is easy to let it fall to the bottom of the list—or never happen at all. We are well intentioned, of course, but we also need systems to make this happen. Therefore, we have to plan for this by including the time to do it in our Weekly Worksheets! Go ahead, take a minute, pull up your Weekly Worksheet and add to your list or block time to do this!

 Reader Reflection: How will you keep positive comments flowing to your students or their families?

WHEN AND HOW AM I SHARING THE DATA WITH STUDENTS AND FAMILIES?

Once the work is graded, entered, and ready to hand back, you'll want to think about WHEN it makes sense to share the data with your students. If you're dealing with a high school midterm that students are on pins and needles about (and maybe they've even already peeked at their platforms and know their grades!), you may want to have one-on-one conferences with individual students. In other cases, you may simply decide to return work to student cubbies, make copies of exemplars for future lessons, or keep papers in a portfolio for parent conferences. This should be determined ahead of time as part of your lesson and unit plans, and done in accordance with district or school policies. Ultimately, we need this time to land on your Weekly Worksheet so that it doesn't sneak up on us in the midst of a field trip week!

Weekly Written Updates

Lindsey uses a simple Parent Contact log (Figure 11.11) to ensure that her outreach is evenly distributed. Lindsey notes, "At least once a month, I try to contact each family. Additionally, I aim to send a positive text to each student to build relationships." If Lindsey doesn't carefully track this, she could end up missing families or opportunities.

	August		September		October		November	
Student	Text	Call	Text	Call	Text	Call	Text	Call

Figure 11.11   Lindsey's Parent Contact Log

Reader Reflection: Continue along the Grading Workload Estimator and complete the final column.

All the Assessments	Frequency of Review	Collection Method	Level of Brainpower Required 3 = major focus brainpower 2 = in between 1 = I can do this in front of the TV with my eyes closed	When and Where Am I Grading?	How Is It Returned?
Math Exit Tickets	Daily	Students submit via Google Classroom.		Each day right after the lesson, so I can adjust for the next day. I need to have access to my lesson plans.	Students get immediate feedback via the Canvas platform!

And of course, go ahead and put this time into your Weekly Worksheet.

Whew! I'm sure that grading makes up the bulk of your time outside of teaching, so I'm glad we figured out how you could balance it all using your Comprehensive Calendar and Weekly Worksheet. Remember, if you change grade levels or schools, or grading systems, or anything, please revisit your process and adjust as needed. You can quickly scan the Grading Workload Estimator and recalibrate. My planning and grading processes looked very different when I taught fourth-grade writing with three sections versus when I taught fifth-grade self-contained all subjects. I needed to do all of my grading in ONE swoop to really standardize essay quality across all 60 plus students. Experiment to find what works best for you and keep adjusting.

THE ROLE OF FORMAL STATE AND NATIONAL TESTING

In addition to your own assessments, you are likely required to administer some types of formal testing, whether it's STEP, MAP, AP Exams, or statewide tests. Whether you agree with them or not, you gotta deal with 'em. So we may as well be Together about it, right?

- **Determine when the actual tests occur.** Don't know? Check district and school calendars. Mark the dates in your Comprehensive Calendar so you can also be sure you lesson plan around these. Lessons often need to be modified during testing windows.

- **Learn about your own role in test administration.** Are you required to cover up materials in your classroom? Make sure you block time in your Weekly Worksheet for this!

- **If you're new to your grade level or subject, make time to learn about the test itself.** Perhaps you need training or support on administering reading assessments for elementary kids. Maybe you want your high school geometry students to take a pretest at the beginning of the year.

TURBO TOGETHERNESS

Grading is truly a window into how our students are learning, and it is arguably one of the most important parts of our jobs. But it can quickly overtake us if we are not intentional about what we grade, how we grade it, and when and where we grade it. Picture efficiently and thoughtfully examining your students' work and then figuring out where your instruction needs to go from there. That is where I hope we can all land; we just have to get it Together!

☐ Consider what and how you grade each assignment.

☐ Decide when, where, and what materials you need to grade.

☐ Determine when and how you will share assessment results meaningfully.

☐ Incorporate grading time into your Weekly Worksheet as you plan each week during your Meeting with Myself.

Or, instead of going step by step, you could just fill out the entire Grading Workload Estimator!

All the Assessments	Frequency of Review	Collection Method	Level of Brainpower Required 3 = major focus brainpower 2 = in between 1 = I can do this in front of the TV with my eyes closed	When and Where I Will Grade the Assessment	How Is It Returned?

Ultimately, I want you to develop an efficient and effective assessment strategy that works for you. Mimi G., in California, describes, "Every morning, I carve out time for a quick exit ticket overview and record the data in a Google Sheet: 'Got it, Almost Got It, Didn't Get It, Big Trends, Next Steps.' I use exit tickets just to drive my instruction, not for grades. I take big tests home on weekends send them home, graded, the next week in the School-to-Home folder. I send out a notice on ParentSquare or RemindApp telling families to check the folder for the test and let me know if they have questions. To track tests and assignments, I use a digital gradebook-aligned Excel sheet."

MAINTENANCE MOVES

- **Grading still taking too much time?** Track your time for a week and see how long it actually takes you. Better yet, do this with a colleague and compare notes. Bonus points for an experienced colleague.

- **Distracted and scrambling for materials while grading?** Make a checklist of all grading materials you need before you "settle in"! Bonus points for packing a delicious snack or making a Grading Bag!

- **Procrastinating even getting started with grading?** Break each planning task into even smaller chunks on your Weekly Worksheet. For example, instead of saying that you will "update English grades," you may need to make that task even smaller. "Grade English exit tickets," "review Period 1 final drafts," "review grammar worksheets."

- **Only grading day by day and not seeing the bigger picture?** Get ahead on a week's worth of plans and place on a Monthly Calendar (it could even overlap with your Comprehensive Calendar!) or move to an annual view.

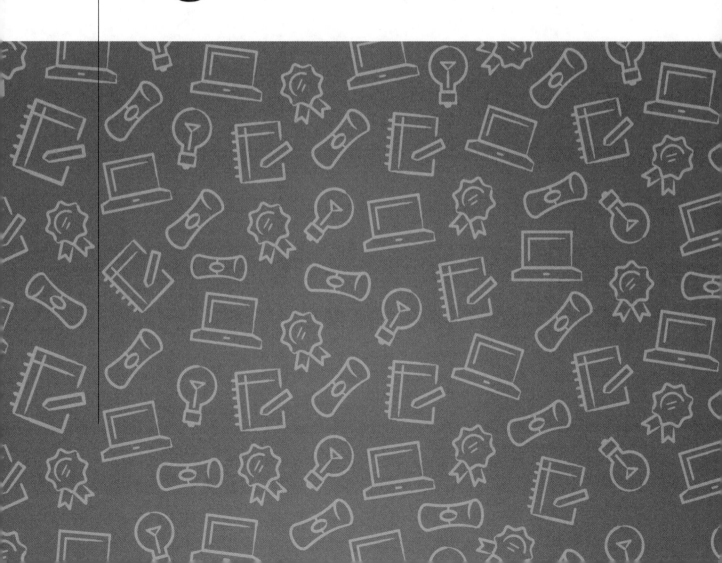

PART 4

Together Your Team

CHAPTER 12

Join 'Em and Lead 'Em: Make the Most of Meetings

SETTING THE SCENE

What *do* you do with those copious ideas you gather in a great staff professional development (PD)? How *should* you best prepare for a grade level or team meeting? I conducted an unscientific study (I do a lot of these . . .), and found that even those of us who are intentional about this sort of thing—diligently taking notes in a beautiful notebook purchased just for the purpose of capturing Meeting Notes—simply don't have the time to go back and review that notebook regularly. And what about creating purposeful meeting agendas to drive collaboration and achieve clear outcomes, instead of meetings that go on and on?

IN THIS CHAPTER, YOU WILL LEARN TO:

- Maximize your time by preparing agendas and prework for meetings

- Involve all team members by sharing leadership responsibilities

- Create clear next steps for notes and action items

Showing up to a meeting unprepared or racing through a laundry list of topics is all to common. We're busy, we're focused on other things, and we haven't had too many good meeting models ourselves. But ladies and gentlemen, there is another way. This chapter will focus on the key steps to take before, during, and after meetings to make the most of your (and others'!) precious time. Working this way takes a little bit of discipline and a commitment to preparation, but it will be helpful when you have more time and energy to focus on what matters most—your classroom!

 Reader Reflection: Let's play Bingo! Please "cover" each statement that applies to you! Evaluate your current meeting practice.

Meeting Bingo!

I **meet regularly** with the people and teams that are connected to my goals—my students!	Our meetings ensure there are ways for everyone's voices to be heard and air time is shared.	The process for **agenda creation and preparation** is clear and communicated. *For example, participants know how to contribute and prepare*
The **logistics are tight**. *For example, invites are sent, the right location or mechanism is selected, equipment is tested*	**FREE SPACE!**	Each topic on the agenda is **well laid out and primed for the anticipated outcome.** *For example, if it is a decision-making item, all possible decisions and recommendations are spelled out.*
The roles and responsibilities are crystal clear. *For example, there is a note-taker, people know if they are contributing*	Meetings **begin and end on time** or trade-offs are made transparent.	The meetings have **airtight note-taking and follow-through mechanisms.**

- If you're a teacher leader, jump to sample agendas to learn more about how to make the most of small group meetings.

- If you're a new teacher, start with the section to develop a plan to track all of the learning you are doing in PD, teacher training, and grad school.

Let's look at a few examples of agenda templates from Together Teachers. You can download the templates from the Wiley website and use them on your laptop, tablet, or desktop PC to take notes electronically, or print and add to your Together Teacher System.

Reader Reflection: Consider all the meetings you have in total. We will work through this Meeting Matrix throughout the chapter.

1	2	3	4	5	6	7	8
What type of meeting is it (1:1, team, staff, etc.)?	What is the purpose of the meeting (information sharing, decision-making, celebrating, etc.)?	Who will create the agenda?	What are recurring or predictable meeting topics?	Where will the meeting be held? What materials are needed?	How clear are the roles during the meeting?	How will notes and next steps be recorded? By whom?	Where will notes and next steps live when they are finished?

CREATE THE MEETING AGENDA

At some point in your teaching career, if not now, you will be responsible for the creation of a meeting agenda. Or maybe asked to give input into how an agenda is created! In this section, we will look at several teacher-generated meeting agendas for various topics and consider benefits of each approach. In each case, you will see the following criteria represented:

- Clear goals and purpose
- Times allotted to topics
- Shared facilitation
- Community agreements
- Next steps noted

And before we just jump to asking people for meetings or showing up at meetings, let's get in the habit of establishing the purpose of the meeting! Is it to review student progress? Plan family conferences? Debrief implementation of new curriculum? Figure it out before you go all in!

Stephanie's Prep and Follow-Through

You probably meet regularly with your department, content area, or some other kind of working group. Because people tend to plan less for meetings with smaller groups, they can quickly go downhill. However, these meetings are also often the lifeblood of the school and *the* opportunity to make things happen.

Let's look at how Together Teacher and grade-level lead Stephanie F. planned, led, and followed through on a grade-level meeting to prepare her third-grade students for Funtastic Friday (a positive reward event at her school) (see Figure 12.1).

In this example, Stephanie set the stage for a very productive team meeting (and you can too, using the Group Meeting Notes template on the Wiley website). Let's break down what Stephanie did to prepare.

- **Set outcomes.** She clearly set the goals of the meeting by defining the outcomes. It is very clear to participants that they will leave with a plan for Funtastic Fridays and will know all they need to prepare for Week One.

- **Aligned the topics and time to the outcomes.** Stephanie then listed the meeting's topics and allocated time to each one.

- **Assigned a facilitator.** To keep meetings moving, someone has to be in charge! Although Stephanie often asks colleagues to facilitate, in this case she led most of the meeting herself.

- **Distributed agenda in advance.** Stephanie emailed this agenda to her team in advance of the meeting so that they all knew what to expect and how to prepare.

Wednesday's Morning Outcomes
◊ Team Exceed will understand the Funtastic Fridays (FF) timeline and have action steps to be completed before our first Funtastic Friday
◊ Team Exceed will divide and conquer all materials needed for Week One.

Time	Topic	Owner	Outcome
8:00–8:05	**Warmer-** If you could have any super power what would it be?	Steph	*get to know each other better.* ☺
8:05–8:10	**Agenda/AIMs**	Steph	*understand the outcomes for today.*
8:10–8:30	**FUNtastic Friday** ☺ • What's this? • Timeline • LP for Fri. Aug. 26	Steph	*understand the FF timeline and have action steps completed before our 1st FF.*
8:30–9:00	**Days 2-5 Materials Check-in** • Owners • Create/Fill our intern request forms	All	*review days 2–5 to see if there are any additional materials that need to be made.*

Figure 12.1 Stephanie's Grade-Level Meeting Agenda

During the meeting Stephanie took notes directly on her laptop. Immediately following, she emailed the next steps to everyone. Stephanie can now start the next meeting by reviewing the status of these next steps. This will ensure accountability and provides clarity on who is doing what. Although this level of preparation and follow-up took Stephanie an extra 10 to 15 minutes before and after her meeting, the time saved by having a focused and productive meeting, and by clearly dividing up the work, will pay off later when the team is not scrambling and can focus on teaching instead.

Describing her approach to meetings, Stephanie said, "I prepare so much because the grade-level meeting goes astray if I do not. We wouldn't end up getting through everything and we'd be unable to achieve solid, clear outcomes. It's also important to prepare so that the team feels it's worth their while. I need a plan for how I want to introduce each topic. Am I giving folks enough think time? Do I need everyone's voice?" Stephanie is doing the heavy lifting with the agenda set-up and follow-through so she can spend the precious meeting time on what matters most to the team.

Diana's Value-Driven Agenda

Diana F., in Philadelphia, shares a meeting agenda (Figure 12.2) that includes many pieces, such as Grade-Level Community Agreements and Group Problem Solving, designed to keep the meeting focused on the objectives and the community's values in mind.

The beauty of Diana's template is that she's included so many meeting element essentials:

■ Team Builder

■ Next steps from previous meeting

■ Goal check-in

■ Problem solving

■ Q&A

GRADE-LEVEL COMMUNITY AGREEMENTS:

-

<School>
<Grade-Level> Team Meeting
<Date>
Note Taker: <Name>
Time Keeper: <Name>

Agenda

Agenda	Details	Notes
<Minutes>	**Teambuilder:** •	
<Minutes>	**Check-in on Next Steps:** 	

Responsibility	Point Person

<Minutes>	**Progress To Goals**

	Goal	Actual
Academics		
Attendance		
Behavior		
Suspensions		

<Minutes>	**Grade-Level Problem Solving & Planning** •
<Minutes>	**Follow Up/Q&A:** Any questions for the team?

Weekly Deadlines	**Upcoming Dates**
• •	•

Action steps and responsibilities on following chart

DOL (See below)

Responsibility	**Point Person**	**Responsibility**	**Point Person**
•		•	
•		•	
•		•	

Figure 12.2   Diana's Grade-Level Meeting Agenda

Now of course, strong meetings are not built on Togetherness alone. Of course, there are many other aspects, such as trust, communication, participation and more. But we are going to stay in our lane over here, and just focus on the Togetherness aspects. However, we encourage you to pay attention to ALL of the things related to building a strong team culture.

Laura's Team Template

There is much to love about the simplicity of Laura's agenda (see Figure 12.3). As you create your own, consider how you are setting it up to be sent out in advance. The formatting of text boxes allows it to be easily digestible before the meeting. Additionally, it is very clear to participants what will be discussed during the meeting.

Laura's eighth-grade meeting agenda rocks because she's included:

- ■ Built-in joy and warmup
- ■ Clear prework for all participants, including prereading and a place to take notes
- ■ Reminders about upcoming events and meetings

FAQ: WHAT IF IT IS A FORMAL MEETING, SUCH AS AN INDIVIDUALIZED EDUCATION PLAN (IEP) OR PERFORMANCE REVIEW?

In the case of a formal meeting with an established protocol, such as an IEP meeting, you may need to rely upon school or district created templates and timelines. For example, if you are a special education teacher, you may need to invite parents a certain number of weeks before the meeting and send out notes in a certain form a required number of days after the meeting. If this is the case, be sure to put all of the deadlines directly into your Comprehensive Calendar! Grace H., a special educator in Denver, notes, "First, we put in the IEP due dates and then look at the tasks in the weeks leading up to them. I block time to schedule the meeting, figure out who has to be in the meeting, and secure permission to evaluate." Her form is demonstrated in Figure 12.4.

8G Team Meeting #1
July 25, 2019

Today's Big Ideas

TWBAT build team by getting to know members of their team more deeply.

TWBAT internalize transition and entrance/exit routines for their grade level by reading the Proc Doc and practicing as one team.

TWBAT prepare for summer school as one team.

Agenda

☐   JOY! (30 Minutes)

☐   Transitions (45 Minutes)

☐   Entrance/Exit (35 Minutes)

☐   Summer School (20 Minutes)

☐   Logistics (20 Minutes)

TEAM

1.   Favorite Photo

2.   Fruit Salad

School Transitions

1.   Read 8th Grade **Transitions** section in Proc Doc

Same	Different

2.   Practice & Tape Floors
    a.   Criteria for Success:

What are the components of a strong transition?	*Strong Transitions KEY POINTS*

(Continued)

Figure 12.3   Laura's Eighth-Grade Meeting Agenda

3. Tricky Transitions – Talk Through & Practice!

Notes/Reminders

Entrance/Exit

1. Read 8th Grade **Entrance/Exit** section in Proc Doc

Same	Different

2. Practice!

Summer School

Questions for LB (Email or Offline)

Up and comings!
KACP PD 7/22- 8/6 pm 8am- 5pm
7/29-7/31 KIPP School Summit in Houston
8/2 KTK-austin Convocation at North Campus
8/5 Meet the Teacher Night
8/7-8/16 Summer School
8/19 First Day of School
9/4 Grade Level HH Location TBD * *Tentative*
Teacher/Upper School dress up days saved to begin after October

Figure 12.3 (*Continued*)

Student name: _____   Date of meeting: _____

Annual IEP Review

NOTE – when scheduling a meeting, schedule it about 7–10 days prior to the IEP deadline to give buffer time to the Enrich Deadline in case it needs to be rescheduled or various things that could come up do come up.

Timeline	Documents and Events	Steps/description	✓
2 weeks prior to the meeting	Notify gen ed teachers	• Email – Ask all teachers and admin that work with the student for feedback (e.g. strengths, areas of growth, ideas or suggestions, accommodations that work well). I use the same Google form all year and give them 24–48 hours to fill it out. Then I politely follow up to all teachers that haven't in a 1:1 email. • For general education classes a student is qualified to have a longer extensive conversation about LRE & goal areas.	
1 – 2 weeks prior to meeting	Grade-Level Probe	• Give a second grade-level probe order to figure out the ROI at the end of 6–8 weeks to use in the meeting for LRE discussion.	
At least 10 days prior to the meeting	Send 10 day notice of meeting	• Schedule and complete notice of meeting in the IEP development event in Enrich. • Print and send home with student for parent.	

Within 2 weeks prior to the meeting	Collect Body of Evidence (BOE) Prep for IEP	• Complete BOE worksheet with all assessment data results and upload into the IEP in Enrich
		• BOE should include
		   o CMAS data
		   o STAR/NWEA/etc. data
		   o ACCESS results
		   o CBM's (probes)
		   o Grades
		   o Observation (for SED or OHI, included with their current BIP)
		   o Screener results if applicable (e.g. math/reading)
		• Interview student:
		   o What do you want to be when you grow up?
		   o What are some things you are good at?
		   o What do you struggle with?
		   o Which classes are your favorites and which do you struggle with?
		   o Strengths/interests?
		• Have an idea of possible goals and hours prior to the meeting
		   o LRE – ROI (and gap analysis if possible)
		   o Look at the agendas to help you plan ahead
		   o Fill out blank BOE form (which has all you may need)	

Figure 12.4   Grace's IEP Meeting Prep List

FAQ: What if I'm running a series of meetings?

Indeed, many meetings are recurring, such as grade-level teams, department meetings, or child study groups. It can help to take the long view when planning these. This way, one meeting doesn't become a cram-fest of everything at once; you can pace out the work instead. Check out this example of one school's scope and sequence for a series of meetings. If you create and share a scope and sequence for a series of meetings, it can help others plan their preparation and involvement. Additionally, if things go off the rails during a meeting, you have an automatic deferral method to another meeting in place!

FAQ: What if setting an agenda like this feels too rigid?

Ooooh, I hear that loud and clear. The key will be creating an agenda that you and your team both feel good about. It may be that you cocreate it and check in to make sure it stays aligned to priorities. It might be that you all take turns leading different sections of the meeting. It might be that a handwritten version on a whiteboard works best for you. Time is a limited resource and no one wants to be in a never-ending meeting without clear goals, but there are lots of ways to be creative about your delivery!

Reader Reflection: Consider all the meetings you have in total. Please complete the first three columns of this Meeting Matrix.

1	2	3	4	5	6	7	8
What type of meeting is it (1:1, team, staff, etc.)?	What is the purpose of the meeting (information sharing, decision-making, celebration, etc.)?	Who will create the agenda?	What are recurring or predictable meeting topics?	Where will the meeting be held? What materials are needed?	How clear are the roles during the meeting?	How will notes and next steps be recorded? By whom?	Where will notes and next steps live when they are finished?

And if YOU are responsible for some of the agenda creation, for example, a weekly grade team meeting, block time in your Weekly Worksheet to get that agenda done each week! You will wow your team with your Togetherness—your meetings will be stronger too!

Determine Materials and Location

During school building times, we often have more choices, such as conference rooms, teachers' lounges, libraries, media centers, or even our own classrooms. During the pandemic era, meetings were limited to video calls only. Depending on what materials you need, such as technology, white boards and markers, or even a photocopier for some real-time work, you may need to shift your location accordingly. Of course, if you are leading a video call across campuses, be sure to send a clear digital invite with the relevant information.

If you want participants to bring certain materials, be sure to specify that in the agenda as well. In the example shown in Figure 12.5, the team at Langston Hughes Academy in New Orleans has a Meeting Preparation and Norms section listed as part of the agenda.

Now that your meeting agendas are up and running, let's shift to staying together DURING the actual meeting.

STAYING TOGETHER *DURING* THE MEETING

Feeling good about your prep? Let's dig in to what happens during your meetings. In this section, we will peek at different ways Together folks think about meeting roles, locations, and needed materials. You want to establish systems that help team members build trust, align on values, and work toward common goals. We love the book *Five Dysfunctions of a Team* for its focus on interpersonal dynamics in meetings. But for now, let's stay in our lane and think more about how to keep Together DURING a meeting.

Establish Meeting Roles

It is neither effective nor fun to feel completely in charge of an entire outcome, nor is it great to be cast as a passive and silent participant. To avoid these extremes, be sure to establish who is playing what role in the meeting, articulate these responsibilities beforehand, and share responsibility for participation and contribution.

Common meeting roles include:

- Timekeeper
- Note-taker
- Culture leader

Langston Hughes Academy Department Meeting Agenda

April 13, 2016—Mrs. Trejo's Room Time 1:15pm to 3:40pm

Meeting Preparation *Please Bring*

☐ Positive Attitude
☐ Pen/Paper
☐ Laptop
☐ Data Analysis COI Completed form
☐ Writing samples

Objectives

1. **Review Spring Data Reflection**

Team Core Values

- **Respect**
- **Team**
- **Collaboration**

School-wide Goals

3-5 Year: Student Retention to Graduation: 80% of 7th graders graduate LHA, 90% of 9th graders graduate from LHA in 4 years.

Annual Site Goals:

1. Writing/Reading Across the Curriculum: Golden Sentence, Annotations, Schaffer paragraphing, Close Reading
2. Cultural Responsiveness, Close our gaps for Males' Writing, Latinos, and African American males ELA. Males and males of color leaving LHA
3. Staff Culture: Students and Staff are aware of monthly pillars and expectations for LHA team.
4. Systems Focus: Technology integration of Schoology, illuminate

Norms

1. *Prompt & Prepared
   a. Begin and end on time
   b. Establish the goal to be achieved in the given time frame
   c. Bring all necessary materials and complete all assignments prior to meeting
   d. Binders and Computers are brought to meetings

2. *Purposeful & Prioritized
   a. Staying purposeful and mindful of our task.
   b. Post it - or parking lot for questions not on topic
   c. Goal Oriented with clear meeting objectives
   d. Kids First- all decisions start with what is best for kids.
   e. Weigh impact of decisions on the entire team.

3. *Professional
   a. What we say in the meeting stays in the meeting (HIPAA Rule)
   b. Being open, active, and respectful
   c. Assume Best Intent
   d. Avoid side conversations
   e. Unified- Once a decision is made it is the decision of the team
      i. Not: "Well, they decided"
      ii. Instead: "we decided" or better, "our goal is to . . ."
   f. Electronics are limited to necessity for the meeting agenda.

Figure 12.5   Preparation Items Listed on Langston Hughes Academy Agenda

Even more important than establishing formal roles is making sure everyone has a voice. That may look like:

- Whirlarounds to hear from each team member

- Doing quick opinion votes to get a pulse on an issue

- Thoughtful prework so those less confident can do their thinking in advance

- Turn and talks

FAQ: What if the meetings I attend are not effective and I have no control over them?

Oooooh, I love this question, and indeed, as professionals, we all occasionally have to attend meetings that are. . . ahem, less-Together. A few thoughts come to mind:

- Can you do any relationship building? Are there people you can connect with that could make it worth it?

- Can you do any strategic multi-tasking? Even just giving yourself a problem to mull over in your brain.

- Can you assist in making the meeting better? Offering to help with some preparation?

Reader Reflection: Please complete the fourth and fifth columns.

1	2	3	4	5	6	7	8
What type of meeting is it (1:1, team, staff, etc.)?	What is the purpose of the meeting (information sharing, decision-making, celebration, etc.)?	Who will create the agenda?	What are recurring or predictable meeting topics?	Where will the meeting be held? What materials are needed?	How clear are the roles during the meeting?	How will notes and next steps be recorded? By whom?	Where will notes and next steps live when they are finished?

NOTE-TAKING DURING MEETINGS

We are all guilty of it: being in a staff meeting getting issued deadlines and just writing the notes in the margin or sitting in incredible PD sessions scribbling important notes and great ideas on a legal pad, then shoving said legal pad in the bottom of our teaching bag and unearthing it only when it is so crumpled that we actually can't even tell anymore what is recorded on it. Who has the time to go back and write anything up? Let's discuss how to put those great learnings to use by being more organized about the notes we take and popping them right into your Together Tools the first time. It will take a little bit more planning, but I promise you that it will be worth it.

The first step is to be very thoughtful about how you take notes. Many of us think and process information through writing, which is helpful in the moment. However, it is *not* helpful when we return to those notes six months later and find ourselves sorting through a lot of jibberish. Let's look at a few ways to make this process easier on ourselves by actually taking on those good ideas. We will talk through the ways Together Teachers take notes during meetings, PD workshops, graduate school courses, coaching meetings, and observational feedback sessions.

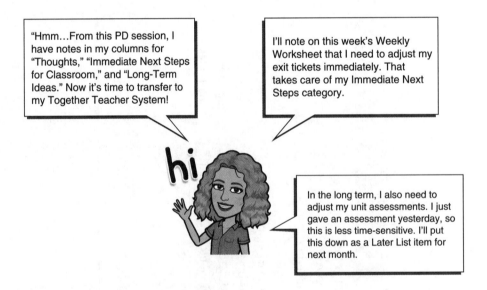

The template in Figure 12.6 is designed to bring to a PD workshop or graduate school course to take specific notes related to a topic. This will essentially become your "cover sheet" for all of the information, papers, and tools that come your way during the workshop or class so that you save yourself the time of having to dig through the materials later to find *that one thing* you wanted to remember! Here's how a few other teachers take notes at PD sessions.

Meeting Topic: _____ **Date:** _____

Participants: _____

NEXT STEPS

Action	By Whom?	By When?	Notes

OTHER MEETING NOTES

Figure 12.6 Meeting Notes Template

Reader Reflection: As you review the samples that follow, please consider:

■ **What are the components of strong note-taking systems?**

■ **What similarities do you notice across all samples?**

Kate's Grade-Level Meeting Notes

Kate creates a post-meeting summary (Figure 12.7) with clear reminders of action steps and FYI (For Your Information) that can easily be read by the Homeroom Teachers. By doing this, Kate ensures that the field trip stays on track, everyone is informed, and it is easy to take action after the meeting!

FAQ: What about on-the-fly meetings? Not every meeting will be a formal sit-down. You may bump into a student guardian at dismissal or get a spontaneous phone call. For these predictably unpredictable meetings, you will want to ensure you have a template in hard copy—if you are on the move—or digitally, if you are online—to capture next steps and take action. Braxton S., in Mississippi, keeps a template for his "unplanned" meetings (see Figure 12.8), so he can catch those To-Dos on the fly!

6/1/2012 Grade-Level Meeting Notes

Notebook:	BT: Blog Interviews		
Created:	6/3/2012 8:00 PM	**Updated:**	6/3/2012 8:02 PM

Team Possible,

I hope you all had great weekends. I enjoyed some QT with the family in Maryland ☺. I am excited for our Sony Wonder/Central Park excursion this week. I am reaching out with some reminders and info about the trip.

(Action Requested, by COB on Monday, 5/23): Please read the below reminders and info about our trip.

REMINDERS:

WHO	Action or deadline	DATE
Homeroom Teachers	show students slide of Sony overview	5/23/2011 - 5/25
Homeroom Teachers	call parents of anyone who did not return slip	Tuesday, May 24, 2011
Homeroom Teachers	BY 7AM: send Kate final list of all scholars who **can't** attend	Wednesday, May 25, 2011

(FYI Only):
1. Attached please find the schedules for the trip. **These is no need to review the schedules (unless you want to) before the GLM on Tuesday.**
2. At the GLM we will discuss the following logistics:
   • Final schedule
   • How to walk from Central Park to Sony Wonder
   • Process of swapping students between Michigan/York and Upenn/Fordham

NOTE: As a correction to my previous email, you will get hard copies of everything on Tuesday at the GLM instead of Monday by COB (I figured it just makes more sense to distribute when we are all together)

Please let me know if you have any questions.

My best,
Kate

Figure 12.7   Kate's Grade-Level Meeting Notes

Braxton's Unplanned Meeting Template

This ensures Braxton can grab his next steps in the moment and not worry about missing any follow-up. This is important as we build relationships with others and our follow-up helps build trust. Let's move on to group meetings!

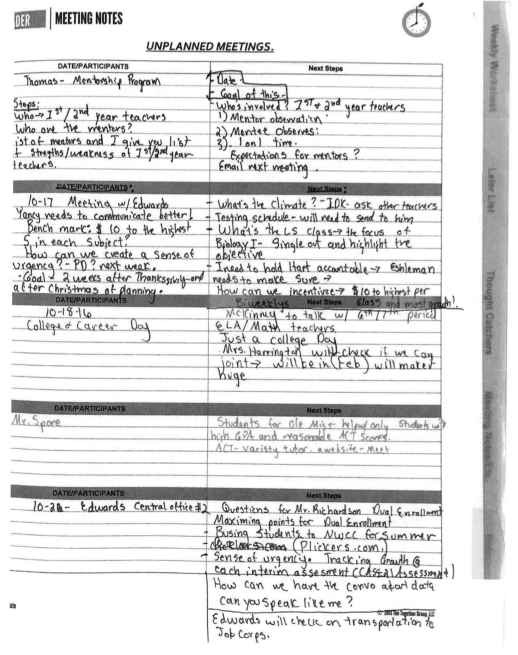

Figure 12.8   Braxton's Unplanned Meeting Notes

Acting on Group Meeting Notes

Group meetings, such as grade levels or departments, can be great—if we ensure the follow-up steps are captured—so we can share the work. You can easily use one of our Together Templates and have everyone take careful notes during the meeting.

We want to be sure that our departments, grade levels, and committees hold strong meetings with consistent and transparent follow-through. For example, if a third-grade team meets about an upcoming field trip, one person can serve as the Note-taker. He or she would either record next steps on the Meeting Notes template or cut and paste the table from the template into an email. Immediately after the meeting, the Note-taker can send all the notes to everyone on the team, to be revisited at the next meeting. The beauty of this process is that if you receive next steps from a colleague in this format, it is very easy to quickly transfer them right onto your Comprehensive Calendar or Later List.

Acting on Professional Development Notes

Julie's Professional Development Notes

Julie G. is an elementary special educator who attended a professional workshop to learn how to help students with attention challenges. She took notes on a simple legal pad but drew a line down the middle. Julie took lots of notes on the left about student memory function and organization, but on the right, she got very disciplined about what she would *do* after attending the workshop. You can see in Figure 12.9 that she noted her immediate next classroom steps:

1 Research three different types of memory

2 Look up "Type to Learn" and "Typer's Deluxe"

Julie needs to make sure that these great ideas then get rolled up into her Comprehensive Calendar or Later List. She can scoop out her next steps during her Meeting with Myself.

FAQ: Notebooks: To Be or Not to Be?
I just love a notebook. I mean, I really love a notebook. The challenge is that what goes in a notebook often doesn't come out. Notebooks are full of great intentions that may never get actualized. If you love your notebook, don't get rid of it. But beware that it can be a place where good ideas get trapped. You may want to consider loose sheets of paper, digital options like OneNote or Evernote, or even digital notebooks, like Rocketbook.

Whether you take notes on a legal pad with a line drawn down the middle like Julie, use a categorized template, or take notes directly on your laptop or iPad (in which case, similar categorization ideas should be used), the overall

NOTES	NEXT STEPS
♦ Use green & red tape on desk to help kids remember how to write left to right (could also mark margins of paper w/green & red markers)	

· 3 kinds of memory
    ↳ Short term
    ↳ Long term
    ↳ Working
	· Research 3 diff. types of memory - what deficits look like/strategies to work with

✳ Students w/attention problems often have trouble w/long term memory ✳ Kids w/organization problems (organizing work on a pg) also have L.T. memory problems · ↳ For kids w/memory problems, try kinestetic & visual cues	· Look up 'Type to Learn' and 'Typer's Deluxe'· 10 Thumbs Typing Tutor - teach kids w/writing difficulties how to type (separate from writing so kids can just focus on typing. (Use for [redacted]? Try out w/him, then pass on to mom)

Figure 12.9   Julie's PD Notes

point is that we all need to do more than jot ideas in the margins or draw stars around ideas we like. When we reenter our classrooms, we won't have any time to revisit our scribbling!

Reader Reflection: Name three strengths of the note-taking systems you just saw:

1

2

3

FAQ: What about group meeting note-taking?

You may already have a Note-taker for the meeting, but even still, people will probably want to take their own notes. Before the meeting starts, be clear who the note-taker is, the purpose of note-taking, and what form the notes will take. For example:

- If the meeting is related to compliance or regulations, you may need someone to take scripted notes in a certain way.

- If the meeting is simply sharing back a decision and next steps, then you may need just a simple Who/What/When chart. You can find samples of both on the Wiley website.

Reader Reflection: Please complete the sixth and seventh columns.

The meeting went well, felt good, and you are excited about what will happen next. But our teacher lives are busy and who has time to go back to all of these notes!?!?! Well, now that we're Together, WE DO! Especially when we build that step to review right into our Meeting with Myself!

Now let's hit our most important step—how we actually take action *after* our meetings.

1	2	3	4	5	6	7	8
What type of meeting is it (1:1, team, staff, etc.)?	What is the purpose of the meeting (information sharing, decision-making, celebration, etc.)?	Who will create the agenda?	What are recurring or predictable meeting topics?	Where will the meeting be held? What materials are needed?	How clear are the roles during the meeting?	How will notes and next steps be recorded? By whom?	Where will notes and next steps live when they are finished?

STORE AND RETRIEVE YOUR MEETING NOTES

This is where it gets tricky. It's extremely easy for notes to get buried in notebooks to which we never return. But imagine the happiness you'll feel when you're wracking your brain to figure out the best way to teach that science concept and you remember: "Ah ha! I went to that amazing weeklong hands-on science seminar last year! Let me open my binder that has those resources in it!" You will save yourself time *and* get great lesson ideas by ensuring your Meeting Notes are part of your Together system. An easy way to do this is to ensure that reviewing Meeting Notes is a step in your Meeting with Myself each week. Ahhhh, yes, that checklist we created together in Chapter 6. Pull it out right now and add this step. I'll wait for you!

Okay, you are back! You have a few options for effectively storing and retrieving your meeting notes.

Options for Storing and Retrieving Meeting Notes

1. Paper (Simple)	2. Paper to Digital (Complex)	3. Digital—Even More Complex
Create binders ordered by topic or content area. Hole punch all materials and handouts. Put your Meeting Notes cover sheet on top of all the handouts and other materials. Transfer next steps to your Weekly Worksheet or Later List. Store binders near where you do your lesson planning.	Transfer next steps to your Weekly Worksheet or Later List. Scan all materials from the workshop or course and store them electronically with your other lesson planning resources, arranged by topic. Use phone apps like Scannable and Genius Scan to turn notes into searchable PDFs. By putting the date in YearMonthDate order—20210809 for August 9, 2021—your materials will sort chronologically, which will be helpful over a long career of teaching.	Take notes directly into Evernote, OneNote, Google Docs, or Word. Transfer next steps to your Weekly Worksheet or Later List. Sort them into your hard drive or within the actual app, using the processes described in the previous column.

Reader Reflection: How will you store and retrieve your Meeting Notes?

1	2	3	4	5	6	7	8
What type of meeting is it (1:1, team, staff, etc.)?	What is the purpose of the meeting (information sharing, decision-making, celebration, etc.)?	Who will create the agenda?	What are recurring or predictable meeting topics?	Where will the meeting be held? What materials are needed?	How clear are the roles during the meeting?	How will notes and next steps be recorded? By whom?	Where will notes and next steps live when they are finished?

TURBO TOGETHERNESS

Whether you are a first-year teacher attending PD or an experienced teacher responsible for an entire grade level, getting meetings right is essential. Done well, meetings keep us moving ahead and helping our students. We can review all the notes during our Meeting with Myself and pop those action steps right into our Together Tools. For example, an action step shared verbally in a staff meeting?! Bam! Pop that baby into your Weekly Worksheet and you will sleep better at night. A long-term idea about the student talent show? Run that future To-Do right over to your Later List! A deadline from your grade-level leader to contribute to the IEP next month? Hello, Comprehensive Calendar! Jump into this checklist to get your meetings off to a great start.

☐ Create a clear agenda with objectives.

☐ Circulate the agenda to meeting participants in advance. If applicable, communicate any pre-work or required materials.

☐ Identify your role in the meeting: Are you leading the meeting? Taking notes? Something else?

☐ Select your note-taking tool. (Paper? Digital? A Together Teacher template?)

☐ Add any follow-up items to your Weekly Worksheet, Comprehensive Calendar, and/or Later List.

Complete the following chart to create a full outline of your meetings.

1	2	3	4	5	6	7	8
What type of meeting is it (1:1, team, staff, etc.)?	What is the purpose of the meeting (information sharing, decision-making, celebration, etc.)?	Who will create the agenda?	What are recurring or predictable meeting topics?	Where will the meeting be held? What materials are needed?	How clear are the roles during the meeting?	How will notes and next steps be recorded? By whom?	Where will notes and next steps live when they are finished?

Sam, a special educator, describes the importance of planning carefully for her meetings with other teachers: "Last year, we had 50-minute meetings, but there was not a template, objectives, or plan. We needed to be more purposeful, but different teachers had different ideas about what to do. After the first year, we moved to a structured template model. I ask teachers to bring student work into the meeting. Things got much more purposeful!"

MAINTENANCE MOVES

Keep track of your meetings for a month. Use the following chart to rank their effectiveness on meeting (heh, heh) the objectives.

Meeting and Date	Objectives	Effectiveness 4 = We met the objectives—and more! 3: We met the objectives. 2: We partially met the objectives. 1: Objectives? What objectives?
Grade-Level Meeting 9/15	• Develop a plan for Back-to-School Night • Divide up preparation tasks	3

Together Tour:

Veronica Urbanik

Veronica Urbanik is a pre-K teacher in Washington, DC.

What is your favorite office supply you use in your classroom? Why?

My favorite office supply in my classroom is my laminator. Our school has a large laminator in the teacher's lounge for bigger projects but for quick jobs my printer paper sized laminator is so quick and easy. The school laminator breaks down often too because it is overused and so I like having mine as a backup. I love to laminate whenever I can so I can save materials for future use to save time and paper.

What is your most used organizational tool to keep YOURSELF Together?

My most used organizational tool is definitely my planner! I use it to keep track of meetings and due dates and to take notes. Because it is a digital planner, I bring it with me everywhere either on my iPad or on my phone. I use it both professionally and personally and so my entire life is in there.

How do you re-Together yourself when unexpected things pop up?

What I have found that works best for me is having a meeting with myself to reset. During the day, there's coffee. During the evening, there's wine. I try to make it a pleasurable experience and not something stressful. I sit down with my planner. I take a few moments to just breathe and then I adjust my calendar and my To-Do list. I look through emails and texts to make sure I am not missing anything. I take notes to reflect on what is working and what isn't. I map out a plan.

What is a time you had to adjust your Together practice and why?

During the pandemic, I had to temporarily switch other to a paper planner for a little while. After staring at my computer screen for hours on end, I could not handle looking at my phone and iPad to utilize my digital planner. I used an old undated planner I just so happened to have so I could give my eyes a break. I wanted my planner to work for me and so the change was good. I ended up getting blue light blocking glasses for $10 on Amazon and have since switched back to my digital planner.

What is your top Together Trick to share with other teachers?

Know. Your. Priorities. And then stick to them. I had the hardest time with this for the longest time. I think as teachers, we sometimes have this mindset that if we aren't 100% all the time, then we are failing. I am learning to let go of or hold off certain things that don't need 100% of me right away.

My friend gave me the greatest advice and I constantly refer to it in my daily attempts at Togetherness.

In life, we are forced to juggle a lot at one time. Some of the things you juggle are "glass" and some things are "plastic." If you drop something that's plastic, it won't break. I can make lesson plan materials that "just get the job done" that aren't aesthetically pleasing. That's a plastic issue (even if it bothers me personally—ha!). But if you drop something that is glass, then the chances are that it may shatter and can't be put back together again.

Determine if the things you are juggling are plastic or glass and you'll see your priorities clearly.

What is your favorite teaching snack?

My favorite teaching snacks are RXBARS. They are these amazing granola bars that don't have many ingredients but taste delicious. They have their fall seasonal flavors out now and their "pecan pie" bar is a must. It's something quick that's filling and not bad for you.

Why does Togetherness matter to you?

To me, "Togetherness" means balance. Personally, it can be hard for me to separate my work life from my home life because everything is so intertwined, especially now that we are teaching from home! Being "Together" means I can be both "Veronica" and also be "Ms. Urbanik" and not feel burnt out by either role because I know my limits for each.

CHAPTER 13

Events, Projects, and Parties: Project Plan Your Way to Success!

SETTING THE SCENE

In addition to ALL of the other things we do as teachers, we often volunteer or are called upon to lead or participate in additional functions that add to student life at our schools. You know, spelling bees, field trips, International Nights, band concerts, and drama productions, the events that we remember most about our own school experiences. Pulling these off can be exhilarating, exhausting, fulfilling, and stressful, all at the same time. We need to involve a number of people along the way, follow policies set forth by our school districts, and take responsibility for student safety and satisfaction. But it doesn't have to be painful. With some serious planning, a lot of anticipation, and tons of communication, school events can be some of the most joyful and memorable parts of teaching.

IN THIS CHAPTER, YOU WILL LEARN TO:

■ Build your vision of a highly successful event

■ Create a Project Plan that lists all necessary steps before, during, and after your event

■ Identify key support tasks and empower others to help you with them

■ Communicate clearly with all parties involved and get the support you need

■ Manage the "day of" with detail and delight

Maybe you've been directing the school play for years, or maybe this is your first year running the talent show. Wherever you are in your event planning journey, it can be helpful to go through each of these steps when an event kicks off. Leave nothing to chance! No one wants rained-out prom pictures. In this chapter, we will take you through planning an event from start to finish—a school Talent Show! You will get the most out of this chapter if you have an event of your own in mind; we'll work through planning it together!

 Reader Reflection: Let's get started by selecting your event.

What is the event?	
When is the event?	
Is it a new event or an old standard?	
How has it gone before?	
What previous materials, if any, can you review for reminders and inspiration?	

Now that we know the basics, it may be time to go digging for any information used in the past for this event—either in files, with actual humans involved with the event in the past, or even talking to your students about it.

DETERMINE A SUCCESSFUL OUTCOME

Say the words "Spelling Bee," "Robotics Competition," "Eighth-Grade Graduation, or "Junior Prom," and we all have different definitions of how those events look based on our own experiences and biases. YOUR definition of an awesome talent show may be very different from mine. So, let's first get clear on our vision and think through how we'll get others on board with it.

Let's say my principal comes up to me and says, "Hey Ms. H.-M., since you are the grade-level lead, I would love for you to plan the middle school talent show this year." Gulp, gulp, gulp. "Okay, cool. On it." Gulp, gulp. TALENT SHOW? With all of those people? Just kidding. I got this.

But before I just start talking to parents and students, I better figure out what a successful outcome looks like so we know what we're working toward. In fact, I even want to put this in writing to ensure I keep everyone on the same page.

Here are some questions I should ask myself and others before I even get started:

What does the event look like if it is going well? How does it feel?	
What are the educational outcomes connected to this event, if any?	
Who else has an interest in this event going well?	
What could go or has gone wrong in the past with this event?	
What is the budget, if any?	
What are school or district policies I need to be aware of?	
Who needs to be communicated with in an ongoing way?	

I'm going to sit down with my principal FIRST. Probably in a separately scheduled meeting to get all of this information from her. And then I need to speak to the teacher who organized the Talent Show last year, and then review any existing materials. Once I understand the past, I can get ready to speak to folks about the future. I should probably speak to parents, students, the PTA, and other teachers who'll have a role.

My Talent Show vision:

Students will showcase their self-selected talents to an appreciative audience of families, teachers, and friends. The logistics will be flawless, and students will feel proud and joyful.

 Reader Reflection: Describe your own event vision.

Okay, the vision is in place. I can see this Talent Show. But it's only January, and the event is in April. It's tempting to wait a few months to get started, but this is a big one, so I need to get started now. I need a Project Plan! And don't worry, after we make the Project Plan, we will transfer those To-Dos by month right on over to that trusty Later List.

Project Plans: A simple list of To-Dos that are grouped together chronologically and assigned to various people involved with the project. Project Plans may come in handy when you are in charge of something that has multiple To-Dos. Good rule of thumb: Any project with more than 10 steps is worthy of a plan.

FAQ: I have no idea what a Project Plan even looks like! Where do I start?! Never fear, we have you covered! At its most basic, a Project Plan is simply a list of step-by-step actions to accomplish a goal laid out across a timeline with owners of each step. If you want to get more complex, you can sort, filter, and all of that.

Figure 13.1 is a peek at one: Our first step will be to build out our Buckets to make sure we are addressing all aspects of the Talent Show!

Bucket	Deadline	Task	Owner	Support

Figure 13.1 Project Plan Template

BUILD OUT YOUR BUCKETS

Let's work backwards from the actual event.

April 18, 7:00–8:30 p.m. Talent Show

What steps will it take to actually pull this off? I'm going to start by thinking about my broad categories, otherwise known as "Buckets."

Your event may not need items in all Buckets (known as "workstreams" in official project management speak), but this is a way to get your brain thinking through all of the steps.

Break Down Your Buckets into Actionable Steps

Let me return to my Talent Show and the facilities Bucket, shall we? I need to brainstorm every step it will take to secure the facility for the night of the show. Although it could be tempting to try and fit all of these steps into a Google Sheet or Excel file, we need to get the content out of our heads before we beautify it. Sometimes it can help to consider the What, Where, When, and Who for each of your Buckets.

- Who is in charge of facilities? Do I have their contact information?

- What is the process for securing facilities at my school?

- When do I need to secure the space by? What facility will I need to use for the Talent Show?

- What OTHER spaces may I need for the Talent Show? A place to store materials? A place to practice?

Reader Reflection: Carefully go through each of the Project Buckets and consider the 4 Ws for each of them. Don't worry about format right now. And don't worry if you don't have the answers to your questions. That can become a step in your Project Plan!

List your own Project Buckets in the following chart and steps to figure how to make it happen! Remember to use the list as a starting point and think of the Ws.

Buckets	Bucket 1	Bucket 2	Bucket 3	Bucket 4	Bucket 5
Who?					
What?					
Where?					
When?					

There are lots of ways you can do this kind of school event planning. It depends on how your brain works, who needs to see the planning materials (if anyone), and the details of the event itself. Here are a few ideas in the order of least to most complex.

As you Build out Your Buckets, you will want to have the following materials handy:

- District calendar with key districtwide dates

- School calendar with other school events. It would not be good to have Bingo Night near the basketball championship!

- Your own personal Comprehensive Calendar, Later List, and Weekly Worksheet. Perhaps even your Thought Catchers!

CREATE A PROJECT PLAN

Now that you have Built Your Buckets, it's time to place the action steps into your Project Plan. Most teachers like to list the steps chronologically, and there are many formats your Project Plan could take. The next image shares some options.

Ways to Organize Your Project

- If your project is very simple with few people involved: Use Post-it Notes on a whiteboard to arrange tasks, or place them on a paper calendar. The challenge with this method is that it is not portable. But if it's just for you, you could take a photo and carry it with you!

- If your project is on the smaller side: Sketch out the plan in chronological order in a notebook or Word or Google Doc.

- If your project is more complex, write a detailed Project Plan using Excel, Google Sheets (Figure 13.2), or other project management software. We have some models here.

- If your event is super detailed, you may also need to distribute a "Day Of" sheet to volunteers. More on that soon.

Because the Talent Show is fairly complex, the Project Plan needs to be shareable. We also want to be able to sort and filter my To-Dos, so I'm going to write this out using Google Sheets.

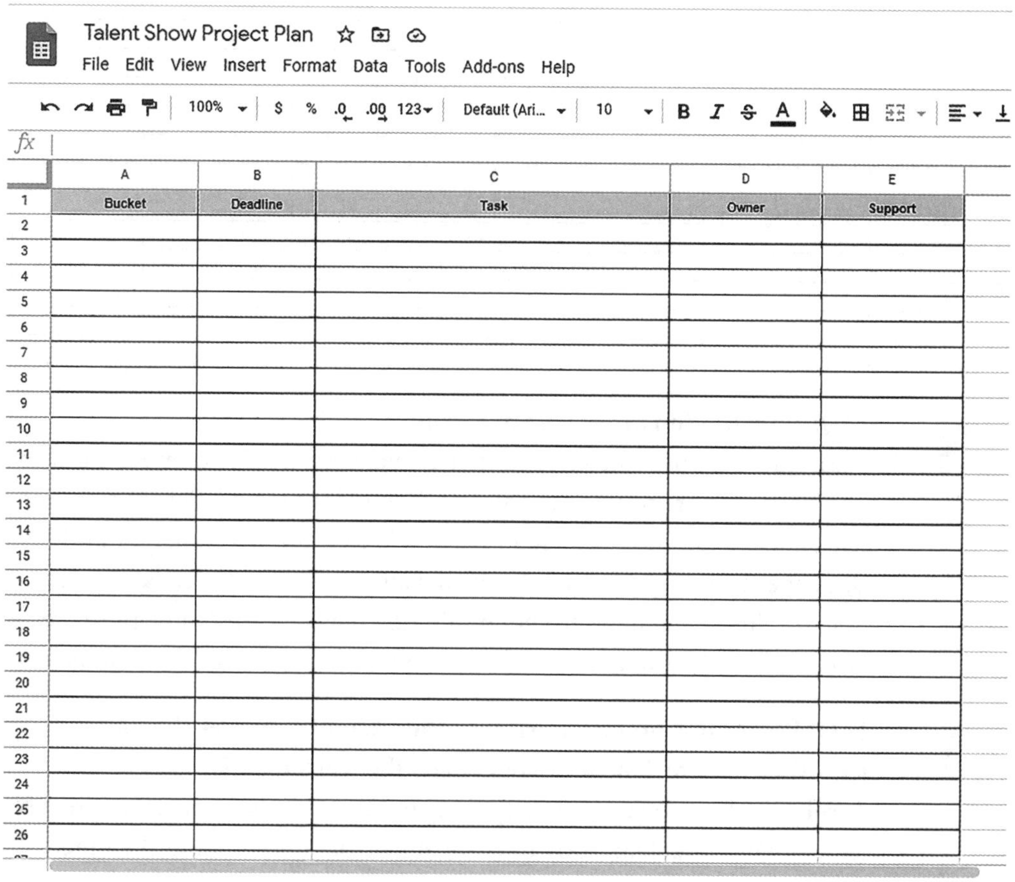

Figure 13.2 Project Plan Template in Google Sheets

Reader Reflection: This is a good time for you to pause and create your Project Plan. List each task.

Don't forget to enter all of the deadlines into your Comprehensive Calendar and block time to work on them over on your Weekly Worksheet. For example, if you need to make some phone calls to vendors during business hours, slot that To-Do during a prep period!

To download this template, head to http://www.wiley.com/go/togetherteacher.

Bucket	Deadline	Task	Owner	Support

FAQ: Why wouldn't I just use a later list?

Great question. In some cases, this may make sense. However, for most Project Plans, our brains need to think through all of the To-Dos as a cluster of steps that should be considered as a whole. Eventually you may want to take all of the dates and put them in your Comprehensive Calendar (if they are true deadlines); but to do the good thinking that is needed, it helps to create a Project Plan when you are initially trying to figure out what needs to be done.

FAQ: Would this process work for other school activities that are less event-driven? Like let's say I coach the track team?

Absolutely! You would just be sketching out the entire season versus preparing for a singular event. Start by thinking about the Buckets, and then break the Buckets down into actionable steps.

Now that you have a draft plan, you can get some much-needed help.

BRING ON THE TEAM

Hopefully you have a little bit of help with your event. In the case of the Talent Show, we can count on a few other people for support:

- PTA president and parent committee
- Student volunteers
- Food vendors
- Facilities staff for space, security, and custodial services

Each of these groups plays a different role, and I need to communicate with each of them in unique ways. This is where that Project Plan comes in handy! Let's sort and filter for who can support each Bucket and/or To-Do.

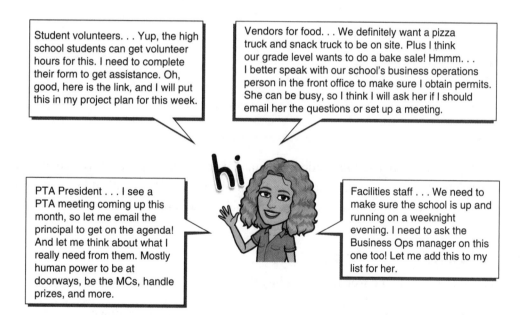

Student volunteers. . . Yup, the high school students can get volunteer hours for this. I need to complete their form to get assistance. Oh, good, here is the link, and I will put this in my project plan for this week.

Vendors for food. . . We definitely want a pizza truck and snack truck to be on site. Plus I think our grade level wants to do a bake sale! Hmmm. . . I better speak with our school's business operations person in the front office to make sure I obtain permits. She can be busy, so I think I will ask her if I should email her the questions or set up a meeting.

PTA President . . . I see a PTA meeting coming up this month, so let me email the principal to get on the agenda! And let me think about what I really need from them. Mostly human power to be at doorways, be the MCs, handle prizes, and more.

Facilities staff . . . We need to make sure the school is up and running on a weeknight evening. I need to ask the Business Ops manager on this one too! Let me add this to my list for her.

Oooooh, I'm so glad I thought all of this through in advance. I've added all of this to my Project Plan, which I will review weekly during my Meeting with Myself! Thinking of all of this in advance will make sure I'm not stuck scrambling and doing everything myself.

Reader Reflection: Who are the people involved in your project? What role do they each play?

Bucket	Deadline	Task	Owner	Support
Facilities		Secure permits and permissions to use auditorium and rehearsal space	Facilities Director	School Secretary
Marketing		Post info on school's Facebook page	Ops Manager	Parent Coordinator

Now that we've set our vision, made the plan, and gotten other people involved, it's time to consider the things that could make the Talent Show go off track. We don't want to be negative but we do want to ensure a plan for possible sticky points.

Being Positively Pessimistic

I don't want to assume the worst, but let's just think . . .

- The school's portable AV system is scratchy at best. What if it goes down?

- There is only one entrance to the cafeteria. What if there is a huge line of attendees?

- Kids LOVE Talent Show prizes. What if we run out?

- We need food to raise additional funds. What if food interrupts the Talent Show?

- What if more families than expected show up and we run out of chairs?

The good news is I think most of these things are solvable. Let me build solutions into the Project Plan.

Bucket	Deadline	Task	Owner	Support
Awards	February 15	Secure and double count the talent show prizes.	PTA President	Grade-Level Leaders
Awards	February 21	Triple check number of talent show entries against prize count	Me!	Grade-Level Leaders

 Reader Reflection: Think about your event. Walk through each moment. What could go off track? List the items. For each one, brainstorm a potential solution or next step to seek help in your actual Project Plan.

Now we have time and space for when something UNPREDICTABLE goes wrong.

WORK THE PLAN

At this point, the bulk of the planning is complete and you are settled back into the regular rhythms of planning, teaching, and grading. But how do we keep our events on track—both for ourselves and for others? And by on track, I mean meeting deadlines and completing To-Dos, so nothing piles up on us! The risk of not doing this is high—our event could collide with report card night, school sporting events, or a friend's birthday.

Revisit and Review

You've entered key dates into your Comprehensive Calendar, so you know what's coming and when. But at least twice a week, pull out your actual Project Plan to adjust dates as needed and block time to work on tasks in your Weekly Worksheet. Pull up your Meeting with Myself checklist and add a step to review the Project Plan each week, especially To-Dos coming up in the next two weeks.

Communicate

If your event is more complex, you may need to hold one or more meetings to ensure that things are moving along with various teams. For simpler events, it may be enough to just keep your eye on the bigger picture. In the case of the Talent Show in Figure 13.3, I'm going to communicate key happenings to everyone involved via a weekly email, and I will also occasionally hold a Project Meeting like the sample you see next.

 Reader Reflection: Do you need event meetings? If so, how often, who should attend, and what is the agenda?

And you guessed it! Add these meetings right into your Project Plan! The plan is made, the team is psyched, and now, the Talent show is getting closer. I need a detailed Day Of plan.

Talent Show Planning Meeting January 22, 3:00–3:30 PM		
Time	*Topic*	*Notes*
5 min	Revisiting the Vision	*Students will showcase their self-selected talents to an appreciative audience of families, teachers, and friends. The logistics will be flawless, and students will feel proud.*
5 min	Quick Updates + Reminders	
15 min	Project Plan Overview: Upcoming Deadlines	
5 min	Next Steps	

Figure 13.3 Sample Talent Show Meeting Agenda

THE BIG DAY—OR NIGHT?

The event is upon you! As you get ready for the rundown, you may be a bundle of nerves. Let's consider how to make things even easier on yourself. For the Talent Show, we are lucky enough to have a team of folks on deck for the actual event. We have a shakedown meeting at 4:30 p.m. before the event starts at 6 p.m.! We all sit in a circle, I hand out our Day Of document (Figure 13.4), and we each read and review our parts. This will help ensure

Friday, May 29th - THE BIG DAY!

Time	Action Step	Notes, if applicable	Point Person
During School	Pull winners for "guess how many" prize	n/a	SBK
During School	Stop by PM HR to check in with talent show participants	n/a	SBK
2:00pm	Order Pizza for planning team	So we don't go hungry! Early dinner around 3:00 ☺	Bridget
3:00pm	Pack up items that need to go with us to Williams, put in SBK's car	"PREP" banner. Other?!	All
4:15pm	Be at Williams	- BW – set up balloons, stationed outside doors to show students inside - Bryan – supporting Andrew and Sabrina with sound - Krista – overseeing space and decoration (and food setup) - SBK – stashing student props in right location, hanging up set-lists, delegating student jobs	All
4:50pm	Dry Run Starts (each performer does 30 seconds–1 minute of talent, to test for tech and flow)	- SBK – gives overview of directions to all students, overseeing stage - Krista and Bridget – managing student flow from backstage to stage - Gattis – managing backstage	All
5:00pm	Dry run continuing, Teachers arrive	- Julia – stationed out front; don't let parents in yet! All - BW joins Julia (Spanish speaker); - Guerin joins to manage backstage - Steph, Elijah – on call/as needed	All
5:30pm	Dry run should be wrapping up around now	- Julia and BW stay outfront - Any teachers present manage students, keep them calm backstage - SBK gives peptalk of some kind. - Extra admins stationed at cafeteria doors so parents don't enter.	All

Figure 13.4 Sarah's Day Of Agenda

we're all on the same page about who is doing what and we can actually enjoy the event and savor the moment. Let's peek at the agenda that Sarah, from Boston, put together for a school Talent Show.

 Reader Reflection: Do you need a Day Of document? Sketch it out below.

Nice work, team! We did it. The kids showed their stuff, their families were proud, and the event is done. Let's take a nap. But before that, let's take time to close out and celebrate!

CELEBRATION AND CLOSEOUT

Last but not least, I need to make sure I update everyone, celebrate their contributions, and codify the materials.

Headline: How was the event? _____

Bucket	What went well? (Let's do this again!)	What didn't go well? (What should we change next time?)
Participants		
Marketing		
Materials		
Facilities		
Families		
Budget		
Staff		

Although it might feel like the last thing you want to do, we promise making time to debrief the event, store and label all materials, and get it set up for next year will save everyone time and stress!

Excellent work! Ready for your next event? Just kidding. Sort of.

TURBO TOGETHERNESS

Project Plans can be daunting to start, but here is how you can get a jump!

☐ Think about an upcoming project and determine if it needs a Project Plan.

☐ Create Buckets for your Project.

☐ Consider the 4 Ws for each bucket: Who? What? Where? When?.

☐ Break your Project Plan into actionable steps.

☐ Determine roles and responsibilities (including an owner and support person for each step).

☐ Create a clear Day Of agenda to share with your team.

☐ Codify and celebrate your project.

You can also just dive into one of our Project Plan templates located on the Wiley website, but we recommend going step-by-step for your first one!

"The level of specificity in our Project Plans for field trips ensured total team accountability for safe, seamless, and highly rewarding trips. Accounting for all logistics so thoroughly and far in advance of our trips allowed us and our kids to reap all of the possible benefits of the trips themselves!"

– Ami P., a third-grade teacher in Brooklyn

MAINTENANCE MOVES

The purpose of good plans is that they allow us to be *more* flexible and responsive to a changing environment. The important thing is not that all of the steps in the plan are completed exactly on time but rather that all of the steps of the project are in one place so that anything that comes up is easy to evaluate against the larger goals.

■ Once per week: Review your Project Plan during your Meeting with Myself

■ Adjust and recommunicate deadlines

■ Add Action Steps to your own Weekly Worksheet!

Rinse and repeat!

CONCLUSION: WHY THE WORLD NEEDS TOGETHER TEACHERS

Whew. You made it. We've been on an organizing, planning, decluttering *adventure* together. You've envisioned your Ideal Week, which shows your hard commitments and limited discretionary time. You've met multiple Together Teachers who've shared their tools, routines, and habits. You've learned more about using specific systems to organize your classroom, and you've finally found your way out from under all that paper on your desk! You've got everything you need to become a Together Teacher; you can serve your students much more effectively *and* lead a full and fulfilling life!

Of course it is *not* that easy. Just the topic of organization can be completely overwhelming, and your blood pressure may spike after you finish reading this book. This is *normal*. The journey to become a Together Teacher will be hard at first. I distinctly remember sitting on the floor of my principal's office (thank you for not firing me, Ms. Bienemy!) during my first year of teaching, crying about how-to-differentiate-my-reading-instruction and not sure how-to-manage-my-seemingly-simple-behavior-incentive-systems and how-on-earth-could-I-keep-all-of-those-materials-together-to-be-a-great-teacher (said with a huge sob and sniffle). Then I had a similar meltdown with my literacy coach, Ms. Lay (but this time I had the dignity to sit in a chair and sob). There was *no way I could do this!* But with practice, I began to believe I could get it Together. Slowly and step by step, Ms. Bienemy and Ms. Lay helped me make a plan for what I needed to do first, second, third, and so on. I used my precious preparation period to script better guided reading lessons. I discovered the magic of two-gallon Ziploc bags, and my students carried their independent reading books in them so that the books were not strewn about their desks and backpacks. I got my classroom library organized by reading level. And I posted a clear schedule of which reading groups met with Ms. H.-M. at which times per day. I remember the moment, several months after my meltdown, when Ms. Bienemy walked through my classroom, where soft music was playing, some students were reading independently, others were writing their reading response logs, and the rest were working with me around a U-shaped table. My journey had started. I could *do* this.

Being a Together Teacher *is* a journey. But you can get there. Picture it. Now *you* will be the teacher with a healthy homemade lunch and the time to tutor the students who most need your help. *You* will walk into school knowing exactly what you need to accomplish and where to locate the materials and supplies you need to execute your well-planned lessons. *You* will have the mind-space to respond thoughtfully to unexpected events that appear over the course of the day.

RETURN TO YOUR TOGETHERNESS INTENTION

Remember that Togetherness Intention you set wayyyyy back in the beginning of the book. Maybe it has changed, maybe it has held true, but let's revisit. Remember, it could be anything from. . . .

READER REFLECTION:

My Togetherness Intention is _____ **because** _____

_____.

Once you have completed your Togetherness Intention, make it bold. Write it on cardstock, make it your screen saver or the wallpaper of your iPhone. When you have a moment of not-Together-enough or overly-Together-procrastination, look at your Togetherness Intention to remember your why. Organization alone never got all of us anywhere; we are looking for it to serve a larger purpose.

Okay, my yoga teacher moment is over. For now!

TEST YOUR SYSTEM: CAN IT SURVIVE UNDER PRESSURE?

Now that you've assembled your Together Teacher System, there comes the incredibly challenging step of making sure that your system can hold up under the pressures of your fast-paced and important job. The test is whether *your* system—be it a paper planner or an apped-out iPhone or something in between—is completely comprehensive and airtight.

The following quiz will help you test the strength of your system. If you find yourself hesitating, give it your best guess. You will likely see a few holes exposed as you go through this process. That's okay! Once we know where the issues lie, we can make changes to address them.

 READER REFLECTION: WHAT NEXT?

6:30 AM	You arrive at school 30 minutes early to get a little work done before everyone else arrives. What do you do with this time?	
7:00 AM	You briefly check your email before you pick up your students from the cafeteria and see a notice from your principal about doing more interventions in the next grading cycle that begins in two months. Where does this go?	
8:00 AM	A member of the office staff pokes his head into your room while you're teaching and lets you know that the deadline for changing your benefits has switched. Where do you put this information?	
9:00 AM	When you're quickly getting a cup of coffee in the teachers' lounge between classes, you see a sign for a professional development session at the district office that you'd like to attend. Where do you put this information?	
10:00 AM	Oh, shoot! You remember that your car registration is about to expire! How do you remind yourself to deal with it later?	

(Continued)

11:00 AM	Your 60-minute preparation period is beginning. You go to make copies for your afternoon classes but the copier's jammed. What do you do?	
12:00 PM	While on lunch duty, you have an idea for your grade team about a student who needs extra support. What do you do with this information?	
12:45 PM	As you walk back from lunch duty, you listen to a voicemail message from a parent informing you of a student absence next week for an important family event. Where do you record this information?	
1:30 PM	In the middle of teaching a lesson about dividing fractions, you have a revelation about a different way to teach it next year. Where do you put this information?	
1:45 PM	You are circulating during independent work time and you notice that one of your students is having a hard time staying awake. This is the third time this week. Where do you note next steps you want to take?	
2:45 PM	You use your shorter, 30-minute preparation period to review exit tickets. As you're grading, you realize that progress reports are due in a *week!* How do you prepare?	
3:45 PM	Your students have been dismissed for the day, you are dead-dog tired, but there is still more work to do. You need to leave by 5:00 p.m.. What do you do with this time?	
5:00 PM	You leave school and head home. Once you arrive, what will you do to relax?	

READER REFLECTION:

- Did you have a clear answer for each of these questions?

- What is your system's biggest strength?

- What is your system's biggest growth area?

There are no exact right and wrong answers for any of these questions; instead they are meant to illustrate the variety and volume of stuff that flies your way each day. What I care about most is that you have designed an effective, simple, portable system that allows you to handle the big and the small, the personal and the professional, and the short and long term.

REMEMBER, TOGETHERNESS IS A JOURNEY

School systems, educational philosophies, curriculum materials, and student needs will continue to change. But the habits outlined in this book will steadily serve you well as professionals working in an unpredictable, on-your-feet, data-rich environments. Although you don't have to put every idea you've learned into place immediately, I suggest that you pick a few that resonated with you and get them up and running right away.

You do not have to take action on everything in this book all at once! Remember: if you tried to implement a new "Be Healthy" campaign, it's unlikely you'd start by exercising every single day nor eat not one ounce of sugar. You'd have more success by taking a more moderate approach—exercising four days a week and having dessert on just three nights. Similarly, you can take a staged approach to becoming a Together Teacher. You have a few options.

Option 1: Read a chapter per month

Test the Together Tools and materials, and ensure the habit sticks before moving on to the next chapter. This book was written in the order we believe it should be implemented. A number of teachers say the following order works for them:

- Month 1: Create a Weekly Worksheet

- Month 2: Make a Comprehensive Calendar

- Month 3: Create Your Later List

- Month 4: Get On the Thought Catchers

■ **Month 5: Create Routines to Support Togetherness**

■ **Month 6: Tidy and Together Up Your Teacher Workspace**

■ **Month 7: Tame the Communications Chaos**

■ **Month 8: Support Student Togetherness**

■ **Month 9: Make Lesson Planning Efficient**

■ **Month 10: Grading, Assessing, and More!**

■ **Month 11: Join 'Em and Lead 'Em: Make the Most of Meetings**

■ **Month 12: Project Plan Your Way to Success!**

Option 2: Be selective about which chapters you read when!

Although each chapter does reference content in other sections, they are also written where you can pick and choose what you need most when you need it. Maybe you know planning grade-level meetings differently would help you? Or you are certain creating a Later List would banish those last-minute scrambles.

Option 3: Read-the-entire-book-in-one-huge-binge

This is not our recommended approach, but sometimes we know this will help people to just get it done. In this case, cozy up with some snacks and beverages and quick skim the entire book with your Reader Reflection beside you. Take a trip to Staples or online to Amazon right after, and build your entire Together Teacher system in one swoop. BAM!

Whichever option you select, the best way to proceed is to review your notes from your Reader Reflection Guide. Next, create a Together Teacher implementation plan for yourself using the following table (also found in the Reader Reflection Guide). This will force you to summarize your notes, and it will also help you pace yourself.

READER REFLECTION: MAKE IT HAPPEN!

Month	Next Step	Tools/Resources Needed

FAQ: WHAT IF I GET THROWN OFF TRACK?

Inevitably, at some point in this process, you will trip on the treadmill. Slowly your non-Together Teacher self may begin to rear its ugly head. You have evening events at school for a few nights, and you get behind in lesson planning. Or you have a weekend family celebration and you don't finish your grading. Or a personal emergency that throws everything off schedule. I want to be clear: this *will* happen. What matters most is that you have a *Plan B* ready to activate. Having *some* semblance of a plan is much better than walking into a week blindly, letting your emails pile up, and tossing all of the grading over the proverbial fence. The backup plan for many educators is a shorter Meeting with Myself or a weekend of re-Together-ing. And then you need to get right back on the organizational wagon the following week.

HOW TO USE THIS BOOK AS A SCHOOL STAFF

- Create Togetherness language in any kind of staff evaluation to set the standard of excellence in your building
- A Together Teacher Training at the start of the school year (we can come to you!) or you can register for an online Together Teacher course
- A yearlong book study for the entire staff or subset of staff
- Solicit best practices from some of the already Together Teachers at your school and host a panel during a staff training

WHY TEACHERS NEED TOGETHERNESS

As I mentioned in the Introduction, I have spent my entire existence surrounded by teachers. I was raised by one and have been one myself. In addition, I have spent two decades of my professional life recruiting, selecting, training, supporting, and evaluating teachers. I am utterly convinced that there is no job more important and more complex than classroom teaching. I'm equally sure that rigorous and intentional practices for planning, organizing, and decision-making will get us better outcomes with our kids and allow us to sustain our good work for more years than we could ever imagine.

I know from my own years in the classroom that tight planning and organization makes your day with your students more enjoyable. Forget fumbling for copies, losing track of which kids are tardy or absent or without their homework, spending prep periods procrastinating

FAQ: WHAT IF I'M A SCHOOL BUILDING LEADER, TRYING TO MAKE MY ENTIRE SCHOOL TOGETHER?

■ Ensure the school has a digital calendar inclusive of the entire year that is easily accessible to staff with clear norms for what lands on that calendar

■ Clear communication agreements with how and when your school uses texts, emails, calls, and other forms of reaching each other

■ Regular weekly efficient communication to teachers about events, expectations, schedules, etc.

■ Consistent naming conventions for any digital storage in Google Drive or Dropbox

■ Easy access to materials for teachers to keep their classrooms together, such as file folders, label makers, cabinets, various storage units, etc.

■ Ways to keep students organized used consistently across students, whether that is a commercial planner or something homemade

■ A consistent communication method to families about any school happenings or updates

■ If possible, a sacred and quiet teacher workspace that is not the teacher's lounge. This is where teachers can keep their professional development books, etc.

■ Easy and clear ways to "check out" any materials teachers need, such as guided reading books, Chrome Books, etc. For example, having each item numbered and inventoried

■ Clear project plans and timelines for school events and happenings

■ Clear leadership team roles and responsibilities and Who to Go to for What

by checking your favorite websites or hanging in the teachers' lounge—only to end up taking all those parent phone calls home. Being a great teacher *and* having a life is completely possible. It takes a little bit of time, a medium amount of discipline, and a wholehearted belief that it *is* possible. Ms. Bienemy and Ms. Lay were kind enough to help me create a step-by-step plan for meeting my students' needs when I found out that my first year of teaching was in a high-stakes testing year. I hope this book has helped you create a plan for making your teaching a little stronger and your life a little easier.

Teaching *is* different from many other professions, but it is not so unique that we have to surrender ourselves to the chaotic and unexpected parts of our work. Students figure out in an instant if you will be the type of teacher who returns the graded midterm on the day you said you would, and if you follow through on their Scholar of the Month outing. Similarly, in a profession that is easily all consuming and never ending, intentionality about planning, work time, and nonwork time helps us have more balance—which is good for *everyone* in our lives. Being organized is certainly not the ultimate goal in teaching, but being Together plays a huge role in ensuring that we can have an impact on kids' lives for a long, long time while doing the work we love.

To download the templates featured in this book, head to http://www.wiley.com/go/togetherteacher.

For regular updates, tools, and tricks, check out The Together Group blog: www.thetogethergroup.com

 Find us on Facebook: The Together Group

Follow us on Instagram: @together_teacher

ACKNOWLEDGMENTS

The second edition of *The Together Teacher* was a long time coming. I should have known when I reread the first edition and saw mention of Blackberries! Since my very first Together Teacher Training in 2007, I've been privileged to visit with hundreds of schools and districts and thousands of dedicated educators. Because of all of those amazing conversations, interviews, and observations, I've been able to curate and narrate effective practices back to you—even more effectively than the first time, I hope!

To the thousands of Together Teacher workshop participants: Thank you for sharing your stories, your results, and your passion. Every time I deliver a training, I'm reminded of your commitment, motivation, and innovation. I'm grateful to everyone who tolerated my emails, visits, questions, and more. I mean, I won't ADMIT that I openly stalked my own daughter's fourth-grade teacher, but. . . . There are too many teachers to list individually, but I am so grateful for how you all have navigated my requests for interviews, documents, and more interviews with grace and enthusiasm.

Many people donated their most precious resource (time) to read entire copies of this book. Most notably, the small but mighty Together Team played a significant role in getting this to the finish line during the pandemic. Kendra Rowe Salas, my longtime copilot, kept every aspect of our trainings running smoothly so I could focus on writing while still delivering high-quality instruction. Longtime editor Marin Smith teamed up with newer details guru Maggie G. Sorby to serve as cowriters, thought-partners, rubric-makers, reflection wizards, and more. All three of these women juggled their own small children and other life responsibilities while brilliantly managing many projects and revising thousands of words.

Amy Fandrei and her wonderful team at Jossey-Bass supported this project from the very start. They joined me at workshops, refined the table of contents, ensured every ounce of text flowed smoothly and every image printed clearly. And lastly, to Josh Lowitz, my pretend boss, here's to another decade together (and Together).

I'm eternally grateful for the community of people who support my home life, especially my dear Inner Wolf Pack, who don't mind early morning text messages, vacation memos with meal plans, and potluck planning documents. And WoMos, thanks for all the gold stars over the past few years. That WhatsApp chain is gold. To Keith O'Doherty, thank you for constantly cheerleading me, for reminding me of my progress, and for keeping me laughing, no matter what. Last but never least, thank you to my kids, Ada and Reed, for helping me see clearly what really matters—and experimenting with unicorn planners to humor their mother. I see a Together Student on the horizon. . .

MAIA HEYCK-MERLIN

Maia Heyck-Merlin is the CEO and founder of The Together Group, the consulting practice behind *The Together Teacher*. She helps schools, districts, and nonprofit organizations create custom methods to get organized to get results. In 2011, she wrote the first edition of *The Together Teacher: Plan Ahead, Get Organized, and Save Time,* published by Jossey-Bass in 2012. Her second book, *The Together Leader: Get Organized for Your Success—and Sanity*, was released in 2016. Most recently, she founded The Together Press and released *The Together Work-From-Home Teacher* to meet the unique and sudden needs of teachers across the country abruptly going remote during the COVID-19 pandemic.

Maia has over twenty years of experience working with teachers, school leaders, operations staff, central office teams, and nonprofit organizations. Before entering The Together Universe full time, she served as chief talent officer and chief operating officer for Achievement First. Before that, she worked at Teach For America in a variety of capacities, including executive director, institute director, and founding director of National Institute Operations. Maia began her career as an upper elementary school teacher in South Louisiana where she taught fourth grade for two years. She was named Teacher of the Year by her school and was selected as a Fulbright Memorial Fund recipient.

Maia holds a BA in child development from Tufts University. She lives in the Washington, DC area with her energetic un-Together children and her two unruly cats. In her free time, she enjoys her life as an amateur triathlete, Girl Scout troop leader, and neighborhood project planner for block parties and vacations.

MARIN SMITH

Marin Smith is a clinical social worker in college and university mental health. In her past life, she taught third grade with the New York City Teaching Fellows program and later worked as a founding kindergarten teacher, academic dean, and principal for Achievement First Crown Heights. Her love and respect for emerging adults was born from the great relationships she enjoyed as a teacher coach. Marin has combined her background in education with her interest in mental health to design coursework, deliver programming, and provide consultancy to teacher training programs at Relay Graduate School of Education, Teach For America Massachusetts, Match Education, and Excel Academy.

Marin holds a BA from Harvard University, an MS in elementary education from Mercy College, and an MSW from Bryn Mawr College. She lives in the Boston area, where she enjoys getting outside with her family, trying new Instant Pot recipes, and texting Maia for advice.

MAGGIE G. SORBY

Maggie G. Sorby is an educator with experience in charter, private, and traditional public school settings. Before joining The Together Group, she served as the chief student supports officer for the Camden City School District in New Jersey. Before that, she lived in Los Angeles, where she worked as a high school history teacher and a nonprofit program director—and, in her spare time, tried to keep up with teenagers as an assistant coach with Students Run LA. Maggie joined The Together Group in 2019 and now spends her days learning from Together educators from across the country.

Maggie holds a BA in international studies from Elon University and an MA in education policy and administration from Loyola Marymount University. She lives in the Philadelphia area, where she enjoys hiking and camping with her husband and two children, reading, and digging around in her sometimes-thriving vegetable garden.

INDEX

A

Academic observation charts, 166, 167f
Achievement First, 6
Action bins, 149, 151
Action tabs, 155
Administrative information,
    availability, 165
Agenda. *See* Day Of agenda;
    Meeting agenda
Anchor Board, 139
Appointments, insertion, 17
Artifacts, collection methods, 265
Assessments, 263, 271f, 344
    formatting, 270–271
Assignments, 203
    Google Classroom, usage, 219f
    posted class assignments, 207, 210f, 211
    posting, Google (usage), 216
Auto-notifications (emails), cessation, 177

B

Backpacks, 1, 7, 129, 220
    checking, 225, 234
    problems, 125, 168, 203, 232, 339
    usage, 155, 222
Behavioral data logs, 167
Big work, calendar component, 21

Binders
    clips, usage, 149, 165
    expectations, 224, 224f, 225f
    International Binder Week, 230f
    whole school binder, challenge, 230–232
Bins, usage, 149, 151, 159–161
Book bins, 160, 160f
Boundaries, 4, 17
Broken-up inbox, 150
Buckets, 327–328
    actionable steps, determination, 327–328
    Project Buckets list, 328
    Project Plan usage, 335
Buffer times, addition, 17
Bulletin Board, 227, 228f
Bullet Journals, 75

C

Calendar, 23–26. *See also* Comprehensive
    Calendar; Digital calendar;
    Together Teacher
    components, 21
    digital calendar, usage, 50
    digital-paper blend calendar, 67–69, 68f
    listing, 77
    multiple calendars, dilemma, 60–62
    paper calendar, 64–67, 65f, 66f

Calendar (*continued*)
    rationales, 74
    review, 63
    system, assessment/rating, 61
Calls. *See* Phone calls; Video calls
Checkboxes, usage, 41, 47
Class
    daily class activities, posting, 204–205
    expectations, 206
    post-class planner expectations,
        227, 229–230
    posted class assignments, 207, 210f, 211
    schedules/syllabi, display, 204–211
    weekly class schedules, digital
        sharing, 205–206
Classroom
    calendar, 211. *See also* Google Classroom.
    library To-Do, inclusion, 89f
    materials, 17, 204, 223
    supplies, 7
    volunteers, usage, 266, 266f
Clipboard
    academic observation charts,
        inclusion, 167f
    lesson plans, inclusion, 166f
    materials, 168
Closing routines, 134–140, 135f, 139f
    design, 140
    planning, 140
Clutter, reduction, 162
Colleagues
    coplanning, 247
    groups, Thought Catchers (usage), 116
    list/phone numbers, 164
Color coding, usage, 47, 71, 73, 76, 271
Communication, 174, 334
    control, 173, 344
    differentiation, 196–197

effectiveness, increase, 108
management system, strength/gap
    (naming), 175
norms, 188f
routines, establishment, 182–187
Comprehensive Calendar, 343
    building, 77–82
    calendars, listing, 77
    creation, 59
    defining, 62–63
    events/FYIs, insertion, 79
    hard deadlines, insertion, 78
    maintenance, 83–84
    options, 75–76
    personal items, insertion, 80–82
    planner-based Comprehensive
        Calendar, 64
    portability, 64
    recurring/one-off meetings,
        recording, 79–80
    storage location, 74–77
    updating, 82–83
Computers, folders (creation), 158
Copy bins, 151
Copy tabs, 155
Corrections, key (creation), 271
Coteachers, Thought Catchers
    (usage), 111–112

D
Daily class activities, posting, 204–205
Daily reading logs, usage, 264
Daily routines, 133–140
Daily schedule, 205f
Daily worksheet, 216–217
Data analysis, 25, 303f
Data entry, 50
Day Of agenda, 335f

Day Of document, usage, 335–336
Deadlines
　clarity, resolution, 94
　consolidation, 64
　lead times, lengthening, 95–96
　missed deadlines, 59
　soft deadlines/hard deadlines, 78
Desk
　calendar, usage, 77
　control, 220–221
　deskless approach, 153
　storage, 221, 221f
Desktop, set-up, 221
Digital calendar, 63, 69–73, 70f, 72f
　usage, 52
Digital Comprehensive Calendar,
　　usage, 180
Digital materials, location, 146
Digital-paper blend calendar,
　　67–69, 68f
Digital Thought Catchers, 120
Digital work, collection, 269–270
Discretionary personal time, calendar
　　component, 21
Discretionary work time, 21
Disorganized teachers. *See* Teachers
Distractions, 13, 133, 139, 185, 258
　filtering, 204
　smartphones, impact, 212
District standards, availability, 164
Documents. *See* Day Of document;
　　Google Doc
　creation, 238, 271
　digital documents, 106
　naming, 158, 162
　sharing, email usage, 175
　usage, 45
Do-Nows, peer grading, 264

E
Efficiency, 2–3
　skill, demonstration, 4
Electronic folders, 157f
Emails, 174, 193–197
　abuse, avoidance, 193–197
　accounts, limitation, 176
　action/response, 181
　advantages/disadvantages, 175
　auto-notifications, cessation, 177, 198
　bankruptcy, declaration, 177
　checking, routines, 184–185
　control, 175–176, 178, 187
　deferral methods, 186
　effectiveness, 189f, 190
　extension, 196–197
　family/friends emails, control, 176–177
　filing folders/labels/tags, creation/
　　deletion, 178, 180
　instructional emails, folders, 179f
　junk email account, usage, 176
　maintenance, 198–201
　offenses, 194–195
　open-ended emails, sending
　　(cessation), 189–193
　organization, 197–198
　phone, syncing, 176
　processing, STAR-D method,
　　186–187, 198
　resistance, difficulty, 183–184
　responding, efficiency, 185
　school usage, 184
　subject lines, 190–192
　unclear messages, dangers, 190
　unsubscribing, 176, 198
Emergency buffer, calendar component, 21
End of week self-meeting, 129f
Energy levels, attention, 25

Events
 buckets, 327–328
 calendar insertion, 79
 celebration/closeout, 336
 consolidation, 64
 Day Of document, usage, 335–336
 outcome, determination, 324–326
 planning/selection, 323, 324
 special events, 62, 247
 Talent Show vision event, 325–326
 tracking, 333–334
Evernote, 120
Exit ticket grading, requirement, 264

F
Families
 contact information, availability, 164
 data sharing, timing/process, 281–284
 parents, teacher contact log, 282f
 students, teacher praise, 281
Family time, teacher allotment, 17
File bins, 151
File tabs, 155
Filing
 folders/labels/tags, creation, 178
 location, trigger (creation), 24–25
Flexibility, skill (demonstration), 4
Folders, 158, 178, 179f, 223f
 hierarchy, 156
 review, 182
 Take Home folder, 223f, 224
Formal state/national testing, role, 284
FYIs, calendar insertion, 79

G
Google Calendar, 23, 69, 76
 assignments, posting, 207, 211
 printed version, deadline recording, 71

student maintenance, 212
 usage, 51, 55, 81, 83, 91
Google Classroom, 211f, 219, 219f
Google Doc, usage, 51, 191, 264
Google Drive, organization, 156, 158f, 159
Google Forms, usage, 275
Google Keep, 120
 Later List example, 91–93, 92f
Google Sheets, 327
 Project Plan template, 329f
Google Tasks, 102, 120
Grade bins, 151
Gradebook
 scanning, 166
 selection, 276
Grade-level meeting agenda, 293f, 294f–295f
Grade-level meeting notes, 308, 308f
Grade tabs, 155
Grading, 263, 344
 assessments, formatting, 270–271
 batches, 276–279
 capacity estimator machine, 265
 chunks, 279–281
 determination, 264–265
 efficiency, 270–272, 279
 maintenance, 286
 materials, checklist (creation), 286
 role, 284–286
 software, selection, 276
 time, consumption, 286
 timing/location, 276–281
 volunteer, usage, 281
 Workload Estimator, 265
Group meetings
 notes, actions, 310
 note-taking, consideration, 312
 small group meetings, 290

H

Habits, highlighting, 182–183

Hanging inbox, 150f

Hard-copy calendar, information
transfer, 69

Hard-copy handouts, digitization, 250

Hard-copy materials
collection, 268
location, 146, 168

Hard-copy testing calendar, placement, 60

Hard deadlines, entry, 78

Homework
key, 272f
student completion, planner
expectations, 229f
tracking log, usage, 167–168

Hyperlinks, usage, 45

I

iCal, usage, 76, 83

Ideal week, 17, 18f–19f, 20–21, 20f
building, 21–26
calendar, 21, 23–26
creation, 13
design, 15–21
questions, 16–17
template, 22f

Ideas
professional development ideas, availability, 164
sharing, 108

Inbox
broken-up inbox, 150f
change, 178–182, 179f
control, 173
control, goal, 176–182
hanging inbox, 150f

Inbox, organization, 149–152

Incoming To-Dos, placement, 100

Incoming work, display, 37

Instruction
design/delivery, teacher role, 2, 13–14
effectiveness, 168
online instruction, 2, 18–19
order, change, 162
writing, approach (change), 194

Instructional feedback, collection, 114

Instructional materials, control, 155–163

Instructional planning routines, 126

International Binder Week, 230f

Interviews, 55, 105, 169, 261, 321

J

Junk email account, usage, 176

K

Kudos board, creation/setup, 149, 152

L

Labeling, 157

Labels
adjustment, 158
creation/deletion, 159, 178, 180

Later List, 89–93, 91f
availability, 101
building, 93–97
classroom library To-Do, inclusion, 89f
creation, 85, 343
defining, 86–89
digital issues, 99–100
Google Keep, usage, 91–93, 92f
maintenance, 102–103
planner-based Later Lists, 90f
planner model, 89, 91
scheduling priority, 93–95, 96–97
template, 88f

Later List (*continued*)
  tool, 97–100, 98t–99t
  updating, 100–101
  usage, 117, 330
  weekly review, 101
Lesson planning, 50
  efficiency, 237, 344
  location, decision, 255–257
  maintenance, 258–259
  materials, 248–251
  work, defining, 244–247, 254
  workload, outcomes (sample), 245
Lesson plans
  clipboard usage, 166f
  electronic organization, 156
  skimming/scanning, 52
  usage, 165–166
  workload (determination), questions
    (usage), 245
Lesson Plan Workload Estimator,
    additions, 253
Lessons, exit ticket grading
    (requirement), 264
Levenger calendars, 75
Little work, calendar component, 21
Lockers, expectations, 220
Logs, usage, 166–167
Long-term To-Dos, 24
  control, 85
  tracking system, rating, 87

M
Mailboxes
  complexity, appearance, 149
  homework assignment distribution, 139
Manipulatives, 3, 155, 160
Master calendar, 61
Mastery tracker, 274, 274f

Materials, 154–155
  organization, 159–160
Meeting agenda, 290, 297f–298f
  creation, 292–302
  criteria, 292
  Day Of agenda, 335f
  distribution, 292
  facilitator, assignment, 292
  grade-level meeting agenda,
    293f, 294f–295f
  outcomes, 292
  preparation/follow-through, 292–293
  preparation list, 299f
  rigidity issue, 300–302
  template, 291, 296
  value-driven agenda, 293, 296
Meeting notes, 311f
  grade-level meeting notes, 308, 308f
  group meetings, notes/note-
    taking, 310, 312
  notebooks, usage, 318
  note-taker, usage, 302
  note-taking process, 306–314
  professional development notes,
    actions, 310–314
  storage/retrieval, 314–316
Meetings
  checklist, 317–319
  cohesion, 302–305
  culture leader, usage, 302
  issues, 112
  materials/location, determination, 302
  maximization, 289, 344
  on-the-fly meetings, notes (usage), 308
  planning meeting, example, 334
  preparation items, 303f
  recording, 80–81
  roles, establishment, 302, 304

running/planning, 300
   template, 306, 307f
   timekeeper, usage, 302
   tracking, maintenance, 317–319
   unplanned meeting template, 309, 309f
   whirlarounds, usage, 304
Meetings Bingo, 290
Meeting with Myself, 132–133
   checklist, 125–127, 140
   end of week self-meeting, 129f
   logistics, 132–133
   preparation, 126–127
   public prep Meeting with Myself,
      127–128, 128f
   review, 332
   timing, 132–133
   Together Teacher checklists, 127–131
   weekly cleanup, 125–126
   weekly meeting agenda, 130–131, 130f
Meeting with Yourself, logistics, 131
Meet with Yourself, 123, 132
Messages
   control, 173
   unclear messages, dangers, 190
Microsoft Excel, 75, 102, 120, 286, 327, 329
Microsoft OneNote, 114, 120, 310
Microsoft Outlook Calendar, 76
Microsoft Outlook, usage, 51, 83
Microsoft Word/PowerPoint, 75, 102
Middle school students, organization
   methods, 212
Missed deadlines, 59
Missing work crate, 232, 233f
Mobile cart, creation/example, 153, 153f
Moleskine planners, 75
Monthly lesson plan overlay, 239
Monthly Overlay, 239
Monthly Plan, 240f

Monthly views, 62, 75, 79
Motivational board, 152
Multiple calendars, 60–62

N
Nonwork activities, 50
Notebooks
   notebook-based/color-coded To-Do
      list, 218–219
   student notebooks, Table of
      Contents, 226f
   usage, 225–227, 310
Notes. See Meeting notes
Notices, 3, 97, 126
Not-together teacher, appearance, 1

O
Objectives tracker, 274–276
Observation charts, 165, 166f
Observation notes, Thought Catchers
   (usage), 113–114
Office bins, 151
Office tabs, 155
One-off meetings, recording, 79–80
Online instruction, 2, 18–19
On-the-fly meetings, notes (usage), 308
Open-ended emails, sending
   (cessation), 189–193
Opening routines, 134–138, 135f, 137f, 140
Organization, 2–3
   system, 8–9, 14–15, 23–26, 99
Outcomes, 324–326

P
Paper calendar, 64–67, 65f, 66f
Paper calendars, 55, 62–64, 75,
   79, 126, 329
Paper clips, usage, 149

Paper management, 167–168

Paper planners, 8, 75, 322

Papers, 203
    collection system, 268–269
    excess, student avoidance, 223
    storage, 269f

Paper Thought Catchers, 120

Parent communication, 18

Parents, teacher contact log, 282f

Parties
    outcome, determination, 324–326
    planning, 323

Personal events, 30, 62, 81

Personal items, calendar insertion,
    80–82

Personal organization system, 8–9

Personal priorities, 4, 16, 32

Personal/professional lives, display, 37

Personal supplies, 152

Phone calls, 82, 105, 191, 201
    identification, 49, 139
    making/returning, 32, 126, 140, 330
    time allotment, 1, 21, 128, 347

Phone/emails, syncing, 176

Physical needs, calendar component, 21

Physical student work, collection, 267

Planner
    expectations, 229f
    post-class planner expectations,
        227, 229–230

Planner-based Comprehensive
    Calendar, 64

Planner-based Later Lists, 90f

Planner/notebook, modification/update, 52

Planning/plans, 2–3. *See also* Lesson
        planning; Project Plan
    colleagues, coplanning, 247
    day/time, determination, 251–254

display, 37

lesson planning, 237

long-term planning, 238–241

meeting, example, 334

pauses, usage, 26

purpose, 337

routines, 123–125, 138f

scenarios, 251–252

skill, demonstration, 3

substitute plans, usage, 257

tote bag, 249f

year-long lesson plan sketch,
    241, 242f–243f

Planning Workload Estimator, 244,
    250, 256–258

Portability. *See* Comprehensive Calendar

Post-class planner expectations,
    227, 229–230

Posted class assignments, 207, 211

Posters, creation/usage, 25, 246,
    248, 250, 252

Post-Its
    deadline usage, 84–85
    electronic Post-it Notes, 14
    idea list, 96
    location, 148
    notebook/planner usage, 98t
    usage, 9–10, 90, 103, 108, 154,
        267, 329

Pre-moves, 267

Preparation periods, 13, 16, 21,
    32, 339

Printers/printing, 101, 105, 132

Priorities, 4, 16, 32–33, 52
    defining, 37

Prioritization, skill (demonstration), 3

Processed folders, 178, 198

Procrastination, avoidance, 258, 286

Professional Development (PD), 5, 17, 62, 200, 289
  attendance, 257
  handouts, 248
  ideas, availability, 165
  notes, actions, 310–314
  sessions, 79, 109, 145
  workshop, 93
Professional library, creation, 155–156
Progress monitoring, 273, 273f
Project Plan, 326, 328–330, 344
  communication, importance, 334
  Later List, usage (reason), 330
  maintenance/process, 337
  people, involvement/list, 332
  revisiting/review, 334
  template, 326f, 329f, 330f
  To-Dos list, 326
  tracking, 333–334
Projects
  Buckets list, 328
  folder, usage, 178, 198
  organization, methods, 329
  outcome, determination, 324–326
  planning, 323
  preparation, importance, 332–333
  team support, 331–333
Public prep Meeting with Myself, 127–128, 128f

R
Rainy-day To-Dos/ideas, 96–97
Reading levels, 111, 154, 162, 164, 339
Recurring meetings, recording, 79–80
Reference folder, usage, 178, 198
Reference information, 163–165
Return bins, 151
Return tabs, 155

Routines, 123, 140, 182–187, 344
  closing routines, 134–140, 135f, 139f
  creation, 123
  daily routines, 133–140
  email checking routines, 184–185
  maintenance, 141
  opening routines, 134–138, 135f, 140
  planning routines, 123–125, 138f

S
Scan Trash Archive Respond Defer (STAR-D) email processing method, 186–187, 198
Schedule
  daily student schedule, 205f
  ownership, 25–26
  virtual learning daily schedule, 206f
  weekly class schedules, digital sharing, 205–206
Scheduled time, calendar component, 21
School
  email usage, 184
  holidays, 62, 67, 239
  leaders, 111–112, 347
  middle school students, organization methods, 212
  school-created planners, 214
  Schoolwide Communication Agreements, creation, 187–188
  staff, reading approach, 346
  whole school planners, 212, 213f
Scripting, value, 244
Seating chart, 167
Seat Sacks
  student Seat Sacks, expectations, 222–223
  usage, 222–223, 222f
Self-awareness, skill (demonstration), 4

Self-care, 26–29
  planning template, 27f
  usage, 13, 152
Short-term To-Dos, 24
Small group meetings, 290
Smart Board clickers, 111–112
Smartphones
  distractions, 212
  synchronization, 23, 76, 99t
  task entry, 15
Soft deadlines, 78
Special events, 62, 247
STAR-D. *See* Scan Trash Archive
    Respond Defer
State standards, availability, 164
Stress management
  plan, 27–29, 28f, 29f
  usage, 26–27
Students
  coaches, hiring, 272
  daily schedule, 205f
  data, 255, 281–284
  desks, expectations, 220f
  digital planner, 216f
  files, 151
  formal state/national testing, role, 284
  goal card, 278f
  habits, 231
  independence, 231
  information, availability, 164
  learning, 231
  mailboxes, homework assignment
    distribution, 139
  mastery tracker, 274, 274f
  middle school students, organization
    methods, 212
  papers, excess (avoidance), 223
  physical student work, collection, 267

planner, 213f
progress, tracking, 272–276
reading levels, questions, 111
Seat Sacks, expectations, 222–223
space set-up, supporting, 220–227
take-home folder, 223f
teacher praise, 281
Weekly Worksheets, 214, 214f, 215f
weekly written updates, 282–283
Student Togetherness
  support, 203, 344
  teaching, 227–233
Student work, 273
  absence, 232
  collection process, determination,
    266–270
  files, 268, 268f
  grading, batches, 276–279
  objectives tracker, 274–276
  tote bag, 277f
Subject lines, 190–192
Substitute plans, usage, 257
Suitcase, emptying, 151
Supplies, 152, 203
Syllabi, 204–211, 207f–209f
Systems, skill (demonstration), 3–4

T
Table of Contents, 226f
Tabs, usage, 155
Tags, creation/deletion, 178, 180
Take-Home Folder, 223f, 224
Talent Show, 325–326
  planning meeting, example, 334
  team support, 331
Teachers
  desk, 147–148, 147f
  disorganized teachers, problems, 3–4

formal state/national testing, role, 284

inbox, tabs (matching), 155

teacher-leader alert, usage, 116

togetherness, importance, 347–348

tubs, 249f

Teacher Workspace, 126, 145–169, 344

Teach for America (TFA), 6

Teaching

materials, availability, 139

schedule, 69, 73, 80

Teaching Station, 146–149, 148f, 151, 168

Technology, usage, 5, 120, 302

Template, search, 51

Testing

formal state/national testing, role, 284

information, availability, 164

Texts, control, 173

Thought Catchers, 107, 111–118,
118f, 343

benefits, 110

brainstorming, 119

colleague group usage, 116

coteacher/school leader, 112f

defining, 109–111

digital Thought Catchers, 120

headings, creation, 122

maintenance, 122

observation notes, 113f–115f

paper Thought Catchers, 120

review, regularity, 121

setup, 119

teacher-leader alert, 116

template, 109f

To-Dos, contrast, 117

tool, selection, 119–120

usage, 110, 114

writing team example, 117f

written update usage, 116

Time

blocking, 52

calendar components, 21

commitments, display, 37

Timed commitments, brainstorming, 52

To-Dos, 37, 42, 93–97

brainstorming, 52

capture/catching, 38, 49

checking, 3

classroom library To-Do, inclusion, 89f

display, 37

handling, 23

incoming To-Dos, placement, 100

list, 33, 34, 218f, 326

long-term To-Dos, control, 85

management, 7

notebook-based/color-coded To-Do
list, 218–219

organization, 24, 30

paper To-Do list, 14

problems, 24

scheduling, 96

Thought Catchers, contrast, 117

tracking, Later List (usage), 117

traffic jam, avoidance, 24

weekly worksheet, usage, 32

writing, 37

Together

meaning, 3–4

template, downloading, 52

Togetherness, 54. *See also* Students

expectations, 233–234

journey, perspective, 343–346

maintenance, 234

support, routines (creation), 123, 344

teacher usage, reasons, 347–348

Togetherness Intention, 9–10

examination, 340

Together Student tools
   school creation, 212–216
   student/family creation, 216–219
Together Teacher
   interviews, 55, 105, 169, 261, 321
   long-term planning, examples, 238–241
   necessity, reasons, 339–340
   reading options, 343–346
   template, downloading, 50
   Thought Catchers, 111–118
Together Teacher Comprehensive
   Calendar, 64–74
Together Teacher Later List, 89–93, 91f
Together Teacher Meeting with Myself
   checklists, 127–131
Together Teacher System
   components/characteristics, 14–15
   paper/electronic option, 8
   testing/survival, 341–343
Tools
   availability, 23
   change, 25
   location, focus, 23
Tote bag, 249f, 277f
Traveling instructional crate,
   154–155, 154f
Trigger, creation, 24–25

U
UnCalendar, 75
Unclear messages, dangers, 190
Unit bins, 161–162
Unit labels, 161, 161f
Unit plans/planning, 25–26, 77, 137, 265
   design, 182
   format, selection, 238
   writing, 245
Unit storage, 162f

Unplanned meeting template, 309, 309f
Upcoming meetings (folder), 179f, 198

V
Value-driven meeting agenda, 293, 296
Video calls, 302
Virtual learning daily schedule, 206f
Visual anchors, 3, 227

W
Web-based calendars, 76
Week (Meeting with Myself), 125–127
Weekly class schedules, digital
   sharing, 205–206
Weekly Long-Term Sketch, 238
Weekly meeting agenda, 130–131, 130f
Weekly overview, 239f
Weekly Worksheet, 50–52
   app, selection/experimentation, 50
   change, 41f
   checklist, criteria, 38, 39, 41, 43,
     45, 47, 49
   content, brainstorning, 51
   creation, 31, 343
   defining, 35–37
   digital version, 53, 180
   examples, 36f, 39f, 44f, 46f, 48f
   maintenance, 54–55
   plan, components, 53
   preparation, 32
   quick hits, inclusion, 40f
   revision, example, 42f–43f
   sections, 35, 37
   student usage, 214, 215f
   template, selection, 51, 52
   tool, selection, 52–53
Weekly written updates, 282–283
What-er/When-er answer key, 34

What-ness/when-ness, orientation, 33–34
Whirlarounds, usage, 304
Whole school binder, challenge, 230–232
Whole school planners, 212, 213f
Work
    completion, 52
    corrections, key (creation), 271
    defining, 127
    digital work, collection, 269–270
    time, addition, 17
Workload estimator, 244, 246, 250
Worksheet, 216–217. *See also*
        Weekly Worksheet
Workspace, 146–153
    bins, usage, 149, 151, 159, 159f
    cleanup, 145, 344
    clipboard, organization, 164–167
    electronic folders, 157f
    folders, hierarchy, 156–157
    Google Drive, organization,
        157–158, 157f
    inbox, 149–152, 150f
    information, availability, 162–164
    inspiration, impact, 152–153
    instructional materials, control,
        155–161

lesson plans, electronic organization,
        156
    maintenance, 168
    materials, 154–155, 158–159
    mobile cart, creation/example, 153, 153f
    new teacher advice, 162
    paper management, 167–168
    professional library, creation, 155–156
    self-care, usage, 152
    tabs, usage, 155
    teacher/teaching desk/station,
        147–149, 147f
    traveling instructional crate, 154–155
    unit bins/labels, 160–161, 160f, 161f
Workstreams, 327
Writing, 23–24, 73–74, 189–193
    team, Thought Catcher example, 117f
Written updates, Thought Catchers
        (usage), 116

Y
Year-long lesson plan sketch,
        241, 242f–243f

Z
Ziploc bags, usage, 154, 339